International Politic

For Molly

International Political Thought

A Historical Introduction

EDWARD KEENE

polity

First published in 2005 by Polity Press

Polity Press
65 Bridge Street
Cambridge CB2 1UR, UK

Polity Press
350 Main Street
Malden, MA 02148, USA

ISBN: 0-7456-2304-2
ISBN: 0-7456-2305-0 (pb)

A catalogue record for this book is available from the British Library and
has been applied for from the Library of Congress.

Typeset in 10.5 on 12 pt Sabon
by Graphicraft Limited, Hong Kong
Printed and bound in Great Britain by
MPG Books, Bodmin, Cornwall

For further information on Polity, visit our website: www.polity.co.uk

Contents

Preface

It is perhaps inevitable that histories of the past reflect an image of the present. Certainly, most surveys of the history of international political thought are powerfully influenced by late twentieth-century ways of thinking about the world; they often project contemporary ideas back into the past, thereby illuminating great 'traditions' of thought which, with a suspicious coincidence, map perfectly onto our current problems and debates. This history is probably no less a prisoner of the present, but it draws upon more recent developments in international relations theory in an attempt to break free from the conventional wisdoms that historians have previously entertained about the subject. In particular, the book builds upon the currently popular idea that the construction of identity is of great importance to the conduct of international relations. Rather than focus attention on theories exclusively concerned with the dynamics of international systems or societies of sovereign states, the book introduces students to the history of international political thought by asking them to contemplate the different ways in which people in the past have thought about their own identity as a community, what differentiates their community from others, and therefore how relations between their own and other communities should be conducted. It is, I believe, only from this starting-point that we can begin to understand the richness and diversity of the history of international political thought, and thereby acquire a better sense of the particular strengths and weaknesses of current ways of thinking.

Several years ago, James Mayall suggested my name to Polity as a possibility to write this book, and I would like to take this opportunity now to thank him for that recommendation. At Polity itself, my special thanks go to Andrea Drugan and Louise Knight for their patience and guidance while working on the manuscript, and my appreciation to the press's two anonymous readers, both of whom, in different ways, taught me valuable lessons about good scholarship. As they will be aware, the final version is very different from the first draft, and I think their criticisms have helped me to improve it considerably. Other people who have contributed to the book's development, either through discussing its topics with me (perhaps unwittingly) or by reading parts of the manuscript, include David Armitage, Peter Borschberg, Bob Hargrave, Kinch Hoekstra, Stephen Hopgood, Andy Hurrell, Benedict Kingsbury, Mark Salter, Jennifer Welsh and Tom Young. I am extremely grateful to all of them. I presented parts of the book to a seminar at the University of Reading and to a roundtable at the International Studies Association and would like to thank all the participants at those events, especially Nick Bisley and Sasson Sofer, who organized them. Finally, I would like to acknowledge how much I have learnt from my students at SOAS, Oxford and Georgia Tech: I thank all of them for their stimulating and invigorating discussions of these and related topics, and particularly want to express my gratitude to Dan Baer for our always enjoyable tutorials. Of course, I take full responsibility for any errors which remain in the manuscript.

These debts are considerable, but nevertheless trivial in comparison with those I owe to my wife, Molly. The book was written during an extremely busy period in our lives. In the absence of any sabbaticals or external funding, it is entirely thanks to Molly's unstinting hard work and patient, loving support that I have been granted the precious time in which to work on this book, and that is a privilege in return for which, with love and immense gratitude, I dedicate it to her.

Introduction:
The Study of International
Political Thought

People who write books on the history of international political thought tend to think that their subject does not receive all the attention it deserves. For example, Torbjörn Knutsen begins his recent *History of International Relations Theory* with an attack on the 'common assumption that the study of international relations has no theoretical tradition', and he ruefully observes that, 'whereas the new student of political theory is introduced to a tradition which begins with ancient Greek authors and evolves continually up to our own times, the new student of international relations is introduced to no comparable chain of classics' (Knutsen 1992, 1). The complaint is not a new one. As early as 1936, Frank Russell had already noticed that 'there is no book in any language ... that attempts to present from the earliest times ... the more significant ideas ... that men have entertained concerning international relations' (Russell 1936, vi). Despite Russell's efforts to fill this gap with his survey *Theories of International Relations*, however, Arnold Wolfers still felt twenty years later that 'what a student of international relations may happen to learn about political thinkers of earlier centuries usually comes to him from outside the programme of his speciality' (Wolfers 1956, ix). The compilers of a 1970 reader came to a similarly gloomy conclusion, complaining that 'the great writers of the past are at present neglected by students of international relations' (Forsyth et al. 1970, 11). As we have seen with Knutsen's work, the problem has apparently persisted until recent years, when a flurry of books has attempted once again to remedy it (Donelan 1990; Williams 1992; Thompson 1994; Doyle 1997; Boucher 1998; Pangle and Ahrensdorf 1999; and Brown et al. 2002).

Nor is Knutsen alone among these in remarking on the still neglected state of the history of international political thought in the discipline at large: Thomas Pangle and Peter Ahrensdorf, for example, begin their study of *Justice Among Nations* by sympathizing with Wolfers, whose lament, they say, 'remains as true today as when it was first uttered almost half a century ago' (Pangle and Ahrensdorf 1999, 1).

Despite this chorus of complaints, it is easy to overstate the degree to which the history of international political thought really is, or has been, neglected. David Boucher, for example, rightly points to the increased levels of interest in international relations theory in universities today, and notes that this has led to more and more students being referred to 'classical theories' as part of their education in the subject, although he too repeats the standard concern that 'no text is available for students to familiarize themselves in detail with such theories' (Boucher 1998 3; he cites only two works in support of this claim, Parkinson 1977 and Williams 1992). Indeed, it may well be the case that historians of international political thought have *always* underestimated the importance that experts on international relations attach to the study of 'classical theories'. The frequency of references in leading twentieth-century theoretical treatises to past thinkers such as Thucydides, Machiavelli, Grotius, Hobbes, Rousseau and Kant certainly suggests that the history of international political thought is regarded at least as an important reference point for current theorizing (see, for example, Morgenthau 1949; Waltz 1959; Hinsley 1963; Aron 1966; and Bull 1977). Even if one disagrees with the interpretations those authors place on the classical thinkers they invoke, it is nevertheless significant that such influential international relations theorists of the late twentieth century have so often felt it necessary to use the history of international political thought in developing and explaining their own ideas. One might well think that classical theories have been abused in the process, but it is hard to say that they have been neglected.

Furthermore, whatever the situation may have been when Russell first complained about the problem in the 1930s, it is clear from the number of works cited in the above paragraphs that there is now no shortage of textbooks on the history of international political thought. In fact, there are plenty of other works on the subject beyond those already mentioned: the list above, for example, does not even begin to scratch the surface of the vast literature that deals with more specific aspects of the history of international political thought (there are too many to attempt any kind of an overview here but, just to give a sense of the range of this literature, a few particularly out-standing examples are Alexandrowicz 1967; Holbraad 1970; Muldoon 1979; Hinsley 1986; Ceadel 1987; Gat 1989, 1992; Linklater 1990; Long and Wilson 1995; Welsh 1995; Mapel and Nardin 1998; Onuf 1998; Schmidt 1998; Tuck 1999; and Berridge et al. 2001). Rather than pretend that the history of international political thought is some kind of unsurveyed wilderness, it is more honest to start out by acknowledging the existence of this substantial body of work. I will not, therefore, begin with the familiar complaint about neglect, but will rather explain how this book differs from the many existing treatments of the subject, and say why the particular approach adopted here has been chosen.

This book's approach

Four features distinguish this study of the history of international political thought from the many others that are currently available. First, it tries to avoid the popular strategy of organizing theories of international relations into 'schools' or 'traditions' of thought, whether in familiar pairings such as realism and liberalism (for example Nye 2000; Doyle 1997 adds socialism to the mix as well), or in more idiosyncratic combinations such as Martin Wight's trio of realism, rationalism and revolutionism (Wight 1991) or Boucher's 'empirical realism', 'universal moral order' and 'historical reason' (Boucher 1998; Pangle and Ahrensdorf 1999 use the standard dichotomy of realism and idealism, but interpret each school of thought in an unconventional manner). The notion that theories can be grouped into schools of thought or intellectual traditions like this has occupied an extremely prominent place in the history of international political thought (Dunne 1993), and, as the above references show, there are relatively few textbooks which try to present ideas about international politics in their immediate historical context, free from the interpretive framework imposed by conventional wisdoms about the traditions and especially the pervasive influence of the school of *Realpolitik* (of recent textbooks, Knutsen 1992 most closely approximates the more chronological and less thematic approach to the study of international political thought that is used in this book; older texts often did the same: see Russell 1936 and, on international legal thought, Nussbaum 1947).

I have tried not to use the terminology of traditions or schools, except in cases where the people under discussion themselves might have used the label. Thus, for example, I might associate Cicero with a 'Stoic' school of philosophy, but I would not place him together with, say, Immanuel Kant in a 'liberal' tradition of thought supposedly united by a shared universalist or cosmopolitan outlook. The book's main aim is to present ideas about international politics in terms of their immediate historical context, rather than with reference to long-standing traditions in which they are supposed by late twentieth-century commentators to have been developed. Consequently, in a way that might seem odd to readers already familiar with the literature on the history of international political thought, terms such as 'realism', and questions about whether or not thinkers such as Thucydides, Machiavelli and Hobbes should be thought of as 'realists', do not really figure in this book. 'Realism' itself does not emerge until the final two chapters, dealing with the nineteenth and twentieth centuries, when the organization into academic disciplines of history, law, politics and, eventually, international relations began to create self-conscious attachments to this and other schools of international political thought. Nevertheless, even though I will try to employ these labels only as historically appropriate, my use of them in order to lend structure to the discussion of what are often voluminous and diverse bodies of work may still overstate the coherence of such groups, and readers should view them with a certain degree of caution.

My decision not to resort to schools or traditions as a thematic organizing device is closely related to the second point of difference: this book concentrates on describing changes in the conceptual apparatus of international political thought, rather than identifying continuities across historical periods. The fact that so many textbooks use the idea of a tradition as their organizing theme very often leads them to stress the continuous nature of international political thought, since to locate a thinker within such a context is usually to identify a link with other thinkers from different times who nevertheless also belong to the same tradition (although some, for example Boucher 1998 and Pangle and Ahrensdorf 1999, do try to acknowledge the significance of the breaks that occur within traditions). It is therefore unsurprising that most current textbooks talk about the 'perennial' character of international political thought, whether in Michael Doyle's claim that 'much of what they [the classical theorists] argued for and about is timeless'; or in Boucher's desire 'to seek in the transitory something which reveals in a systematic and coherent manner the more fundamental springs of action'; or in Pangle and Ahrensdorf's determination to take seriously their subjects' claims 'to have pierced the veils created by historical tradition and culture, and thus to have penetrated to the initially hidden grounding of the unchanging nature of man' (Doyle 1997, 9; Boucher 1998, 12; Pangle and Ahrensdorf 1999, 7; see also Thompson 1994 for an even stronger assertion of the perennial character of international political thought).

By contrast, one consequence of this book's focus on the immediate historical context within which ideas about international politics have been developed is that it highlights – indeed, it deliberately accentuates – the discontinuities between particular historical periods. The narrative is organized not around traditions as much as around moments of crisis in the theory and practice of international politics, when old beliefs ceased to exercise their grip and new ideas began to come to the fore. I should make clear that this is a historiographical choice, rather than a matter of trying to achieve greater factual accuracy. Continuist and discontinuist histories both rely on interpretive frameworks to select and make sense of the facts that they relate, and it is difficult to say that one or the other is better at telling a history of international political thought 'as it really happened'. Nor, although I will do so here, is it the case that one should always favour a focus on change over continuity; continuist comparisons across time may offer valid, interesting and useful insights as well, as is evident from many of the textbooks mentioned earlier (Nardin 1992 also offers a good defence of the 'traditionalist' approach). Because of the widely shared bias in favour of an approach organized around traditions or schools, however, thus far the history of international political thought as a whole has failed to strike a proper balance between these two historiographical themes, and more attention needs to be paid to methods which help us to appreciate the importance of change and discontinuity in the field. The two approaches offer different insights into the history of international political thought, and therefore stand to make different contributions to how we use our knowledge of that history to help us think about the world we live in today. The fact that so much work has been done along broadly continuist lines indicates that we may be depriving ourselves of certain valuable benefits that could be provided by a different way of approaching the subject, as I will explain in more detail later.

The third major point of difference is that for the most part this book avoids talking directly about theories at all; it is more concerned with identifying and explaining the fundamental ideas or concepts that thinkers have used to make sense of their international political environments. The book is therefore rather unusual in that it contains few interpretive summaries of the 'classic works' produced by 'great thinkers', which are often the core of existing textbooks on international political thought. Kenneth Thompson's analysis of the 'fathers' of international thought is perhaps the most extreme example of this kind of approach (Thompson 1994), but many others insist that one should pay close attention to what Doyle describes as 'the time-tested classics of ways of war and peace' (Doyle 1997, 17; see also Boucher 1998; Pangle and Ahrensdorf 1999; and Brown et al. 2002).

While students of the history of international political thought certainly should be encouraged to read the 'time-tested classics' in the field, that does not necessarily mean that the main task of an introductory textbook is to explain what those classic texts say. A useful analogy might be to compare the task of learning how to read treatises on international politics to the challenge of learning to read literature written in a foreign language (in many cases, of course, this is literally true). One would not try to learn, say, German by reading critical interpretive commentaries on great works of German literature. That might come eventually, but one would presumably begin by engaging in the more humble, and more straightforward, task of learning German vocabulary and grammar. In a similar way, only when one understands the conceptual vocabulary with which thinkers in the past built their theories about the world is one in a position not only to read and appreciate their arguments accurately, but also to evaluate the interpretations of those arguments that are presented in most of the textbooks currently on the market. In short, rather than saving students from the bother of actually reading the primary texts, which I suspect is often the unintended result of books that comment on great works in the conventional manner, this introductory textbook aims to provide the tools with which students can read and interpret primary texts for themselves, and that requires a focus on the key concepts that thinkers in the past have used to make sense of international politics, the most basic building blocks of the arguments they constructed.

Fourthly, this book is different because it adopts a broader focus than the conventional fixation with the international politics of the European states-system, as supposedly created by the Peace of Westphalia in 1648 (although some, notably Wight 1991 and Boucher 1998, do touch on these broader themes). This widens the conceptual vocabulary with which the book deals beyond the relatively small group of ideas that are normally considered important to the history of international political thought. In other words, alongside the familiar ideas about the nation-state, sovereignty and anarchy which are associated with the modern states-system, the book attaches equal importance to other concepts that have been just as fundamental in structuring intellectual speculation about political relations between peoples or communities, although they are often ignored by more conventionally minded historians because they do not fit easily with the focus on the states-system (Salter 2002 is a notable exception). Ideas about barbarism, religious faith, civilization, culture, racial difference and imperial hierarchy, for example, will appear as major elements in the picture of international political thought presented here. I want to expand on this particular point now at more length, since it raises the important, even primary, question of what exactly 'international political thought' is. Then I will return to the more methodological questions raised by my intention to highlight discontinuities in the history of international political thought rather than overarching traditions, and to focus on the meaning of concepts rather than the logical structure of the arguments made by 'great thinkers' in 'classic texts'.

What is international political thought?

Most existing textbooks on the history of international political thought begin from the assumption that the field is defined by the question of how relations between sovereign states are conducted under the condition of anarchy. To give just one example from many, Martin Wight begins his influential study *International Theory* with the assertion that 'international theory is the ... tradition of enquiry about relations between states, the problems of obligations that arise in the absence as distinct from the presence of government, the nature of the community of which states are members, and the principles of foreign policy'; he goes so far as to say that 'one cannot talk properly about international relations before the advent of the sovereign state' (Wight 1991, 1). This obviously limits the scope of the enquiry in terms of the conceptual vocabulary that is attributed to theorists of international politics. As Knutsen observes, it 'makes the "state" the primary object of the discussion and it makes "sovereignty" the primary concept' (Knutsen 1992, 2). It also narrows the historical and geographical context within which scholars seek to understand the evolution of international political thought. To quote Knutsen again: histories that concentrate on the sovereign state tend to be 'inordinately preoccupied with Western events and with European theorists' (ibid.), and they tend to be particularly concerned with the development of both since the sixteenth or seventeenth centuries, when the sovereign state first came to dominate other forms of political organization in Western Europe (Spruyt 1997). Other places and periods are viewed as important only in so far as they obey a logic that seems to bear comparison with the anarchic dynamics of the modern states-system. Thus the 'city-state' system of ancient Greece frequently appears as a historical example in textbooks on international politics; the Roman empire hardly at all (but see Buzan and Little 2000 for an exception).

The assumption that relations between independent sovereign states are the defining theme of international political thought reflects the influence of a long-standing belief among historians that the transition from the medieval to the modern age was marked by the decline of putatively universal institutions – the Catholic Church and the Holy Roman Empire – and the rise of absolutist states claiming independent authority, sovereignty in other words, over their own specific territories and populations. Many textbooks on the history of political thought operate with a similar idea of the distinctive features of the modern way of thinking about politics more generally: George Sabine's influential *History of Political Theory*, for example, is organized around precisely this shift from the medieval 'theory of the universal community' to the modern 'theory of the national state' (Sabine 1961), and the sovereign state continues to play a central role in more recent scholarship on the history of ideas (but see Muldoon 2000 for a vigorous and perceptive attack on the conventional wisdom here). In fact, this point of view is now so deeply ingrained that one might wonder why there is a problem here at all. Any historical enquiry has to be limited in some way, otherwise it will become unmanageable. In that context, it seems hard to argue with the proposition that the concept of state sovereignty has played an exceptionally prominent role in modern thinking about international politics, or with the claim that European theorists' attempts to make sense of their system of sovereign states ought to occupy a substantial part of any proper enquiry into the subject.

Nevertheless, while it is beyond the scope of this study to say whether or not the modern state is an appropriate focus for historians of political theory, the fixation with state sovereignty and international anarchy has been immensely damaging to our efforts to understand the historical development of international political thought. In the first place, despite its claim to speak to modern ways of thinking about the world, this focus does not do justice to modern thinkers' wide range of political experience. For many of them – John

Locke, John Stuart Mill and Mohandas K. Gandhi, for example – the most practically important international political feature of their world was the existence of a colonial or imperial system that operated according to a very different logic than mutual respect for state sovereignty. Why should we assume that living in a system of sovereign states constituted the definitive experience of political modernity, when for so many people modernity was more closely associated with the experience of imperialism, whether as ruler or ruled? To say that international political thought is speculation about relations between sovereign states is, in effect, to deny one of the central themes of modern thinking about international politics: the effort to understand imperial systems. Even if it is legitimate to focus on modern ways of thinking alone, that in itself does not provide a justification for concentrating on theories associated with the states-system.

It is also dangerous to treat speculation about international politics as bound up exclusively with what Knutsen refers to as 'Western events', such as the Peace of Westphalia. The views of eighteenth-century *philosophes* such as Denis Diderot, for example, are almost impossible to understand without taking their fascination with non-European societies seriously, an interest they shared with 'Enlightened' thinkers across Europe, among numerous others. Of course, one might think that how they interpreted other societies' ways of life was shaped by their own Eurocentrism, but that is a quite different thing from saying that we should focus on theories about the development of the European states-system in isolation from the rest of the world. At the very least, we need to realize that very many theorists of international politics have had a global perspective rather than a purely European one; the wider view is by no means a product of the late twentieth-century communications revolution and a process of 'globalization'. A few historians of international political thought do devote some time to this issue (see, for example, the interesting discussion of the 'theory of mankind' in Wight 1991). It is all the more puzzling, then, why these same commentators often persist in saying that international political thought is centrally concerned with relations between states, when these crucial questions are usually much better understood in the context of theories of imperial or colonial administration (as Wight 1991 acknowledges).

To begin by selecting relations between sovereign states as our defining theme, then, risks reading many works on international politics out of their practical imperial and global context, quite apart from the fact that it is inevitably prejudicial to those scholars who are then dismissed as unconcerned with international relations in the proper sense because they lived in a world before a portion of continental Europe was divided into territorially sovereign states. Numerous medieval Christian thinkers, for example, were well aware of the existence of political, legal and cultural differences between peoples within Christendom. It seems silly to exclude their attempts to construct peaceful and orderly relationships between different nations (*'diversae nationes populorum'*: see Reynolds 1997, 257) from the corpus of what counts as international political thought, simply because most of them lacked the conception of each nation's sovereign independence that we regard as an attribute of a properly modern state. No enquiry can be comprehensive, but the conventional way of proceeding imposes a lens that both narrows and distorts our view of the subject to an unnecessary degree. We need to find a better way of defining the scope of the enquiry.

Rather than beginning by asserting the centrality of the concept of the sovereign state to international political thought, this book starts from the proposition that all theories of international politics involve a prior definition of how communities – and that word is left undefined for the moment – differ from one another, and therefore constitute distinct entities whose relations with one another need to be understood. Such definitions are often assumed rather than explicitly argued, but the identification of what belongs to a particular community and what is alien to it is extremely important because these very often furnish the theorist with a preliminary sense of what factors might be significant to the relations between communities, usually with important implications for the further development of their understanding of the structure of world order more generally (see Walker 1992; Brown et al. 2002, 6–8). One of the main themes in this book is therefore a description of how ways of understanding the similarities and differences between communities have changed over time, as new concepts structuring these divisions have come to the fore and as the meanings of old concepts used for the purpose have been altered. The word 'community' is deliberately left as an empty category at this stage, because we need to wait to see how different peoples at different times have filled it in. It is only once this vital concept is specified, once the idea of a community is defined, that we can begin to understand the structure of the international political thought of a given period.

Of course, one way of drawing boundaries between communities is to focus on territories that are governed by authorities which are administratively and juridically independent from one another. That, in a nutshell, is the point of the idea of state sovereignty (see Walker

1992). This is often linked to the belief that within each sovereign state resides a group of people who are united not just as citizens but also by a collective identity as a nation; hence the concept of the nation-state, which plays an extremely prominent role in most surveys of modern international political thought (see Mayall 1990). Nevertheless, while it should not be forgotten that historically the idea of the nation-state has been an important answer to the question of how communities differ from one another, it is only one among many ways in which the boundaries of communities can be and have been understood. This theme will be picked up repeatedly throughout the book, and it would anticipate too much of what is to come if it were developed in detail in this introductory discussion. One or two of its keynotes may be sounded, however, to give a preliminary sense of the kind of approach that I am adopting and the insights into the nature of international political thought that one can expect it to yield.

If we stay with modern international political thought for the moment, where the concept of the territorially sovereign nation-state is often supposed to reign supreme, at least one other idea has played a vital role in defining the boundaries of communities in international relations: the concept of 'civilization' (see Robinson 1929; Bagby 1963; Gusdorf 1971; Braudel 1994; Elias 1994; and Salter 2002). Textbooks on international politics and international law from the nineteenth century, for example, habitually make distinctions between 'the family of civilized nations' and 'barbaric' or 'savage' peoples. These distinctions had immense implications for the conduct of political and legal relationships between the communities. With only a handful of exceptions, virtually everyone in the 'civilized world' believed that they should behave one way in their dealings with other 'civilized' states, and another way in their dealings with 'barbarians' or 'savages'. Indeed, whether or not a community was perceived as 'civilized' was very often vital in making decisions about whether or not that community should be recognized as a sovereign state in the first place: 'barbarians', as John Stuart Mill put it, 'have no rights as a nation' (Mill 1882, 3.253; see also Gong 1984). In that respect, the distinction between civilized and barbaric peoples was even more fundamental to modern international political thought than the drawing of territorial boundaries between different sovereign states.

If we focus only on the concepts of the nation or the sovereign state, the idea of a specific 'family of civilized nations' cannot be understood, and the world beyond it, against which it was to some extent defined, effectively ceases to exist. But there is no good reason why modern ideas about how to conduct relations between 'civilized' and 'barbaric' peoples should not be included in our consideration of the history of how people have thought about international politics. The only possible objection is that one might worry that, if we were to broaden our account of what counts as 'international politics' in this way, our enquiry would lose all its focus and coherence. The field, it might be argued, is potentially vast, and we need familiar signposts to guide us; it is simply impossible, one might say, to understand anything at all unless we impose on ourselves the kind of simplifying restrictions provided by the focus on 'international politics' as 'relations between sovereign states'. That may be the case, but it is something individuals will have to judge for themselves after reading the book. Obviously, I have not set out to write a history of international political thought that is completely unintelligible. I think that it is perfectly possible to cope with the fact that, at different times, people have held different beliefs about what their community looked like, and to examine how these beliefs have influenced their views about the conduct of political relations between communities, without completely losing oneself in the vastness of human history. To repeat, though, only the reader can judge whether this book is a successful illustration of that view.

Before leaving this issue, it is worth noting that most historians would probably agree that the point of studying the history of international political thought is to learn something that is relevant, useful or valuable to us today. Very few believe that the subject has only antiquarian interest, and I certainly do not think that is the case. So what does that imply about how we should approach the subject? Here, I would point to two important themes in contemporary international political thought which lend further support to my view that we should broaden our attitude to what the history of the subject contains beyond the conventional focus on state sovereignty. First, many people believe that the sovereign nation-state, while not necessarily about to disappear, is at least no longer the defining institution of world politics today: one comes across talk of integration, regionalization, globalization and so on every day (see, for example, Hovden and Keene 2002). Whether or not these people are right, and it is hard to believe that they are all wrong, this provides a *prima facie* reason why our histories of the past should no longer be so anxious to extract the sovereign nation-state from the vast array of different forms of community which have existed in the world. People who lived in a world which they thought was composed exclusively of sovereign nation-states naturally wrote histories which reflected that belief; if we no longer think we live in such a world, then our histories should also be ripe for change. Secondly, and not unrelated, a central concern of much current theoretical speculation about international politics is that we need to understand how identities are constructed in order to understand how international relations work (Walker 1992; Lapid and Kratochwil 1996; Ruggie 1998; Wendt 1999; and Zehfuss 2002). This book does not seek to make any kind of contribution to that theoretical project, but the story it tells is one which will, I hope, be of more interest and use to readers who find such an approach valuable than a conventionally minded history of international political thought.

To sum up thus far: while the concept of the sovereign state certainly ought to form an important part of our enquiry, it is wrong to place the state right at the heart of the analysis such that it plays a defining role with respect to the entire history of international political thought. That fails to do justice to the wide range of different ways of thinking about international politics that have been developed in the past in an effort to make sense of relationships between what the people at the time recognized as distinct communities, albeit ones that were not fully independent states in the administrative or juridical sense implied by the orthodox conception of 'sovereignty'. My proposal, then, is that we should broaden the scope of our enquiry by starting from the more general proposition that all intellectual speculation about international politics originally involves some way of identifying what it is about communities that makes them different from one another in the first place. Each chapter of this book tries to explain the various ways in which such differences were framed in a particular historical period, and will outline their implications for the development of more concrete ideas about how political relations between communities were to be conducted. The concept of state sovereignty is an important way of marking such distinctions, and there is an interesting group of theories with which it is associated, but it is hard to see why we should choose to treat sovereignty as exclusively defining even the modern way of thinking, particularly when alternative ideas, such as the concept of civilization, were just as fundamental to how modern thinkers selected certain attributes of communities as significant for the purposes of understanding their appropriate relationships with one another. Ideas about civilization, barbarism, national character, culture, race and even climate will therefore figure as prominently in this book as ideas about sovereignty.

Why and how to study the history of international political thought

The above discussion of ideas such as sovereignty and civilization in modern international political thought reflects the point that was made earlier concerning this book's focus on the meaning of the basic concepts out of which theories are constructed, rather than on the logical structure or the quality of the arguments of the theories themselves. As I have already said, this is linked to the fact that the book deliberately avoids trying to identify broad, overarching traditions of intellectual speculation about international politics, but chooses instead to concentrate on the context within which ideas developed, and even accentuates the discontinuities between different periods to sharpen our sense of how a particular idea 'belongs' to a particular context. I now want to explain why the book is written in this way, indicating how readers should approach the narrative presented here and what they can expect to get out of it.

To begin with, it is worth briefly noting that in the last twenty years or so a methodological controversy has opened up in the history of ideas largely thanks to the work of John Pocock and Quentin Skinner (Pocock 1972, 1975, 1987; Skinner 1978, 2002 (vol. 1); see also MacIntyre 1966; Pagden 1987; Tully 1988; Richter 1995; and Hampsher-Monk 1998). The core of their approach to the history of ideas is to argue that texts need to be located in an appropriate historical context before their meaning can be properly understood, and that texts should not be treated as if they were interventions in timeless grand debates about perennial questions of justice, freedom, equality and so on. It is beyond the scope of this study to explain in full the philosophical reasons why Skinner and the rest believe this to be the case (Skinner 2002, vol. 1, is probably the best starting-point for further reading here), but it is necessary to give some idea of how this approach works and what its point is in comparison with older approaches to the history of ideas. I will try to do that now.

Unlike many conventional historians of ideas, Skinner argues that one should not set out to tell the history of an idea as if it was a single coherent and more or less timeless abstraction, towards the development of which various great minds were each making their own contributions. Indeed, he maintains that 'there is no history of the idea to be written' in this sense: 'There is only a history of its various uses, and of the varying intentions with which it was used' (Skinner 2002, 1.85). His point, in essence, is that political theorists develop their ideas within an already existing language for talking about politics, which provides the meaning that a given idea has for them, and which connects to an already existing structure of social order by performing ideological functions of legitimating existing practices (this calls into question the notion that there is a clear distinction to be drawn between how people think about international politics – the theory – and how people conduct themselves – the practice). The way that thinkers use ideas to build arguments about their world may therefore be conceived as making 'moves' within a 'language game', which can often have powerful implications for the conduct of social or political relations by helping to change the structure of the language within which their ideas develop. According to James Tully, one of its leading exponents, this approach to the history of ideas therefore involves five main steps: firstly, 'to situate the text in its linguistic or ideological context'; secondly, to examine how the author of the text is 'manipulating the available ideological conventions' in order to justify one particular solution to a pressing political problem of the time; thirdly, to study 'minor texts' in order to work out the 'conventions of the reigning ideologies', and so better to understand the significance of the intellectual moves carried out by 'major texts'; fourthly, to analyse how particular ideologies perform a normative role by legitimating certain forms of social action and stigmatizing others; and, finally, to explain 'how ideological change comes to be woven into ways of acting', how what was once a new and strange idea becomes a commonplace practice (Tully 1988, 8–16).

I should point out at once that this book is not intended to be a worked-out application of this method to the study of the history of international political thought. For a start, it covers too wide an area to permit the detailed examination of specific linguistic and ideological structures within which theorists have responded to international political problems in the way that a Skinnerian approach would demand. That is because the book is not itself meant to be a study of the history of international political thought, but rather an *introduction* to the field, the purpose of which is to put readers in a position where they are better able to carry out this kind of research for themselves. It is asking a lot, to put it mildly, of students coming to the subject for the first time to expect them immediately to embark on the immensely detailed research involved in Skinnerian methods, especially on minor texts as examples of ideological conventions.

This book is therefore intended to give readers a sense of what the linguistic contexts of different periods in the history of international political thought look like, so as to make it easier for them to engage in a more situated reading of the classic texts that conventionally form the basis of speculation about the subject; or to provide a starting-point, and perhaps a critical foil, from which or against which readers may begin to conduct the more detailed study of the conventional linguistic or ideological structures of international political thought that we require in order to achieve a proper historical understanding of the field. In each period, I have highlighted what I think are some of the 'commanding heights', so to speak, of the language within which people developed their ideas about how international relations should be conducted by providing an overview of what some key elements of each period's conceptual vocabulary meant and how they were used at the time. It is then up to the reader him- or herself to examine the texts – both major and minor – and construct an interpretation of their meaning in light of the structures I am describing here; that more detailed research task is, I believe, beyond the scope of an introductory textbook conceived in this way.

One reason why I think it is necessary to write an introductory and very wide-ranging textbook like this is to provide a clear alternative to existing textbooks, which do not properly prepare students to go on to do this kind of work. In fact, they may even be positively harmful. By providing interpretive commentaries on great works within what are usually represented as extended traditions of thought, these textbooks encourage scholarship to focus on a few 'great thinkers', and virtually to ignore the study of minor thinkers whose work is so important to understanding the ideological conventions of a particular period. As I will note on more than one occasion, the literature on the history of international political thought is somewhat uneven, with large bodies of work on a handful of key figures – notably Thucydides, Machiavelli, Grotius, Hobbes, Kant, Burke and Hegel – and very little on anyone else.

Moreover, when it comes to studying even these celebrated thinkers, existing textbooks seldom encourage students to think about the moves that they are trying to make within a given 'language game', or even to speculate on what their immediate intellectual and political environment might look like (although some, notably Knutsen 1992 and Boucher 1998, are less at fault in this respect than others). Instead, they encourage students to believe that the really interesting questions within the field revolve around the critical analysis of standard interpretations of the canonical thinkers (e.g., was Hobbes really a realist, as is commonly supposed?) or in describing what is at stake in the debate between different traditions (e.g., how does Hobbes's theory differ from that advanced by 'liberal' thinkers, such as Kant, and which is right?). They therefore actually work *against* the further development of the Skinnerian approach to the history of ideas within international political thought. This is perhaps a reason why the more historically oriented scholarship that has been done in the history of political thought over the last two decades has had relatively little impact on the academic literature on the history of international political thought (Onuf 1998 and Tuck 1999 are notable exceptions, but perhaps ones that prove the rule).

One might well ask why we should adopt the more 'historical' approach to the history of ideas advocated by Skinner at all. In particular, conventional textbooks often claim that, by focusing on how really exceptional minds have tackled perennial problems of international politics – such as why wars happen, or how to ensure peace, or what kind of moral obligations we have to people from other nations – we can learn better ways of thinking about the similar questions that we still face today (see, especially, Thompson 1994 and Doyle 1997). What, by contrast, does a more historically oriented approach have to offer? Obviously, it does not pursue the same idea that the arguments made by thinkers in the past are directly relevant to our current situation. Its main purpose is to illuminate our contemporary intellectual situation by establishing *contrasts* rather than affinities with the past, to call attention to the fact that at different times thinkers have conceptualized international politics and expressed their views on the subject in quite different ways. Some might argue that this is just a semantic distinction, and that, for example, when sixteenth- and seventeenth-century scholars such as Grotius talked about the *ius naturale* (natural law), or when eighteenth- and nineteenth-century scholars used a distinction between civilized and uncivilized peoples, there is no harm in translating both ideas into a language with which we are more comfortable today, perhaps one that revolves around a concept such as universal human rights. In effect, that is precisely what a continuist approach does: it suggests that, although peoples from different periods have been using different words to describe the world, really they mean the same things and can therefore be compared with one another. My contention, however, is that changes like these in the words that people use to think and talk about international politics ought to be highlighted rather than explained away. I agree with Alasdair MacIntyre's point, made in a slightly different context, that a major change in the vocabulary that theorists use 'marks a difference between two forms of social life' (MacIntyre 1966, 2). And, as he continues, 'To understand a concept, to grasp the meaning of the words which express it, is always at least to learn what the rules are which govern the use of such words and so to grasp the role of the concept in language and social life' (ibid.).

When we read books that were written several hundred years ago, or even barely fifty years ago, it is therefore quite proper that we should be struck by the fact that they contain numerous ideas about international politics that are now hard to accept and sometimes appear downright peculiar; or that they often express prejudices, notably about race and gender, that were once respectable terms of philosophical, diplomatic and legal discourse but would be quite out of place in a polite discussion today. We should not try to conceal these differences by focusing on the ways in which thinkers from the past speak to our current problems, but rather use the changes in the vocabulary of international political thought that they represent to help us understand the different 'forms of social life' out of which they developed and which they played a major role in constituting. In that sense, a vital task for any history of international political thought should be to help us understand the various kinds of international order that have existed in the past, and so illuminate what is different about the specific kind of international order in which we live today. A continuist approach will inevitably fail in this endeavour because it is dedicated to the opposite goal of eliding differences in language, vocabulary and historical context so as to make concepts and theories comparable across time, thus effacing the connection that each specific constellation of ideas has to a unique form of social life. One of the key opportunities that the study of the history of ideas provides – the better understanding of different historical periods – is therefore automatically closed off if one adopts a continuist focus on perennial questions, great thinkers and long-standing traditions.

Another virtue of the more historical approach is that it helps people develop their own ideas for themselves, whereas studying great thinkers or traditions tends instead to help them to think like somebody else. If, for example, one is told that historically there have been two traditions of thought about international politics – let us say Hobbesian realism and Kantian liberalism – then really the only scope left for thinking about the subject is to decide whether to become a Hobbesian or a Kantian. A critically minded person might want to develop an entirely different point of view, of course, but a history which just explained what realists and liberals have said about the world would not really prepare somebody for that task either. Even multiplying the number of traditions in an attempt to provide greater precision does not solve the problem. All that does is create a confusing proliferation of labels, but it does not change the fact that readers are left at the end with no alternative but to sign up to an 'ism', or perhaps a 'neo-ism', rather than think for themselves.

According to Skinner, a contextual approach reflects a different way of thinking about the contemporary relevance of the history of ideas. We cannot expect to find solutions to our current problems in the history of international political thought, but we can hope to discover

> the extent to which those features of our own arrangements which we may be disposed to accept as 'timeless' truths may be little more than contingencies of our local history and social structure. To discover from the history of thought that there are in fact no such timeless concepts, but only the various different concepts which have gone with various different societies, is to discover a general truth not merely about the past but about ourselves. (Skinner 2002, 1.89)

By appreciating that people did think differently in the past, and thus by challenging our belief in the 'timelessness' of the problems we face and the concepts we use today, we place ourselves in a better position to think beyond the constraints of our immediate intellectual and political environment. Furthermore, studying how different scholars have responded to their own particular environments gives us a chance to improve our understanding of our own context and how it shapes the way we think about the world. That does not mean we can or should ignore the specific context in which we find ourselves at present, but it will make us more conscious of the intellectual constraints this imposes and perhaps give us a glimpse of what a completely different way of thinking might look like, although it would then be up to us to work out how those insights might be applied to our own situation. Studying the history of ideas thus becomes less an opportunity to marvel at how 'first-class minds' have thought about the world, and more, as Skinner puts it, a way 'to learn to do our own thinking for ourselves' (Skinner 2002, 1.88).

This message is particularly relevant in view of how the academic discipline of international relations developed in the second half of the twentieth century. Partly (but not entirely) because of the dominance of a continuist perspective on the history of international political thought during that period, it has become conventional to describe the international system as a 'realm of recurrence and repetition' (Wight 1966a, 26), where scholars have always been grappling with essentially the same questions about the problem of anarchy and the dominating influence of power over morality in international affairs. In some respects, this is an even worse situation than that which Thomas Kuhn confronted in the natural sciences (Kuhn 1976). In science, an appreciation of discontinuity in the traditional notion of great leaps forward through brilliant discoveries at least allowed for a sense of intellectual change and development, albeit one that rested on questionable foundations, as Kuhn showed in his study of scientific 'paradigms'. But whereas science has conventionally depicted itself as a cumulatively improving field of enquiry, continuist histories of international politics have led to a depiction of the field as essentially static and unchanging. Even the most sophisticated and nuanced histories often do little more than present us with two or three traditions that stretch back throughout time, even as far as ancient Greece. This helps to secure the dominance of the principal approaches to the study of international politics that developed during the later twentieth century – indeed, the entire history of international political thought is now conventionally cast in their image – but it systematically prevents us from gaining a proper appreciation of the fact that these have historically not been the only ways in which people have thought about international politics, and so does little to encourage us to think for ourselves in fresh or original ways. Continuist histories of international political thought are, in this respect, inevitably uncritical; discontinuist approaches are not necessarily critical, but only they have the ability to present us with this opportunity.

To conclude this introductory discussion, one should not expect this book to provide a detailed explication of what a relatively small number of key thinkers have argued in a canon of classic treatises on international politics; nor should one expect to see questions about the relative merits of those theorists discussed or an analysis of whether they belong in one tradition of thought or another. I believe that the study of the history of international political thought needs to be brought more closely in line with recent developments in the history of ideas more generally, and, to that end, I think that we need to turn our attention away from these kinds of enquiry, and begin instead to conduct detailed examinations of the linguistic, ideological, political and social contexts within which these authors wrote their texts. This book therefore concentrates on trying to give readers a sense of the changing contexts within which theories of international politics have been developed, by selecting what I think are especially important components of the conceptual vocabularies of theorists in different periods, and trying to explain how those concepts were understood by people at the time. This is not, in itself, a study of the history of international political thought; rather, it is intended to serve as a more effective introduction to research in that area than the textbooks which we currently have available. It does not aim to provide exemplary models of how to think about the world, but tries to develop an appreciation for the ways in which linguistic, ideological and political contexts shape and limit how we think about the world, while also making clear that those contexts can and do change, and that theorists have not been completely uninvolved in such developments. With that in mind, the book will end with a brief discussion of two of the most important elements of the conceptual vocabulary of international relations theory today – the ideas of an international system and an international society – in order to invite readers to think more self-critically about the contexts within which we try to come to terms with the international problems that we currently face.

All the chapters are organized around a similar pattern. Each begins with a brief overview of how the period under discussion is seen in contemporary textbooks and an indication of some of the issues which are currently neglected. Each then goes on to consider how identity and community membership were understood in that particular period, concentrating in turn on the distinction between Greeks and barbarians, the idea of world-citizenship, religious beliefs about faith and spiritual community, and then, in the last three chapters, the concepts of the sovereign state, human nature and civilization. Having set out these basic terms of the international political discourse of the period, each chapter proceeds to consider how other concepts were used to frame questions about the proper ways in which communities conceived in this way should relate to one another. Thus, for example, the next chapter examines how ideas about nature and custom were used by Greek historians and philosophers to think about how Greeks should behave towards each other and how they should deal with barbarians. Because the focus is on discontinuities in the history of international political thought, relatively little effort is made to identify overarching themes across the chapters. Some connections are certainly present – the nineteenth-century liberal concept of civilization, for example, was rooted in eighteenth-century ideas about progress and civilization – but it is possible to treat each chapter as an individual unit, and if one is interested in a particular period there should be no problem with jumping ahead to that particular chapter.

1

Barbarians, Custom and Nature

Most textbooks on the history of international political thought begin with ancient Greece, and in that context most focus on the work of the Greek historian Thucydides. As Chris Brown, Terry Nardin and Nicholas Rengger comment, 'Alone among the writers of antiquity, Thucydides has earned himself a niche in conventional scholarship on International Relations' (Brown et al. 2002, 20). One or two textbooks begin instead with the two great classical thinkers of the political theory canon, Plato and Aristotle (Williams 1992), and a few have taken the welcome step of including in their accounts a wider range of classical thought, such as Stoic theories of the 'world-city' or *cosmopolis* (Boucher 1998; Pangle and Ahrensdorf 1999). But most continue to see ancient international political thought as synonymous with Thucydides' *History of the Peloponnesian War*. Even Brown, Nardin and Rengger, who are dubious of the conventional view that Thucydides is the first great 'realist' theorist of international politics, reinforce this focus by making his work the longest single section in their chapter on ancient thought: twenty-six pages, in comparison with just two and a half for Cicero and three and a half for Plato. This is true of recent critical scholarship more generally. As David Welch has remarked, 'identifying realist "misreadings" of Thucydides has become something of a cottage industry' (Welch 2003, 307: see Gustafson 2000; Bedford and Workman 2001; and Kokaz 2001). Although, thanks to this work, the conventional wisdom that Thucydides was a realist has been rigorously and often critically investigated, the spotlight is still fixed on him and other classical thinkers are correspondingly neglected: there is, for example, no 'cottage industry' of Herodotus or Tacitus scholarship in international relations, critical or otherwise, despite the fact that these historians dealt extensively with themes that are not obviously less 'international' than Thucydides' analysis of the Peloponnesian War.

As I explained in the introduction, this textbook concentrates on concepts rather than thinkers or theories or traditions, and I am therefore not going to devote as much time as one might expect to relating the key moments from Thucydides' history (which is readily available in translation: see, for example, Thucydides 1998), or to answering the question of whether his account of the Peloponnesian War represents an early form of realist theorizing through its analysis of the relationship between power and morality in international politics. Instead, the purpose of this chapter is to explain the meaning, or various meanings, of the main concepts which Thucydides and his contemporaries used to make sense of their political environment. To begin, I will look at the way in which ancient thinkers conceptualized differences between peoples, because this provides a crucial foundation for their ways of thinking about their political relations with one another. In fact, it is especially important to ask how ancient thinkers made these distinctions, because they were in some respects surprisingly different from the ways in which modern theorists have viewed their world. Skin colour, for instance, which many late nineteenth- and twentieth-century thinkers have treated as an extremely significant axis of difference, did not figure nearly so prominently in ancient thought. As Frank Snowden says, 'the ancients did not fall into the error of biological racism; black skin colour was not a sign of inferiority; Greeks and Romans did not establish colour as an obstacle to integration in society' (Snowden 1983, 63). Nor was this exclusively a property of Greek or Roman thought: there was also, for example, 'a basic absence in ancient Egypt of racial prejudice' (Bresciani 1990, 231).

The fact that they did not systematically discriminate on the basis of skin colour does not, of course, mean that the ancients were free from prejudice altogether. On the contrary, a common Egyptian epithet for foreigners was 'vile', and ancient peoples typically sought to emphasize their superiority over their neighbours by describing them in highly negative terms. They simply stressed other differences as important in making these judgements from the ones that modern thinkers highlight. While being relatively 'colour-blind', for example, the Romans were extremely 'fashion-conscious'; they were fascinated and appalled by the northern barbarians' habit of wearing trousers (Sherwin-White 1967, 5–6, 58–9). More generally, an important concept for making distinctions between peoples was conveyed by the word *barbaros*, or barbarian (pl. *barbaroi*), which the Greeks used from roughly the fifth century onwards quite indiscriminately to describe all foreigners that they encountered; it was subsequently adopted and Latinized by Roman writers (*barbarus, barbari*). In terms of its origins, some scholars have speculated on the possible irony that this word may have been borrowed by the Greeks from their eastern neighbours, since it is similar to a Sumerian word for foreigners, *barbaru* (Hall 1989, 4; Lefkowitz 1996, 10), but there is a general agreement that the Greeks used the term because it reflected the sound that foreign languages made to their ears ('bar-bar'). It had a pejorative connotation, not simply implying that barbarians had a different language from Greeks, but that they lacked a proper language altogether. John Coleman suggests that *barbaroi* might best be translated as 'gibberish people' in order to capture the sense that the Greeks gave the word (Coleman 1997, 178). After a brief discussion of ways of conceptualizing foreigners in the ancient world more generally, I will look at this Greek idea of barbarians, asking how it was constructed and what implications it had for the conduct of relations between Greeks (*Hellenes*) and barbarians.

This latter question requires us to consider two other concepts which played an exceptionally prominent role in Greek thought about *why* Greeks and barbarians were so different, and also about how relationships among Greeks or between Greeks and barbarians should be conducted: the ideas of *phusis* (nature) and *nomos* (custom or convention). These concepts were of long-standing importance in Greek thought, but a debate about their relative merits came to the fore around the fifth century BCE – not coincidentally, about the same time as the concept of *barbaros* began to enter common use – particularly in the thought of a group of philosophers known as the Sophists. Nature and custom played an extremely prominent role in Greek thinking about international politics, whether in the historical writings of people such as Herodotus and Thucydides, or in the philosophical works of Plato, Aristotle and their successors (see Guthrie 1969). Of course, it would be a serious mistake to interpret the Greek debate about the relationship between *phusis* and *nomos* in terms of how *we* understand them. Instead, we need to make an effort to think about these concepts as the Greeks did before we can properly appreciate how they influenced their ideas about international politics. In this regard it is worth noting that some of the best recent work on Thucydides has developed interesting new insights into his theory of international politics precisely by examining the unusual ways in which he used the concepts of *phusis* and *nomos* in comparison with his contemporaries (Bedford and Workman 2001; Kokaz 2001); this illustrates the value of trying to understand their conceptual development as an introduction to classical thought more generally.

Ancient views of the foreigner

The ancient Egyptian word for the world beyond the boundaries of the pharoah's empire was 'chaos' (Hall 1989, 4). As Edda Bresciani says, they 'contrasted Egypt, where everything was perfectly in order, with the "foreign lands", the kingdom of the "different", and of disorder' (Bresciani 1990, 222). Of course, this distinction performed an important ideological role. As the pharoah was the bringer of order to chaos, his authority automatically extended over all other peoples in the world, and it was seen as inevitably beneficial for them to submit to Egyptian rule and to adopt Egyptian customs and manners. In this lay their only hope of enjoying the benefits of order, the favour of the gods and eternal life.

At the same time, however, the Egyptians did recognize other peoples as having organized societies of their own, and as the legitimate holders of a certain place in the world, albeit one that was subordinate to themselves. An Egyptian hymn to the god Aten relates: 'Thou settest every man in his place . . . Their tongues are separate in speech, and their natures as well; their skins are distinguished, as thou distinguishest the foreign peoples' (cited in Bresciani 1990, 223; although see also Morkot 2001, 227). The division of the world into different communities thus at least had divine approval. Moreover, so long as they accepted the primacy of Egypt, foreign peoples could even sometimes be welcomed into the Egyptian community. Although Nubians and Asians were often forced into servitude after being conquered, captured nobles were sometimes, after a process of cultural assimilation, integrated into Egyptian society, where several achieved positions of considerable status (Bresciani 1990, 241). An important alternative role was service in the Egyptian army, which was the particular speciality of Nubians. Indeed, as Snowden remarks, 'black soldiers commanded the respect of peoples beyond Nubia at various times from the second millennium BC until the early Roman Empire' (Snowden 1983, 68). Nor did they always have to abandon all of their customs to belong: 'Most foreigners who settled in Egypt to become soldiers or members of the royal bodyguard continued to wear national costume', for example (Bresciani 1990, 224).

The Egyptian attitude towards the foreigner is not a particularly unusual one for the ancient world. Ancient peoples who were successful conquerors, and those are often the ones whose records and monumental inscriptions have survived, generally seem to have adopted an image of the foreigner as not only culturally different, but also inferior. They could still be quite flexible in their attitudes towards foreign customs and practices, however. Indeed, some ancient empires were even less assimilationist in their treatment of foreign peoples than the Egyptians. The Persian empire created by Cyrus the Great around the middle of the sixth century BCE, for instance, was heavily dependent upon the cooperation of local elites, and, 'rather than appearing to be outsiders bent on overturning the existing kingdoms and societies, the Great Kings endeavoured to appropriate local traditions to their advantage . . . and to present themselves as protectors of the sanctuaries' (Briant 2002a, 79). Later Persian rulers actually based their claim to greatness on the number and diversity of the peoples under their rule, extolling this feature of their empire rather than making any claim to have made all their subjects conform to a single form of religious worship, legal system or cultural practice. As Amélie Kuhrt says, 'It is a recurrent theme of the royal inscriptions to dwell on the variegated nature of the king's subjects' (Kuhrt 2001, 105; see also Briant 2002a, 179). The Greek historian Herodotus commented that 'The Persians welcome foreign customs more than any other people. For instance, they decided that Median dress was more beautiful than their own, and so they wear it. They wear Egyptian breastplates for their wars' (Herodotus 1987, 97). So long as subject-peoples continued to pay tribute to the Great King, the Persians not only allowed them to maintain their own religion and customs, but even paid some the compliment of adopting their customs in the royal court itself.

Persian attitudes towards foreign customs were quite influential within the ancient world, and in the next chapter we will see that they can help us to get a sense of how ancient imperialism worked. To get a real grip on ancient images of the foreigner, though, it is inevitable that we must enquire in some detail into the specific way in which Greeks perceived non-Greeks, particularly through their concept of the 'barbarian'. A major reason for adopting this focus is simply that it is from Greek texts, riddled with Greek prejudices, that the bulk of our information about the ancient world comes. John Cook observes that, from about the sixth century BCE on, the Greeks 'were developing prose writing as a literary medium in a way that no other ancient people had thought of doing; and one of the branches of literary activity that they made their own was the writing of history' (Cook 1983, 12); there is no real Persian equivalent of Herodotus or Thucydides. To the extent that our knowledge of international politics in the ancient, pre-Roman world comes from Greek histories, and archaeology is often the only other substantial source (but see Briant 2002a, 5–9, 18–21), our understanding of much of the theory and practice of ancient international relations is inevitably refracted through the interpretive lens that the Greeks adopted.

The development of the Greek idea of the barbarian

The concept of the barbarian is notable by its absence from the earliest Greek literature: the Homeric poems. A likely reason for this absence is given by Thucydides: 'He [Homer] does not even speak of barbarians, in my opinion because the Hellenes [i.e., the Greeks] had not yet been comparably distinguished by a single name'; instead they appear in the poem as several different peoples, Danaans, Argives and Achaians (Thucydides 1998, 5). The idea that all foreigners could be lumped together as 'barbarians', in other words, grew up in parallel with, and could only exist in juxtaposition against, the development of a Greek sense of their shared Hellenic identity. Homer pictures the Achaians and Trojans as different peoples with significantly different customs, and they fight a protracted and bloody war with each other, but they are not contrasted as *Hellene* and *barbaros*; that distinction had to come later (although many commentators believe that the picture of the Trojans in the Homeric poems is a negative one that anticipates subsequent Greek ideas about barbarians: see Hall 1989 for an explanation and critical analysis of this interpretation).

During the fifth century BCE, a new sense of the Greeks as a distinct and unified people (*ethnos* or *genos*) began to take shape (Coleman 1997, 177). Thucydides saw it as based on a linguistic connection: 'all speaking the same language' (Thucydides 1998, 5). Herodotus, though, was somewhat more eloquent on the subject. His history describes an Athenian appeal to the Spartans for help in the war with Persia on the basis of a 'common Greekness', which depends on the facts that 'we are one in blood and one in language; those shrines of the gods belong to us all in common, and the sacrifices in common, and there are our habits, bred of a common upbringing' (Herodotus 1987, 611). Blood, language, religion and custom, in other words, are the foundations of the Greek Hellenic identity, and it is accordingly along these axes that the identity of the barbarian is conceived (Hall 1989, 5n.).

Blood, language, religion and custom do not all carry quite the same weight, however, as Thucydides' narrower focus on linguistic identity suggests. For example, when Herodotus talks about custom, he reveals the diversity inherent within the barbarian world. He continually refers to customs where one foreign people differs from another: the Egyptians are different from the Scythians, who are different from the Persians, who are different from the Thracians, and so on (Harrison 2002, 7). He seldom judges the different practices he encounters, but simply reports them. After all, he remarks, with the possible exception of the Persians, who, as we have seen, borrow freely from the customs of foreign peoples, most people inevitably prefer their own: 'if there were a proposition put before mankind, according to which each should, after examination, choose the best customs in the world, each nation would certainly think its own customs the best' (Herodotus 1987, 228). Herodotus' belief not only that customs differ from place to place, but also that it is impossible to judge between them, is an important element of his remarkably tolerant attitude towards barbarians, and one to which we will return in a moment. The image of the foreigner as 'barbarian', however, is a homogenizing identity: it embraces all foreign peoples, *despite* their different customs, religious beliefs and ethnic characteristics, in one single identity, which is defined as the opposite of the *Hellenes*, another homogenous identity.

Framing the difference between Greeks and barbarians

There are three ways in which this more monolithic sense of an opposition between Greek and barbarian was constructed: the first is linguistic, the second to do with innate qualities of the Greeks, and the third political. First, the Greek construction of the 'barbarian' was most often built around language. In the Greek view, barbarian peoples had different ethnic bloodlines, both from the Greeks and from each other, they had different customs, and they had different gods, but they all spoke gibberish, and in that respect were all alike. The Greek emphasis on language is somewhat unusual: as Edith Hall says, 'No other ancient people privileged language to such an extent [as the Greeks] in defining its own ethnicity' (Hall 1989, 5; although see also Bresciani 1990, 245, for an illustration of the importance of language to the Egyptians). This was partly because, in matters of religion and custom, the Greeks, rather like the Persians, tended to be flexible about borrowing from other peoples (Coleman 1997, 185), and the boundaries between them and other peoples were correspondingly blurred in that respect. Language was one of the few things which they felt really marked themselves out as different. Barbarians, in essence, are people who talk differently from Greeks, in a way that invites contempt and ridicule. It is this, more than their different ethnicity or customs, that really distinguishes them as 'barbarians' in the original Greek formulation of the concept. Of course, barbaric peoples were able to communicate within their own language groups, and therefore perhaps should not have been lumped together under a common identity on this basis. There is also evidence that the Hellenes themselves spoke a number of distinct dialects: linguistically speaking, 'Greek' was 'an abstract concept which subsumed all different varieties, much as a federal government subsumes the component states' (Davies 2002, 167–8). Indeed, the diversity of dialects inherent within Greek linguistic unity perhaps explains why it was so important to them to assert the 'barbaric' identity of all non-Greek speakers, and why the unintelligible language of foreigners became such a popular basis for parodying them in Greek theatre (as well as Hall 1989, see Bacon 1961). In any case, there is no doubt that Greeks themselves had a strong sense of possessing a shared language, and one that was fundamentally different from all barbarian tongues.

The second axis along which the Greek–barbarian distinction operated concerns the personal qualities of each group of people. Herodotus says, for example, that 'the Greek stock from the most ancient times has been distinguished from the barbarians for its cleverness', although he does make this observation in the midst of telling a story about how the Athenians were duped by a simple trick (Herodotus 1987, 59). The Persians, on the other hand, at least by the time of their invasions of Greece, are associated with a love of pleasure: 'Wherever they learn of enjoyments of all sorts, they adopt them for their own practice' (ibid., 97). James Redfield suggests that this reflects a persistent comparison in Herodotus' narrative between 'hard, simple' peoples and 'soft, complex' peoples, with the former always triumphing over the latter in war; this is linked with the notion that their luxurious lifestyle has served to 'soften' the Persians, explaining their defeat at the hands of the 'hard' Greeks (Redfield 2002, 40–3; see also Hall 1989, 126). Plato later adopted a similar story about the weakening of the Persian empire, as their very hardness, and resulting success at conquest, led them into decadence (Briant 2002b, 195).

'Softness', however, is certainly not an intrinsic quality of all barbarians: some, the Thracians and Scythians for example (Hall 1989,

137), are generally acknowledged by the Greeks to be fierce warriors. Nor is it something intrinsic to barbarians, but something that varies depending on one's circumstances and environment: luxury and heat soften a *genos*; privation and cold harden it. Nevertheless, that does not prevent the Greeks from persistently presenting themselves as clever, hardy and courageous, with barbarians, especially the Persians, depicted in opposite terms. The two ideas of cleverness and 'hardness' come together in Aristotle's images of Greeks and barbarians – somewhat later than the Herodotean and Thucydidean idea we have discussed so far – where the Greeks' uniqueness is seen to rest precisely on a combination of these qualities, explained in environmental terms that echoes a long line of Greek thought, stretching back at least to Herodotus:

> The peoples of cold countries generally, and particularly those of Europe, are full of spirit, but deficient in skill and intelligence; and this is why they continue to remain comparatively free, but attain no political development and show no capacity for governing others. The people in Asia are endowed with skill and intelligence, but are deficient in spirit; and this is why they continue to be peoples of subjects and slaves. The Greek stock, intermediate in geographical position, unites the qualities of both sets of peoples. It possesses both spirit and intelligence: the one quality makes it continue free; the other enables it to attain the highest political development, and to show a capacity for governing every other people – if only it could achieve political unity. (Aristotle 1958, 296; see also Coleman 1997, 190–1)

Thanks to geography and climate, then, the Greeks strike a happy medium of being both 'intelligent' and 'spirited', and it is this which not only allows them, unlike Asians, to resist tyranny, but also endows them with a capacity to rule others, unlike Northern Europeans.

Aristotle's image of the Greek–barbarian distinction points towards a third, political, theme, which is reinforced if we consider the timing of the idea's rise to prominence. Herodotus depicts the notion of a common Greek identity as emerging in the context of the Athenian-led struggle against the Persian invasions of Darius and Xerxes. The Greek–barbarian distinction, then, is used to inform the Hellenes exactly what they are fighting for in resisting this invasion, and to rally support from the other cities to the Athenian, or 'Greek', cause. In this context, the defining characteristic of the barbarians is that they are subjects of a tyrant, *turannos*, or slave-master, *despotes*; the

Greeks, by contrast, are free citizens, *polites*. The 'invention', as Hall describes it, of the barbarian was thus a crucial part of an Athenian attempt to create an 'ideology binding together democratic Athens and her empire' (Hall 1989, 154). So pervasive was the link between barbarism and despotism that, even within the Greek *polis*, the adoption of foreign customs and practices came to acquire a clear, and insidious, political meaning. When Thucydides mentions Greek rulers who are plotting to establish a tyrannical grip over their cities, for example, he describes them as adopting 'Median garb', while the signal that someone is planning a coup is 'his flouting of convention and his imitation of the barbarians' (Thucydides 1998, 63). To be a barbarian is either to be a despot or to submit to despotism; either way it is inappropriate for the freedom-loving Greeks.

To sum up thus far: despite the occasional inversion of the distinction, with the use of what is sometimes called 'negative ethnocentrism' to extol foreigners' virtues as an example to Greeks of how they should behave (Hall 1989, 211–23; Coleman 1997, 194–9), to most Greeks in the fifth and fourth centuries BCE, the foreigner was a 'barbarian' who talked incomprehensible gibberish, lacked intelligence and was habitually under the thumb of cruel tyrants, who treated him more like a slave than a free man, perhaps deservedly so. The Greeks were different in every respect: they were lucid, rational and fiercely jealous of their independence. It is easy to see that, in this image of the foreigner, the Athenians had created something that was the reverse of their own self-image as democratic citizens, and had done so in large part because of the pressing need to convince themselves and the inhabitants of other Hellenic cities of the need to stand together against the might of the Persian empire.

We have touched only lightly on Greek ideas about why differences between themselves and barbarians existed, and what implications they thought such patterns of different and shared identities had for the conduct of relations among Greeks, and between Greek and barbarian communities. This is the issue to which I will now turn. The best way to approach it is by considering a conceptual opposition that acquired a very central position in Greek writing from about the fifth century on: the distinction between nature (*phusis*) and custom (*nomos*). I will begin by trying to draw out the implications of one of Herodotus' most famous remarks: that 'custom is king'. Then, I will discuss the gradual shift towards seeing nature as the basis for understanding the differences between Greeks and barbarians, and the proper conduct of their international relations.

'Custom is king'

Before the fifth century BCE, Greek thinkers had made little distinction between nature and custom. Customs, legal ordinances and social conventions were believed to have come from the gods, and were therefore hard to distinguish from natural phenomena, which were also thought to have had a divine origin. This point of view, however, was undermined by two developments. Firstly, during the sixth century BCE, Ionian philosophers (often known as the 'pre-Socratics') had begun to argue that nature consisted of more or less random interactions between material elements such as fire, water, earth and air. It was thus becoming increasingly plausible to posit a distinction between the material world of nature and the normative world of customs and laws. Secondly, the international political circumstances of the Greek world changed dramatically during the fifth century BCE, most notably with the Persian invasions. New contacts between Greeks and barbarians forced the former to ask whether their own customs, which differed so much from those of other peoples, could indeed be seen as part of a god-given natural order. As W. K. C. Guthrie puts it, the encounter with the barbarians made it 'increasingly obvious that customs and standards of behaviour which had earlier been accepted as absolute and universal, and of divine institution, were in fact local and relative' (Guthrie 1969, 16). Later, the trauma of the Peloponnesian War reinforced this point of view because it led many Greeks to the dismal conclusion that even the customs, laws and conventions traditionally shared among the Greek cities could not be divinely sanctioned, since they seemed to have little efficacy of their own to restrain people from committing terrible and unethical acts on behalf of their own particular city.

The implications of the Persian wars for Greek thinking about justice are of course most powerfully illustrated by Herodotus, who realized that these variations in custom reflected the fact that barbarians had quite different ideas about justice from those held by the Greeks, and that it was hard to find unobjectionable grounds for treating one as right and the other as wrong. He recounts, for example, how Darius, the Persian king,

> called together some of the Greeks who were in attendance on him and asked them what they would take to eat their dead fathers. They said that no price in the world would make them do so. After that Darius summoned those of the Indians . . . who do eat their parents,

and ... asked them what price would make them burn their dead fathers with fire [a customary Greek practice]. They shouted aloud, 'Don't mention such horrors!' These are matters of settled custom, and I think Pindar is right when he says, 'Custom is king of all.' (Herodotus 1987, 228)

With this new awareness of the extent to which laws and customs differed from one place to another, many philosophers began to argue that 'there is no natural standard of justice at all' (Plato 1997, 1547). Probably the most famous exponent of this position was Protagoras, a teacher of philosophy who, perhaps not coincidentally, also worked on the drafting of constitutions for new Athenian colonies. Protagoras' central claim was that 'the most unjust person ever reared in a human society under law ... [is] a paragon of justice compared with people lacking education and law courts' (ibid., 761), meaning that anyone who has the benefit of living in a society with its own laws and customs – even, presumably, a barbarian one – will inevitably be more just than people who live simply according to the dictates of their natural conscience. Thus, according to Protagoras' most famous statement, 'man is the measure of all things'; or, to put it another way, 'the requirements of morality ... are embodied in the laws (*nomoi*) of political communities' (Nill 1985, 7).

Sophist conceptions of nature

But this point of view raised another question, which assumed increasing importance during the Peloponnesian War: precisely how were customs and laws to be enforced, if they depended on men rather than the gods? In fact, Herodotus' quotation of Pindar to the effect that 'custom is king' is suspiciously brief, and the full quotation suggests a rather different meaning: 'Custom, king of all things mortal and immortal, leads the way, *justifying the most violent course by the hand of superiority*' (in Herodotus 1987, 228n.; emphasis added). Several philosophers – most notably the Sophists Gorgias and Callicles – argued that behind the fabric of custom lay a natural principle after all: that the strong always dominate the weak, and are justified in so doing because, 'both among the animals and in whole cities and races of men, [nature] shows that this is what justice has been decided to be: that the superior rule the inferior' (Plato 1997, 828). We can also find a direct counter-point to Herodotus' account of the Persian wars in Thucydides' history of the Peloponnesian War. In the most famous example Thucydides gives, the Athenians brusquely warn the delegates from the much weaker city of Melos that 'of men we know, that by a law of their nature wherever they can rule they will' (Thucydides 1900, 2.173), and elsewhere they tell their Spartan opponents that 'the world has ever held that the weaker must be kept down by the stronger' (ibid., 1.53). Customs, then, were merely a reflection of the interests of whoever happened to be in power at the time; their justification depended on the natural principle that the strong rule the weak.

Looked at more closely, however, Thucydides' history reveals that many Greeks were uncomfortable with Gorgias' and Callicles' proposal that this 'law of nature' represented a principle of *justice*. In the debate with the Melians, the Athenians' position is based not on the claim that it is just for the strong to rule the weak, but on the quite different assertion that justice is irrelevant to the Melians' situation because it 'only enters where there is equal power to enforce it' (Thucydides 1900, 2.169). Similarly, in the other example mentioned above, the Athenians follow up their assertion that 'the weaker must be kept down by the stronger' by asking the Spartans whether justice by itself could ever exercise a constraint on people strong enough to get their own way by force (ibid., 1.53). This suggests that the Greeks typically saw the natural principle of rule by the strong as having more to do with *expediency* than justice. Its importance in Thucydides' history was an indication of how much Greek ideas about ethics were in crisis during the Peloponnesian War, as people were forced into desperate actions on behalf of their own city that violated traditional conventions (see Bedford and Workman 2001). Thucydides perceived that, without a conception of nature operating behind it, custom alone was an extremely fragile basis on which to base appeals to justice; but what else did nature teach, other than the frankly *un*ethical principle that 'the strong do what they can, the weak do what they must'?

Nature, justice and relations with barbarians

With the Athenian project of uniting the Hellenic world behind them in tatters, Plato produced a different argument: that the problems confronting the Greek cities were largely the result of the fact that 'the way things are at present . . . seems to be against nature' (Plato 1997, 1084). In his early works, he even went so far as to propose that force should be used to make people do things in accordance with natural justice that were 'contrary to what has been written down and ancestral custom' (ibid., 340). For most Greek philosophers of the fifth century BCE, nature was also the source of the differences between Greeks and barbarians. According to Plato, the Greeks ought to see each other as 'natural friends' and stop fighting amongst themselves, but they should regard non-Greeks as 'natural enemies' and 'treat the barbarians the way Greeks currently treat each other' by waging war against them (ibid., 1098). His pupil Aristotle took this line of argument further, proposing that Greeks were 'naturally free' but barbarians were 'naturally slaves' (Aristotle 1958, 16).

Greeks as natural friends

Plato's key move was to argue that 'it is God who is pre-eminently the measure of all things, much more so than any man' (Plato 1997, 1403). A great deal is packed into this one proposition. Firstly, it was obviously a direct rejoinder to Protagoras, indicating that one could not look to man-made customs, laws and conventions as the ultimate source of ethical principles. On the contrary, nature was held up as the appropriate place to look for justice: according to Plato, the standards inherent in nature should be used to assess the customs and laws of particular cities, and to imagine how the ideal *polis* ought to be constituted. Secondly, by saying that it is *God* who is the measure of all things, Plato made it clear that his understanding of nature was primarily deistic, rather than materialistic like that of Gorgias or Callicles. This approach saved him from having to equate natural justice with the principle that the strong dominate the weak because of their superiority in power. His conception of nature was still hierarchical, but it was based on the idea of the soul (*psyche*), and hence the proposition that 'to produce justice is to establish the parts of the soul in a natural relation of control, one by another' (ibid., 1076).

Plato conceptualized the soul in terms of an image of 'the natural union of a team of winged horses and their charioteer' (Plato 1997, 524). The horses represent different kinds of feeling and passion: one is 'a lover of honour with modesty and self-control', while the other is a 'companion to wild boasts and indecency' (ibid., 531). The charioteer, who has the difficult task of controlling these very different horses, is the intellect: 'the soul's steersman' (ibid., 525). This explains what Plato meant when he said that justice rests on a 'natural relation of control' in the soul. The just man's intellect controls his feelings and passions and directs them towards a rational goal, in the same way that a charioteer controls and steers his horses. Moreover, to determine what counts as a rational goal, it is only the intellect that can properly grasp the 'intelligible but not visible' Forms of which perceptible objects are approximate representations (ibid., 1128). Although these Forms are invisible, and exist in a perfect and unchanging world of their own, Plato regarded them as truly natural; he saw tangible material objects, on the other hand, merely as artificial and mutable copies of the Forms. In Plato's hands, the concept of nature therefore came to refer to something unchanging and non-material, which can be known only by the intellect and not by the senses. Among other things, this implied a contrast between the perfect, immutable Form of natural justice and actually existing customs that are man-made and constantly subject to change over time and from one place to another.

One political conclusion that Plato drew from his conception of the tripartite soul was its extension to the idea that there are three different types of men; some are naturally inclined towards philosophy, some towards honour and some towards profit (Plato 1997, 1189). It is only the philosophical man who is capable of 'studying the things that are' – that is to say, of understanding the rationally intelligible but invisible Forms that embody the real nature of things – and hence of working out laws that would conform to the perfect, natural Form of justice (ibid., 1190). Therefore, Plato contended that neither individual cities nor the human race as a whole would enjoy justice, 'Until philosophers rule as kings or those who are now called kings and leading men genuinely and adequately philosophize' (ibid., 1100). It is natural for the superior to rule the inferior, in other words, but this proposition is now understood in terms more of intellectual or philosophical superiority than physical strength or power. Although it rested on a theological conception of nature, this was by no means a simple throwback to the earlier belief in a divine order endorsing existing customs. As I have noted, Plato was quite prepared to contemplate the possibility that people should be forced to do things contrary to their ancestral customs in accordance with natural justice, although he moderated this position in his later works, and accepted that in practice custom might provide 'a second legal standard . . . not the ideal standard, but the next to it' (ibid., 1502).

By relying on a conception of nature that stressed the essential and unchanging qualities of the natural Form of justice, and consequently undermined the standing of the ancestral customs which differed from one place to another, Plato's theory of justice has the appearance of being universally applicable. Every city, indeed every kind of government or rule, ought to be organized in accordance with the same principles, so as to be consistent with the natural Form of justice.

However, Plato not only discriminated between different kinds of Greeks, namely philosophical, honour-loving and profit-loving ones, but also between Greeks and barbarians. He believed that the small Greek *polis* was the appropriate venue within which a man could hope to live a just life, and his conception of the ideal city was certainly *not* a vision of a wider community embracing all Greeks, still less Greeks and barbarians. Referring directly to the Persian wars, for example, Plato praised Athens and Sparta for their success in avoiding both slavery and what he saw as the equally horrible fate of 'a complete mixture of the races – Greek with Greek, Greek with barbarian, and barbarian with Greek' (Plato 1997, 1382). More significantly, Plato regarded barbarians as 'natural enemies' of the Greeks, while the Greeks were 'natural friends' to each other (ibid., 1097). This was a crucial proposal at the time, since Plato was anxious to address the political crisis of the 'civil wars' between Athens and Sparta. By asserting the naturalness of friendship between Greeks, he was in effect saying that the ideal *polis* would not engage in war with other Greek cities; the Peloponnesian wars were unnatural since they violated the friendship that each Greek ought to feel towards another, and they were consequently unjust. Moreover, by depicting Greeks and barbarians as natural enemies he offered an alternative outlet for the military activities of the just city. In effect, he was suggesting that the rival Greek cities should forget their internal disagreements and focus instead on the common project of fighting the barbarians.

From the point of view of international politics this is clearly an extremely important line of argument, but unfortunately the only reason Plato gave to explain the distinction between natural friends and natural enemies was that to be good for a Greek meant to 'consider Greece as their own and share the religion of other Greeks' (Plato 1997, 1097–8). We have seen this at work in the Greek idea of the barbarian, but it is awkward for Plato to the extent that, in its appeal to a sense of 'shared religion', it appears to be an invocation of the similarity of Greek customs; however, Plato was using it to claim that friendship between Greeks was *natural*, and the same for their emnity with barbarians. We find here, and not for the last time, a degree of overlap between the concepts of nature and custom, arising precisely at the point where relations with barbarians come under scrutiny: shared customs – i.e., similar religious practices – are used as evidence of the naturalness of friendly association between Greek peoples; by the same token, differences in custom become the basis for 'natural' enmity between Greek and barbarian peoples. Plato did not develop this argument in great detail, but we will find it more thoroughly worked out if we turn to Aristotle's work, albeit not in a way that lends it much greater coherence. Here, it is used to defend the contention that barbarians are naturally slaves while Greeks are naturally free, and therefore that despotism – which literally means ruling others as if one was a slave-master (*despotes*) – was an unjust institution in the Greek *polis* but was perfectly justified when applied to barbarians.

Barbarians as natural slaves

Aristotle retained Plato's belief that nature did not consist simply of random interactions between material elements, but that it was an order with a rationally intelligible purpose or *telos*. He also continued to argue that nature was hierarchical, describing this as a principle 'of the whole constitution of nature' because, 'where there is a compound, constituted of more than one part but forming one common entity . . . a ruling element and a ruled can always be traced' (Aristotle 1958, 12). The crucial difference between Aristotle's and Plato's conceptions of nature, however, concerns the theory of the Forms. Plato, as we have seen, made a radical distinction between the unchanging Formal realm of nature discernible only through reason and the changeable world of material things open to the senses. Aristotle, on the other hand, contended that 'forms . . . are conceptually, but not factually, detachable from the material in which they occur' (Aristotle 1957, 1.127). Matter and form, in other words, are analytically separable from one another, but there is no distinct world of Forms as Plato had supposed.

As we have seen, Plato's theory of the Forms was consistent with the idea that nature was eternal and unchanging. By locating matter and form together in visible things, however, Aristotle was deliberately making central to his understanding of nature the fact that everything experiences change. Indeed, he used this idea to provide a definition of the concept of *phusis*, proposing that 'nature is the principle and cause of motion and rest to those things in which she inheres primarily'; 'anything', he went on, 'that has in itself such a principle . . . may be said to "possess a nature" of its own inherently' (Aristotle 1957, 1.109). The potential that each natural thing has to change into something else, according to Aristotle, is determined by its own particular *telos*, the end towards which it is constantly striving. Its *telos*, in turn, depends on the particular form it contains and shares with other members of its species. Thus, 'by nature', in the sense of the general order of the universe that imparts a potential for change to all entities, everything 'possesses a nature of its own', in the sense of its own specific function or purpose. The crucial question, then, is how we can know the specific nature that each thing possesses, and hence understand the changes that it will undergo as it develops towards its *telos*. Here, because of his belief in the *factual* inseparability of matter and form, Aristotle committed himself to the method of studying the appearances of things in order to deduce an understanding of their true natures: 'the things most obvious and immediately cognizable by us are concrete and particular, rather than abstract and general; whereas elements and principles are only accessible to us afterwards, as derived from the concrete data when we have analysed them' (ibid., 1.11). Unlike Plato, who thought that knowledge of the Forms could not be achieved through the senses at all, Aristotle's mode of enquiry begins with empirical observation of the way things are in the world, from which the forms shared by certain species of things are to be deduced by examining their tendencies to develop into qualitatively different kinds of entity.

For ethics and politics, the central issue concerns the nature and *telos* that humans possess: what is the specific function that man has been designed by nature to fulfil? Despite their contrasting methods, Aristotle agreed with Plato that reason is the defining attribute of human nature, in contrast with the natures of animals or plants, and that the function of man is therefore 'the active exercise of the soul's faculties in conformity with rational principle' (Aristotle 1968, 33). He developed this general idea in a number of ways, noting, for example, that by virtue of reason humans possess 'a perception of good and evil, of the just and unjust', and when this is added to the fact that individual human beings are not capable of survival when they live in isolation from others, it suggests that there is by nature 'an immanent impulse' in people to associate with others in a *polis* (Aristotle 1958, 6–7). He also commented that friendship 'between members of the same species' is a 'natural instinct' that is 'especially strong in the human race', supporting this claim with an observation that seems to take in the whole of humanity, even extending beyond Plato's 'natural friends' the Greeks: 'when travelling abroad one can observe that a natural affinity and friendship exist between man and man universally' (Aristotle 1968, 453).

But at the same time Aristotle maintained that there was a natural difference between Greeks and barbarians so significant that the latter were 'naturally slaves' while the former were 'naturally free' (Aristotle 1958, 16). His justification of the naturalness of slavery begins with a rehearsal of the broadly Platonic doctrine that 'it is

clearly natural and beneficial to the body that it should be ruled by
the soul, and again it is natural and beneficial to the affective part of
the soul that it should be ruled by the mind and the rational part'
(ibid., 13). Again like Plato, Aristotle then extended this to relations
between people on the grounds that 'What holds good in man's inner
life also holds good outside it' (ibid.). Having demonstrated that the
existence of a ruling element and a ruled is, by nature, a 'general
principle' that must 'hold good of all human beings generally', he
concluded that 'all men who differ from others as much as the body
differs from the soul, or an animal from a man (and this is the case
with all whose function is bodily service, and who produce their best
when they supply such service) – all such are by nature slaves' (ibid.).
As Aristotle recognized, he was in effect suggesting that barbarians
are not fully human, since a natural slave only has the ability to
participate 'in reason to the extent of apprehending it in another,
though destitute of it himself' (ibid.).

To make this argument hold, we need to be told why barbarians
differ from Greeks as much as an animal does from a man, in the
sense that, while Greeks have the truly human function of acting in
conformity with reason, barbarians merely have the lesser function
of 'bodily service'. Although more fully developed than Plato's
account of the enmity between Greeks and barbarians, Aristotle's
explanation of this point is still not systematically worked out, which
rather suggests that the assumption that barbarians were destitute
of reason was so widely shared among his contemporaries, perhaps
because of their perceived incapacity to talk a proper language, that
he felt little need to labour the point. In his discussion of natural slavery at the beginning of the *Politics*, he relies entirely on the observation that there is 'no naturally ruling element' among barbarian
peoples because they make no proper distinction between women and
slaves; since they have no natural rulers among themselves, they are
all fit to be ruled, indeed mastered despotically, by non-barbarians:
i.e., Greeks (Aristotle 1958, 3). It might be noted that even this slender
support for the idea of natural slavery is rendered questionable
moments later, when he observes that barbarians *are* in fact ruled
by kings, like early Greeks and even the gods (ibid., 4), but the main
point is that a barbarian custom – the way they treat women – is
used by Aristotle here as evidence about the nature barbarians possess, and hence to support the claim that their function is merely
'bodily service' rather than living in accordance with reason. This
is consistent with Aristotle's empirical method of enquiry, as outlined
above, but it obviously blurs the line between nature and custom.

One could easily dismiss Aristotle's whole line of argument as simply absurd, or as an ideological rationalization of a logically indefensible practice, but I think that would be a mistake (on this issue, see Schofield 1990). The point we should focus on here is not whether or not Aristotle's thesis is acceptable in terms of how *we* think about slavery, but rather how he is able to use the concepts of nature and custom – as understood by Aristotle and his contemporaries – to defend the proposition that barbarians are destitute of reason and hence natural slaves. I want to highlight two particular features of Aristotle's and Plato's treatment of natural justice in this respect. The first is the difficulty both have in maintaining any kind of coherent distinction between nature and custom when considering the Form or nature of human beings, especially when contemplating the differences between Greeks and non-Greeks. In Aristotle's work, where this argument is made more explicitly, it seems to follow as a consequence of his method: by committing himself to the study of empirically observable phenomena – the appearances of things – he is forced to analyse two different kinds of concrete data with regard to human nature. On the one hand, he makes observations about how human beings in general differ from plants and animals, which leads to his claim that reason is a quintessentially human attribute; on the other, he uses evidence of how Europeans, Asians and Greeks differ in their treatment of women, their institutionalized forms of rulership and the degree of spirit and intelligence they display in their everyday lives and relations with one another. The latter line of argument blurs the boundary between custom and nature, in the sense that (as with Plato) variations in custom – how women are treated, for example – are used as evidence that different peoples have different natures.

The second point concerns Aristotle's inference that differences in the customs of Greeks and barbarians are evidence of the *inferiority* of the latter. One of the novelties in Aristotle's account, compared with Plato's, is that the former justifies Greek mastery of the barbarians, whereas Plato had only suggested the naturalness of separating different peoples into their own political communities, between which there would be a condition of enmity but not necessarily one of justifiable despotism. Plato, in fact, can be read as suggesting that Greeks should have as little to do with barbarians as possible. This suggests that important changes in how Greeks viewed the status of barbarians took place between the fifth and fourth centuries BCE. For Herodotus, they were simply people who happened to live in a different way from the Greeks, although many of his contemporaries did adopt a much more negative view of barbarian servility, in order to stress the contrasting freedoms of the Greeks. By Plato's time, these differences were coming to be seen as a reason for hostility between Greeks and barbarians, perhaps in order to encourage Greeks to be more benevolent towards one another. For Aristotle, however, barbarians are inferior because they live according to alien customs that supposedly reveal them to have a nature and a *telos* that is in some respects lower than that of proper human beings (as defined in terms of the capacity for reason). The claim about the inferiority of barbarians is crucial for Aristotle, because it is part of his argument that Greeks are fully human, naturally free, and hence should not be governed despotically themselves. By treating barbarians disparagingly, in other words, Aristotle is able not just to say that Greeks ought to be good to one another, but to extol the qualities of the 'Greek stock' in general, and so to provide a justification for their freedom and equality as citizens in the *polis*.

A final point that is worth mentioning is that Aristotle's concept of natural slavery implies that barbarians' inferior status cannot change, since it is a reflection of the *telos* that they have by nature. However, if its source is merely different customs, why could barbarians not be introduced to new customs that would allow them to participate in institutionalized forms of association similar to the Greek *polis*? In its appeal to factors such as the coldness of the European climate, and the intermediate geographical location of the Greeks between Europe and Asia, Aristotle's argument echoes Herodotus' explanation of differences in custom by reference to physical phenomena. But Aristotle uses these phenomena, and their reflection in the different customs peoples have, as evidence of intrinsic *natural* qualities in the peoples themselves, rather than as an explanation for divergences in custom alone. Of course, Herodotus did not need to extend his analysis of the effects of climate to peoples' essential natures, even had he recognized that they possessed such a thing, because he had already handed custom a leading role in defining ethical behaviour and proper relations between Greeks and barbarians: custom is king of all things. Aristotle, on the other hand, was committed to the Platonic belief that nature was at the root of justice, and was therefore forced to extend the argument beyond changes in custom to embrace barbarians' ultimate purpose in life. Might the intrinsic nature of barbarians change, then, if they were simply to live in a different part of the world? Is the Asian characteristic of being 'deficient in spirit' simply the result of living in a hot country? Herodotus, having stopped short of attributing different natures to different peoples, did not have to answer these questions. Aristotle's theory of natural slavery poses them, but gives no satisfactory answer. As we will see in the next chapter, they were given a fuller consideration by many Stoic philosophers and Roman thinkers.

Conclusion

The word that the Greeks used to describe foreigners, *barbaros*, has obviously enjoyed a long history. Like so many other terms of Greek political discourse, most obviously the *polis* itself, it has become part of the modern political vocabulary. That should not, however, lead us to suppose that Greeks thought of *barbaroi* in exactly the same way that later scholars might conceptualize 'barbarians'. The importance that the Greeks attached to the purported linguistic inferiority of the barbarian, for example, indicates that some aspects of identity were more important to Greeks than they were to become for later scholars, while others were less so. The Greeks laid much less stress on the barbarians' incapacity for social organization and coordination, a central theme in nineteenth-century accounts of barbaric peoples, while nineteenth-century lawyers would have been unlikely to exclude a people from the 'family of civilized nations' merely on the grounds that they spoke 'gibberish'.

Moreover, as regards how Greeks and barbarians should relate to one another, Greek teleological ideas about nature helped to shape a distinctive way of thinking about the role of barbarians as, in Aristotle's formulation, 'natural slaves', fit only to be ruled despotically. This connected closely with the general pattern of Greek thinking about the identity of foreigners, which used an account of the servility of barbarians and their tendency to live under autocratic rulers to sharpen a contrast with the freedom-loving and democratic Greeks, modelled in the self-image of the Athenians. Not all Greeks were committed to this point of view, and, as I have indicated, it had an especial importance to the project of justifying Athenian imperialism (which was, it might be said, of a significantly different character from the Persian imperialism which Athens was urging its fellow *Hellenes* to resist). Nevertheless, this idea of the barbarian, and its connection with the ideas of custom and nature, which played so important a role in explaining the origins and assessing the significance of differences between Greeks and barbarians, does provide a useful framework within which to understand the specific arguments constructed by historians such as Herodotus and Thucydides or philosophers such as Plato and Aristotle.

Further reading

The collection of essays on Thucydides in Gustafson 2000 is a good introduction to both orthodox and critical scholarship on ancient ways of thinking about international politics. To get a real sense of Greek international political thought, though, it is probably better to begin with Herodotus: David Grene's is a very readable translation, which conveys an excellent sense of Greek attitudes towards the diversity of different communities in the ancient world (Herodotus 1987), and Thomas 2000 is an excellent commentary on Herodotus' work in this respect. More generally, Hall 1989 is a seminal analysis of the Greek concept of the barbarian, with Harrison 2002 a good more recent reading on the same topic. Guthrie 1969 is still a useful introduction to Greek philosophy from the period, with Nussbaum 2001 a seminal recent study; Collingwood 1945 and Lloyd 1979 are both helpful studies of Greek scientific conceptions of nature. Thucydides 1998 is still a reasonable starting-point for understanding international relations within the Greek world, but Bederman 2001 is a valuable addition, providing a much more developed sense of the legal structure of order among the Greek city-states. There is a less developed literature on non-Greek theories and practices of international relations. Nevertheless, Briant 2002a is a seminal treatment of Persian imperialism, and Buzan and Little 2000, Alcock et al. 2001 and Liverani 2001 are useful surveys of a range of ancient international relations; Briant and Alcock are especially valuable for their insights into the wider intellectual environment of the period.

2

World-City, Empire and Natural Law

The previous chapter ended with a brief sketch of Aristotle's argument that barbarians were 'natural slaves'. Even as he was developing this position, however, a new attitude towards foreigners was beginning to gain popularity among Greeks, one that undermined the concept of the 'barbarian' on which Aristotle's theory rested. In contrast with the sharp distinction between *Hellenes* and *barbaroi*, the centrepiece of this new philosophy was that both were 'citizens of the world' (*cosmopolites*). As Plutarch later summarized it, the new belief was that 'our household arrangements should not be based on cities or parishes, each one marked out by its own legal system, but we should regard all men as our fellow-citizens and local residents, and there should be one way of life and order' (cited in Long and Sedley 1987, 429). This more inclusive, less dismissive attitude towards foreigners was not entirely without precedent in the ancient world. We have seen already that some imperial rulers, such as the founder of the Persian empire, Cyrus the Great, had been relatively tolerant in their attitude towards the various customs and religious practices of the peoples they had conquered, and had even made a virtue out of the cultural variety of their empire, so long as everyone obediently paid tribute to the Great King. But the toleration of difference or celebration of variety, with or without the payment of tribute, is very different from a belief that everyone in the world shares a single identity as world-citizens. In that regard, cosmopolitanism represented a significantly new attitude towards foreigners, and thus a new way of thinking about the nature of communities and their relations with one another.

Given the dominant position of realism within twentieth-century thought, the idea of a *cosmopolis* might seem to us now like an idealistic fantasy, and it is of course perfectly possible to argue that no such association actually existed in the ancient world. It was not, however, a complete pipe dream, and there was one feature of international politics in the ancient world which made it appear a genuine possibility. Although maybe not entirely seriously, the Roman poet Ovid punningly declared that Rome was 'at once a city (*urbis*) and a world (*orbis*)', and many of his contemporaries took their empire to be at least an approximation of the 'world-city' envisioned by the philosophers. In Roman ideas about the legal framework holding their empire together and the process through which non-Romans could acquire Roman citizenship, one can therefore detect a practical dimension to what otherwise might have looked like a purely hypothetical position. In its practical application, Roman *imperium* exposes significant problems with, or departures from, the ideal of a 'world-city' predicated on universal fellowship and equality which is suggested in the quote from Plutarch cited earlier. To become a member of this world-city, one had to become a Roman: that is to say, one had to acquire a specific identity primarily defined in terms of Roman religious and customary practices, as well as the Latin language and Roman legal codes. And, despite the cosmopolitan attitude of some Roman thinkers, against the identity of the Romans, the old concept of the barbarian was maintained, defining those people who were non-citizens of Rome, and thus in a sense cut off from Roman/world-citizenship and the rights that it conferred. The concepts of *Romanitas* and *humanitas* could easily blur into one another, just as the *humanum societas* on which the ideal world-city of the philosophers rests sometimes fits rather uncomfortably into the straitjacket of the Roman *orbis-urbis*. How the Romans actually built their 'world-city' therefore reveals further important and interesting features concerning ancient ways of thinking about community and its implications for the conduct of international politics, this time within the context of an imperial system, rather than the somewhat more parochial 'city-states' of ancient Greece. I will explore two of these in particular here: the institution of the Roman citizenship, and the Roman idea of a code of natural law, *ius naturale*, and the 'law of nations', *ius gentium*. Juxtaposing these with the continuing hostility that many Romans displayed towards barbarians (*barbari*) will help us to get a proper sense of exactly how 'cosmopolitan' the ancient theory and practice of the *cosmopolis* really was. Finally, to conclude this chapter, and to act as a bridge into the next chapter, I will look briefly at the impact of another universalistic world-view – early Christianity – upon the Roman empire, examining the assimilation of ideas about Christian and Roman identity and making a preliminary assessment of the degree to which the rise of Christianity and the division of the Roman empire, together with the crisis that Rome experienced in the West, mark a significant discontinuity in the history of international political thought.

Before examining the idea of world-citizenship, it is pertinent to mention the relative neglect that Rome has suffered in the history of international political thought, considering the popular view of Roman imperialism as a major source of elements of Western political theory and practice. Because international relations theorists are most often interested in finding historical examples that help them to understand the dynamics of systems of independent sovereign states, they have typically paid much more attention to the international politics of the Greek 'city-states' than the international order constructed under the aegis of Roman imperialism (Buzan and Little 2000 is a notable exception). This is reflected in the history of international political thought by the focus on Thucydides, which I discussed in the previous chapter, who is seen as *the* historian of the Greek city-states; indeed, his neglect of the role of the Persian empire in the Peloponnesian War is notorious (see Grant 1995). To their considerable credit, some historians (Boucher 1998; Pangle and Ahrensdorf 1999) have begun to correct this by including Ciceronian Stoicism in their analysis, but the vast majority seldom look beyond the world of the *polis* when trying to describe ancient international political thought (see, for example, Williams 1992).

Barbarian or citizen of the world?

After generations fending off the threat posed by the Persian 'barbarian', in the mid- to late fourth century BCE, under the leadership or *hegemony* of Alexander the Great – a Macedonian, and therefore of somewhat dubious Hellenic pedigree himself – the Greeks for the first time managed to attain for themselves a position of imperial power over large numbers of Asian peoples. Once the pressure to stigmatize the barbarian in order to stimulate Hellenic unity was reduced, once the question was no longer how to resist the barbarian but how to rule him, what then for the Greek image of the foreigner? Aristotle lived during this later period, when the Greeks, not the Persians, were the conquerors of Asia. He served as tutor to Alexander the Great, and many have interpreted his account of the Greek stock as having 'a capacity for governing every other people' as a reflection of this imperial Hellenistic moment. In this context, too, many commentators have read Aristotle's belief that barbarians are so destitute of reason as to be 'natural slaves', fit only to be ruled despotically, as a kind of blueprint for Alexandrine empire.

Persian and Hellenic empire

But the pupil did not do as he was told. As Plutarch much later remarked: 'Alexander did not do as Aristotle advised – play the part of a leader to the Greeks and of a master to the barbarians, care for the former as friends and kinsmen, and treat the latter as beasts or plants . . . he behaved alike to all' (cited in Coleman 1997, 193). As one might expect, this strategy was not tremendously popular with Alexander's own followers. The historian Arrian reports that his Greek troops complained: 'you have made Persians your kinsmen' (Arrian 1933, 2.239). Alexander's reply – 'all of you I regard as my kinsmen' – revealed the extent of his departure from earlier Greek ways of thinking about barbarians, and, as Arrian says, he then prayed for 'harmony and fellowship in the empire between Macedonians and Persians' (ibid., 2.239–41).

To a certain extent, in his benevolent treatment of the conquered Persians Alexander was merely following the established way of being a 'Great King' in the Persian empire. As we have seen, in building his empire, Cyrus had boasted of his respect for the religion, laws and customs of the peoples he conquered, and this was an integral part of his strategy for maintaining his rule over a vast empire with a relatively small group of Persian soldiery. Alexander pursued exactly the same approach, and for virtually identical reasons: 'The picture of Alexander as a restorer of traditions, one who is greeted as a liberator, recurs at every stage' (Briant 2002a, 853). That, at least, is the picture presented by the Greeks themselves, although in some respects it is rather puzzling, given the fact that there would have been no traditions to 'restore' if the Persian Great Kings had themselves generally pursued a policy of respecting the customs of their subject cities. The conventional story of Alexander's 'Babylonization' probably conceals a much more convoluted reality of old loyalties within the Persian empire breaking down, and allegiances shifting to Alexander when he seemed to be in the ascendant. In this regard, the suddenness of Alexander's triumph partly reflects the inherent vulnerability of the Great King's position: 'The Persians had never attempted to attack the recognized traditions of their subjects: the multiethnic Empire remained multicultural, as is shown, for example, by its extraordinary linguistic diversity. . . . The unity of the Empire was thus accomplished by means of the uncontested, but personal, supremacy of the Great King' (ibid., 868). To bring down the empire, then, all Alexander had to do was capture or kill Darius, the Great King. At a stroke, Darius' death dissolved the political bonds of the empire. But, of course, Alexander's own early death, in 323 BCE, meant that the equally fragile personal bonds holding together his own empire were as quickly sundered, leading to its division into several more or less independent kingdoms, most of which were eventually to come under the domination of the new power rising in the Mediterranean: Rome.

Lurking behind the Alexandrine vision of empire, however, there was a new way of thinking about foreigners which distinguished itself from earlier beliefs, whether the negative Athenian conception of the gabbling, effete and servile barbarian, or the more *laissez-faire* attitude of the Persians towards the religions and customs of their subject peoples. Even if Alexander's statement – 'all of you I regard as my kinsmen' – was just a piece of rhetoric invented by Arrian, it is still significant for the way it displays a different perception of foreigners which had clearly become important in the ancient world, at once both more inclusive than the Persian view and less exclusive than the earlier Greek view. It reflects a belief which began to gain ground in Greek philosophy during the fourth century BCE that, to repeat Plutarch's commentary: 'we should regard all men as our fellow-citizens and local residents, and there should be one way of life and order.' Rather than there being lots of cities, there was just one 'world-city' or *cosmopolis*, and rather than being divided into Greeks and barbarians, all peoples were its 'world-citizens': *cosmopolites*.

The idea of world-citizenship

One of the earliest statements of the idea of a world-city was advanced by the Cynic philosopher Diogenes, who was highly critical of established customs in Greek cities and chose to ridicule them by comparing them with the practices of barbarians. He suggested, for example, that 'there was nothing out of place in taking something out of a temple or in eating the flesh of any animal; nor even anything unholy in tasting human flesh, as was clear from foreign customs' (cited in Schofield 1991, 141). Diogenes liked to describe himself as 'citiless, homeless, without a country' and as a 'citizen of the world' so as to emphasize his rejection of membership in any actually existing Greek *polis*. This is often interpreted as a negative, purely destructive attack on established Greek customs and legal conventions (for a critical discussion of this point of view, see Moles 1996), but Diogenes' criticisms of the traditional *polis* and his contrasting idea of 'world-citizenship' were developed in a more positive way by the Stoics. Although the break-up of the Alexandrine empire into the monarchies of the Hellenistic period forestalled one attempt at building a world-city along these lines, Stoicism proved to be an extremely popular philosophy in Rome, not least because the image of the *cosmopolis* provided a pleasing philosophical rationale for their vast empire.

There were at least two distinct Stoic conceptions of world-citizenship at work in Roman thought. First, many Roman Stoics believed that the good man would be one who used his powers of reason to the point where his 'knowledge and understanding is co-extensive with the complete structure of the Universe', and in this process 'of fitting himself into the Whole, has gone beyond his own body, beyond his family or nation, to become all-inclusive: he is, in a sense, God' (Christensen 1962, 68). This idea of the 'Stoic sage' implies that the universal city would be composed exclusively of the wise, or at the very least of initiates into the teachings of Stoic philosophy. It would be a *cosmopolis* comprised of *cosmopolites* in a very specific sense: namely, world-citizens who had achieved a state of higher consciousness and wisdom that carried them beyond the confining attachment to any one earthly city, and towards a direct personal identification between themselves and nature or the cosmos. This implied a complete disregard for one's actual position in life within the local city, and an almost mystical sense of oneness with the universe that could in principle be achieved by anyone, Roman or barbarian, emperor or slave. The implications of this point of view were used to develop an ethical philosophy that concentrated on disdain for worldly pleasures and an ability to resist unflinchingly the vicissitudes of fortune. It represents a more spiritual kind of community, downgrading the importance of actually existing earthly communities.

Secondly, however, many Stoics used the concept of a *cosmopolis* in a rather more concrete sense, concentrating on the capacity for speech and rational thought as universally shared features of human nature. (This, of course, was not original; elements of the position can certainly be discerned in Aristotle's, and in even earlier Greek, thought.) Rather than emphasize the 'Stoic sage' who had achieved consistency with nature as a whole in his or her own personal way of life, Cicero pointed out that a bond *already* existed between all men based on reason. This led to the less mystical view that 'the world is as it were the common dwelling-place of gods and men, or the city that belongs to both; for they alone have the use of reason and live by justice and law' (Cicero 1933, 273). Since by nature all people were equal and united through the common faculty of reason, merely differing with respect to the various customs or conventions they observed, it made sense then to argue that a single code of natural law (*ius naturale*), identifiable through the common exercise of reason, should regulate relations within the universal human society (*humanum societas*). One by-product of shifting the concept of 'world-citizenship' in this way, from something attained by the wise to something already shared by everyone on the basis of the capacity for reason and speech, was that the moral significance of the bond between 'world-citizens' was diminished, to the point where it became merely one among many human relationships. In Cicero's words, 'there are a great many degrees of closeness or remoteness in human society', and he argued that one could have different kinds of ethical obligations to others accordingly, with one's duties to other world-citizens less important than one's duties towards members of one's own family or local city (Cicero 1956, 57).

Specifically, Cicero took the 'bond of connection' in human society as a whole to imply a basic principle of generosity to strangers on the grounds of a 'common right to all things that Nature has produced for the common use of man', with the important proviso that the institution of private property laid down by 'civil law' (i.e., the law of a particular city or state) be respected (Cicero 1956, 55). However, 'to proceed beyond the universal bond of our common humanity, there is the closer one of belonging to the same people, tribe, and tongue', and he went on to assert that 'it is a still closer relation to be citizens of the same city-state [*civitas*]; for fellow-citizens have much in common – forum, temples, colonnades, streets, statutes, laws, courts, rights of suffrage, to say nothing of social and friendly circles and diverse business relations with many' (ibid., 57). Unlike the genuinely universal attitude described by Plutarch, this betrays a strong attachment on Cicero's part to the customs of his own, local, city, even at the expense of the universal city of human society.

It is hard, in fact, to read Cicero without gaining the impression that he was at least as proud of being Roman as he was of being human. The achievements of the Roman people were, he pointed out, truly remarkable: 'Spaniards had the advantage over them in point of numbers, Gauls in physical strength, Carthaginians in sharpness, Greeks in culture, native Latins and Italians in shrewd common sense; yet Rome conquered them all and acquired her vast empire because in piety, religion and appreciation of the omnipotence of the gods, Rome was a *nonpareil* (cited in Balsdon 1979, 2). Nor was Cicero above using rhetoric about the vile practices and general inferiority of barbarians if it helped him to win a law case (Sherwin-White 1967, 17, 59). But how could a Stoic such as Cicero simultaneously maintain the idea that all men were members of a universal human society because of their connection through reason and speech, while adopting the attitude that the Romans were distinct from and superior to barbarians?

This question is related to another: how clearly did Cicero distinguish between what it meant to be Roman and what it meant to be human? Here, it is interesting to reflect on the meaning of the concept of *humanitas*, which is obviously essential to the idea of a '*humanum societas*' that he used. In his account of the activities of the general Agricola, the historian Tacitus comments that Agricola introduced the British barbarians to numerous aspects of the Roman way of life: 'As a result, the nation which used to reject the Latin language began to aspire to rhetoric; further, the wearing of our dress became a distinction, and the toga came into fashion. . . . The simple natives gave the name of '*humanitas*' to this factor of their slavery' (Tacitus 1920, 207). Sometimes this term is translated as 'culture' (in ibid.), at others as 'civilization' (see Burns 1994, 2). In either case, it is clear that, despite its appeal to *humanitas*, it does not refer to something universal so much as to specifically Roman customs. The line between Roman custom, humanity and natural law was blurred both for 'simple natives' and for a sophisticated world-citizen such as Cicero. The implication is obvious: despite the fine Ciceronian praises of 'reason and speech', these alone were not sufficient either to found a truly substantial 'bond of connection' between the entire human race, or to furnish the principles of the natural law that would provide order in the human society. Although one did not have to become an all-knowing 'Stoic sage' to qualify for world-citizenship, some criteria were nevertheless set for the attainment of this status, and this became part of a project of 'Romanizing' barbarians so as to fit them for the demands of the world-city in which they now found themselves.

The Stoic conception of nature

We will examine Cicero's idea of a code of 'natural law' that binds together all the members of the world-city more closely in a moment.

First, though, it is worth noting that this idea highlights the importance of the conceptualization of nature to the Stoic way of thinking
about community and their attitude towards foreigners. In effect, the
core Stoic argument is that, although custom may divide humanity,
nature unites mankind through the universally shared natural faculties of reason and speech. This idea that nature provides a universal
bond, which may or may not be attenuated by differences in custom
or convention, is not a brand-new Stoic invention. In the fifth century
BCE, for example, a Sophist philosopher called Antiphon had already
observed that:

> The laws of our neighbours we know and revere: the laws of those
> who live afar we neither know nor revere. Thus in this we have been
> made barbarians with regard to one another. For by nature we are all
> in all respects similarly endowed to be barbarian or Greek. One may
> consider those natural facts which are necessary in all men and pro-
> vided for all in virtue of the same faculties – and in these very matters
> none of us is separated off as a barbarian or as a Greek. For we all
> breathe into the air by way of our mouths and noses, we laugh when
> we are happy in our minds and we cry when we are in pain. (cited in
> Hall 1989, 218–19)

This is obviously similar to the Stoic image of a common humanity
founded in nature, and with its sense that it is differences in 'mere'
custom that create an *artificial* distinction between Greeks and barbarians. Antiphon's position was not, however, commonplace among
the Sophists, and it certainly was not one which would have been
endorsed by most philosophers or historians in the fifth century BCE.

Phusis polis *and* cosmos

The Roman Stoic philosopher Cicero admitted that, as the Sceptics
had argued, it was 'foolish' to suppose that 'everything is just which
is found in the customs or laws of nations', but unlike the Sceptics he
then went on to assert that 'Justice is one; it binds all human society
[*humanum societas*], and is based on one Law, which is right reason
applied to command and prohibition. . . . Justice does not exist at all,
if it does not exist in Nature' (Cicero 1959, 343–5). Stoicism, then,
involved a radical downgrading of the traditional ethical significance attached to custom, and a consequent elevation of nature as
the source of all goodness in the world. In this, it corresponded to
Platonic and Aristotelian ideas about the importance of the concept
of *phusis* to the ethical determination of principles of justice. As we

saw, however, Plato and Aristotle had thought that it was natural for people to live in their own city, among people who shared their specific language, customs, religious beliefs, and perhaps also ties of ethnicity.

Stoic cosmopolitanism therefore required a radically new use of the idea of a *polis* to argue 'that the universe is in the proper sense a city, but that those here on earth are not – they are called cities, but are not really. For a city or a people is something morally good, an organization or group of men administered by law which exhibits refinement' (in Schofield 1991, 24). The Stoics retained the positive moral connotations associated with the *polis*, but changed the refer- ent of the concept from established cities such as Athens to the uni- verse as a whole and the entire society of mankind. In what sense, then, did they see the universe as a city? And why was this the only proper use of the concept of a *polis*, in that it was only the universe that qualified as 'something morally good'? To answer these ques- tions, we need to look more closely at the Stoic conception of nature or *phusis*.

Unlike Aristotle, the Stoics combined the Platonic idea that nature has a *telos* with the pre-Socratic idea that nature is unified through the existence of a single all-pervading element. They believed that this element was a mixture of air and fire which they called *pneuma* or 'fiery breath', treating it as 'both a physical component of the world and an agent capable of rational action' (Long 1986, 155). *Pneuma*'s main property as a physical thing was 'tension', another pre-Socratic concept. This meant that it provided the force that made matter cohere so as to form specific objects – all existing things, in other words, are simply 'hunks of matter or regions of space in which a (partial) tensional field obtains' (Christensen 1962, 65) – and, since *pneuma* pervaded the whole universe, its property of tension operated at a general level as well, making 'the cosmos into a single cohesive unit' (Sambursky 1959, 5). Moreover, by claiming that *pneuma* was a rational agent, the Stoics suggested that not only is every existing thing imbued with different parts of the same spirit in a cohesive universe, but also that the changes that all things experience are part of a single movement towards the same cosmic purpose.

In short, while Aristotle highlighted the particular natures or spe- cific forms possessed by individual things, the Stoics regarded nature as a cohesive and unified rational agent acting in and through every- thing. For Aristotle, the main purpose of studying the physical world was to distinguish, classify and understand the natures that different species have, and hence the various functions or essences that they strive to realize, through an analysis of the qualitative changes all things experience. By contrast, for the Stoics, everything was part of the natural order of the cosmos, and the point of philosophical specu-lation was to grasp the cosmic purpose of nature as a whole. Their understanding of ethics was intrinsically bound up with these ideas of the cohesiveness of the universe and the existence of an ultimate cosmic purpose, upon which they based the proposition that there is an identity between the good, nature and the universe; in effect, all of these terms refer to the same things. 'The Stoic ontology assumes only one substance, the whole of Nature; this one substance realizes its corresponding form completely, namely in the gradual unfold-ing of the structure of Fate. . . . Therefore the Universe or Nature is good in the primary Aristotelian sense, and nothing else is good' (Christensen 1962, 64; see also Long 1986, 179). The main thrust of Stoic teachings on ethics, then, was simply that the good man should live 'according to nature'. This helps us to see why the Stoics regarded the universe, rather than earthly 'cities', as the only morally good thing, and hence as the only *polis* in the proper sense of the concept. Since nature and the good were more or less interchangeable terms for the Stoics, and since nature was universal, any concept that denoted moral goodness – like the *polis* – was itself imbued with the quality of universality.

The idea that foreigners should not be thought of as 'barbarians' but rather as fellow 'world-citizens' thus rested on a transformation of the idea of nature which had lain at the root of much Greek thought about the *polis*. The city was still a natural institution, indeed, one might say it was still *the* natural institution within which humans should live. But unlike the Aristotelian belief that it was really only Greeks who were suited by nature to live as free citizens within the *polis*, this capacity was now extended to everyone, on the grounds that *pneuma* was a unifying force running through all people; differences in climate and different kinds of customs and beliefs were incidental in comparison with the strength of the pneu-matic bond that unified everyone within the universal rationality of the cosmos. Differences in custom and language could thus be ren-dered less significant, but, as we saw with Cicero's formulation of the idea of the world-city, that did not deny them altogether, nor did it prevent the persistence of a belief in the special bond that existed between members of a particular city. What transformed this into a workable scheme for international order was the identification of the ideal *cosmopolis* with an existing city-based empire, within which much more narrowly defined institutions of citizenship and natural law provided a resolution of the tension between the universal and particular cities, with each taking on something of the character of the other.

Empire, citizenship, natural law and barbarians

Stoic cosmopolitanism relied on the proposition that everyone should be considered as a 'citizen of the world', and therefore should be governed by a single universal legal code, rather than by the numerous and various laws or customs of their particular cities. To the extent that Rome approximated to this ideal of the world-city, our key questions, then, are how Roman citizenship was extended to non-Romans, how those people who still lacked Roman citizenship were regarded, and what kind of legal code the Romans developed to govern everyone within (and beyond) their world-city. Here, then, I will examine what was involved in the practice of extending the Roman citizenship – a process which began in a small way during the republican era, but which really took off under the principate that Augustus established after his defeat of Mark Antony – the construction of the ideas of 'natural law' and the 'law of nations' as supplements to the Roman 'civil law', and finally the persistence of the idea of the 'barbarian' as a way of describing peoples who had not attained Roman citizenship. First, though, to appreciate the wider international political context within which these concepts were situated, we need to consider exactly what the Roman 'empire' was, and what Romans understood by the crucial concept of '*imperium*'.

The idea of imperium

Although our popular image of Roman imperialism today is perhaps of a tightly controlled empire ruled with the iron fist of Rome's formidable legions, Roman *imperium* did not involve a single, cohesive, unified administrative structure of direct Roman rule over subject peoples. The Romans did create a system of 'provinces', within which Roman governors exercised administrative authority, but this was only one of several different kinds of relationship between Rome and other communities. Some cities within the empire, for example, were granted the status of being 'free', meaning that they did not have to garrison Roman troops or provide tribute, and were able to keep their own civil laws. The usual terms the Romans used to describe kings whom they had conquered, or with whom they signed usually rather one-sided treaties of virtual clientship, were *amici* or *socii* – friends or allies – but seldom subjects.

To be precise, by describing their position as imperial, the Romans were invoking the military term for a commander, *imperator*, and the idea of *imperium* simply meant 'exacting obedience, compelling other peoples to obey orders' (Lintott 1993, 22). The meaning of this term gradually changed, as the office of its holder – the *imperator* – changed:

> *Imperium* . . . has a semantic range running from 'a command', through 'the power (with its attendant religious rights) of a Roman magistrate or general' to 'hegemonic power held over other peoples and places'. It acquired the additional sense of 'territorial empire' only in that period of maximum expansion, a generation before that of Augustus. (Woolf 2001, 313)

Nevertheless, the Romans generally did not want to be involved themselves in the comprehensive, day-to-day administration of 'subject peoples': they preferred to exercise their influence through indigenous rulers where they could. And the price for being part of the empire was that 'the Romans expected their commands to be obeyed, even when they allowed a great deal of *de facto* autonomy and frequently exercised power by indirect means' (Lintott 1993, 41). To understand how this rather fragmented system worked, I want to look more closely at two key issues – citizenship and law – before concluding with some general remarks about Roman attitudes towards barbarians and their practical treatment of the relationship between nature and custom.

The institution of Roman citizenship

The evolution of the institution of citizenship during the process of Roman expansion can be described in terms of three stages. First, initial grants of citizenship were made to those inhabitants of Latium (a region in central Italy to the west of the Appennine mountains) who celebrated common religious festivals with the Romans and shared their language: the Latins (see Salmon 1982, 3–5). The Romans had for some time been part of the military alliance of Latin city-states, establishing their hegemony in this league through war and territorial aggrandisement. In a final settlement agreed in 338 BCE, after several revolts within the league, 'the Romans made the first large breach in the older conception of a city-state by the grant of Roman citizenship to several other Latin city-states', effectively incorporating them into Rome itself (Sherwin-White 1973, 59). However, non-Latin states covered by this settlement or others around the same time were treated differently: they were not granted full citizenship, but only received certain specific rights among those included in citizenship proper. For example, a political community might be recognized as a Roman municipality, and, while remaining administratively distinct from Rome, its inhabitants might have rights to do business with Roman citizens, or to be granted complete citizenship if they chose to move to Rome itself.

In the second stage of the evolution of Roman citizenship, these partial citizens' rights acted as a channel towards the acquisition of full citizenship by Italian peoples with whom, unlike the Latins, the Romans originally had no shared cultural or linguistic affinities. However, the Romans were still careful to grant citizenship to non-Latins only 'after a probationary period during which these peoples were brought under the influence of Romano-Latin discipline and culture' (Sherwin-White 1973, 61). Gradually, the term Latin 'passed from being a geographical and tribal or sub-national concept to the idea of a social and political status or class' (ibid., 114). The so-called Latin Rights were therefore in principle extendable to anyone, and 'became one of the favourite weapons in the store of Rome for the gradual elevation of provincial communities to a parity with herself' (ibid.).

This paved the way for the third stage, which involved grants of Roman citizenship beyond Italy, initially to areas with a considerable degree of Roman or Latin colonization, but increasingly towards peoples who were still regarded by many as barbarians. Such grants did not begin until after the collapse of the republic, and were closely connected with Augustus' efforts to construct a more unified legal system encompassing the empire as a whole. This policy generated new affinities between Rome and the provinces, and sometimes between non-citizens and the emperor himself, who began to be worshipped as a god in certain places. The process was markedly accelerated under the emperor Claudius and his successors. In the imperial period, the key to citizenship, rather than possession of a specifically Latin culture, increasingly became a rather more diffuse idea of 'loyalty to Rome . . . marked in the West and in the Danubian provinces by a process which, though commonly called Romanization, is really self-Romanization; in the hellenized East loyalty takes a less material form, its conspicuous characteristic or badge being devotion to the emperors' (Sherwin-White 1973, 222).

What is most striking about this whole process is that it represents the gradual identification of the Roman city and the Roman world – *urbis* and *orbis* – until they mean, in effect, the same thing. The emperor, in turn, ceased to be regarded merely as a *princeps*, or first citizen, but became the *dominus mundi*, or lord of the world, and the route to Roman citizenship, through acceptance of a process of 'Romanization', in effect became a frequently travelled route to a certain kind of world-citizenship. Interestingly, this attaches relatively little importance to ethnicity in the sense that we would perhaps understand it today, as rooted in a common biological descent:

> Roman ethnicity was unusual in the ancient Mediterranean world in the relative unimportance given to descent. Descent from Romans did confer membership of the Roman people, but citizenship was liberally awarded to former allies, subjects, and even some defeated enemies and ex-slaves. (Woolf 2001, 316)

Thus, 'the fact that Roman ethnicity was thought of largely as a matter of custom, cult, and language had important implications for the recruitment of individuals and communities to the Roman people' (Woolf 2001, 316). To become 'Roman', in other words, required above all a change in behaviour – in customs, religious practices and language – which was perceived as essentially unrelated to the ethnic characteristics of particular peoples. While ethnicity was not totally unimportant to Romans, and while they certainly noted the different physical characteristics of different ethnic groups, such as skin colour, these were not seen as matters of particular *political* significance. Wearing Roman clothing and speaking Latin were much more important as indicators of fitness for membership in the Roman world-city than any physical qualities that might be perceived as part of the 'natures' of different peoples.

Natural law and the law of nations

Access to the status of a citizen had important legal implications. People possessing Roman citizenship were subject to the *ius civile*, the civil law code made by and for Romans. Non-citizens, however, were in a more ambiguous situation. The attempt to bring numerous different peoples into one political order posed a crucial legal question: what code of rules should be applied to dealings between Roman citizens and non-citizens, or between non-citizens from two entirely different communities, but nevertheless living within the empire and often administered by Roman governors and judges? To answer this question, Roman jurists employed a distinction between the single legal code that was believed to govern mankind as a whole (including Roman citizens and non-citizens) and the various legal codes that had been developed within particular cities.

> All peoples with laws and customs apply law which is partly theirs alone and partly shared by all mankind. The law which each people makes for itself is special to its own state. It is called 'state law' (*ius civile*), the law peculiar to that state. But the law which natural reason makes for all mankind is applied the same everywhere. It is called 'the law of nations' (*ius gentium*) because it is common to every nation. (Tribonian 1987, 37)

The key problem here is that the distinction between the Stoic idea of a law of nature (*ius naturale*) and the jurists' notion of a law common to all nations (*ius gentium*) was never made clear. In keeping with Stoic doctrines, it was often asserted that this law was simply the product of right reason. But in practice, the actual way of working out its content was more often claimed to be derived from the universality of custom, and sometimes from the universalization of Roman legal principles. These two sources – natural reason on the one hand, and universal or Roman laws and customs on the other – were seldom properly distinguished.

As an example of the former, Cicero distinguished both the law of nature and the laws of nations from the 'statutes of particular communities', even when these agree on a particular rule 'with one accord' (Cicero 1956, 291); following his philosophical orientation, he saw them as derived from principles of right reason rather than any kind of customary institution, even one that was universal. However, while Roman jurists more generally also regarded natural law as having great importance, when they used the concept it was not to talk of 'the law or reason of God, but of the nature of things on the ground, things as they are, things for which common sense, the facts of life, the essence of business relations, and so on, "naturally" suggest the appropriate legal treatment' (Kelly 1992, 60). The jurist Gaius, for example, was quite happy to treat both 'the law that natural reason establishes' and the laws which are 'followed by all peoples alike' as synonymous (Gaius 1946, 1.3). Although Gaius' comment suggests that the Roman lawyers had done some kind of survey of the various codes of civil law in the empire, and constructed a synthesis of all the features they shared in common, actually they had done nothing of the sort, and showed relatively little interest in other legal systems (Kelly 1992, 62). In fact, the *ius gentium* was 'a body of native Roman rules which were (exceptionally, because in principle Roman law was applicable only to Roman citizens) applied in disputes either between foreigners on Roman territory, or between a Roman and a foreigner' (ibid.; see also Gaius 1946, 2.12–13).

This helps to explain why we find the ambiguity as to whether the *ius gentium* is derived from right reason alone, or from the observation of universally shared customs – a similar quandary to that which we saw earlier in Greek thought. To some extent, the Romans had worked out a code on the basis of what seemed 'natural' – i.e., the product of 'right reasoning' – in relations between people who were not citizens of the same political community. At the same time, however, perhaps as a way of justifying this code, the Roman lawyers typically explained it as if it were the product of a synthesis of everything held in common by different legal systems. Was it, then, natural or conventional? The answer would have to be 'both'. It was simultaneously regarded as something natural, in the sense of being based on reason rather than 'opinion', and as conventional, in the sense that it was supposed to be the embodiment of universally observed customs, or of Roman conventions that seemed universally applicable.

Romans and barbarians

Thanks to this linkage between the natural law and the Roman institution of the *ius gentium*, the spread of the world-city could be seen as following the process of the universalization of a particular, Roman, set of customs. The most important consequence of this concerns the way in which attitudes towards the granting of citizenship gradually shifted from a standard based on cultural homogeneity towards ideas about the social and political requirements to engage in civic life. Throughout the history of Rome there were always 'barbarians', in the sense of people lacking in Roman citizenship or outside the structure of the Roman empire altogether, but the attitude towards them that emerged was not that they were insurmountably different from Romans (as in Plato's idea of 'natural enemies'); neither was it equivalent to Aristotle's theory of their natural inferiority and servility. It would certainly be true to say that most Romans tended to think of barbarians as alien and inferior, but, as the institution of citizenship evolved, barbarism came to be seen as something other than a natural condition; it was simply (using the same kind of premiss as Aristotle himself) a consequence of one's natural or cultural environment, and therefore something that could be changed, given the right kind of stimuli.

Indeed, barbarians not only *could* change, many frequently *did* change, through a social and political process involving the acquisition of Roman customs and, often, language. Admittedly, this did not apply to everyone. Romans made distinctions between different kinds of barbarians, regarding their suitability for Romanization. Caesar, for example, 'sees the Gauls as a barbarian people with some unpleasant and several extraordinary customs, but also as one whose ways were not of a totally different order from that of the Graeco-Roman world: *homines imperiti* and *barbari* [simple and barbaric], but not *feri* [savage]. That epithet is reserved for the Germans' (Sherwin-White 1967, 29). The opportunities for Gauls and other 'simple' peoples to acquire the status of Roman citizens were correspondingly greater than those which existed for peoples, such as the Germans, whom the Romans dismissed as 'savage'. This is hardly an all-embracing notion of the natural equality of human beings, but the distance between it and the points of view we found in Plato and Aristotle is nevertheless considerable. Allied to the Stoic theory of the world-city, the Roman practice of teaching barbarians *humanitas*, and hence how to be world-citizens, and their imposition of a code of natural law regulating relationships in a putatively universal human society, constituted a revolutionary change in both the theory and practice of international politics, even if it was one marked by the imprint of the specific customs that the Romans deemed essential to true *humanitas*.

The rise of Christianity and the division of the empire

One aspect of the Roman customs which new citizens often acquired was religious; a part, but only a part, of Roman civic identity revolved around the proper worship of the Roman polytheistic pantheon of gods. And, although they made few direct connections between religion and politics, beyond matters of augury and prophecy, a few Romans did try to use their polytheistic religious beliefs to explain and justify the diversity that they recognized continued to exist within (and beyond) their *imperium*. The emperor Julian, known to early Christian writers as Julian the Apostate, said, for example:

the creator is the common father and king of all things, but . . . the other functions have been assigned by him to national gods of the peoples and to gods to protect the cities, everyone of whom administers his own department in accordance with his own nature. . . . Come tell me why it is that the Celts and the Germans are fierce, while the Hellenes and the Romans are generally inclined to political life and humane though at the same time unyielding and warlike? Why the Egyptians are more intelligent and more given to crafts and the Syrians more unwarlike and effeminate, but at the same time intelligent, hot-tempered, vain and quick to learn? . . . Whence come these differences of characters and laws among the nations? (cited in Momigliano 1987, 154)

It may well be significant that Julian offered this analysis of the link between polytheism and diversity at a relatively late period within Roman history, well after the rise of monotheistic beliefs (from which he was not, himself, altogether free). He was trying, unsuccessfully as it turned out, to reverse the process through which Christianity had already been accepted as the official faith of the empire. Earlier classical thinkers, as we saw in the previous chapter, would most probably have explained the differences to which he refers not in religious terms at all, but rather in terms of the effects of climate and physical environment. Julian's attempt to salvage polytheism, indeed, is in itself a striking testimony to the way in which religious differences were becoming more vital to identifying and explaining linguistic, cultural and ethnic differences in the later Roman empire, after the rise of Christianity.

In fact, Christianity developed within *two* Roman empires, one in Western Europe and the other centred on Constantinople in the East. It is tempting to view the deposition of the last truly Roman emperor in the West in 476 CE – the splendidly named but ill-fated Romulus Augustulus – as the end for Rome altogether. But, as John Moorhead points out, from the point of view of the Roman empire as a whole, 'if losses were going to happen' to their empire in the fifth century, 'they occurred where they should have':

The borders in the East stood unchanged, excepting only the Balkans, still enclosing the most desirable parts of the old Empire . . . containing three of the old Empire's four largest cities; it boasted many free, property-owning farmers; and its intellectual sophistication was evident from both a continuing tradition of philosophical thought and a far greater incidence of Christian heresy than occurred in the West. (Moorhead 2001, 125).

Looking at events in Italy from their capital in Constantinople – previously called Byzantium, hence the name commonly given to the later Roman empire in the East of the 'Byzantine empire' – the Easterners were themselves dismayed by the loss of Rome, perhaps even more so than many of the Western Romans who had already given up the struggle there. Nevertheless, their remnant of the empire retained enough vitality not only to keep the Roman traditions alive, but at least in the years before the rise of Islam even to add a new assertiveness to the imperial power and its scope. It was only after Islam's astonishing conquest of the bulk of Roman provinces in the Near East during the eighth century, especially Egypt and Syria, two of the wealthiest parts of the old Roman empire, that the Byzantine empire withdrew on itself to become little more than a relatively minor power within Near Eastern politics, and one that was typically on the defensive.

The Roman empire in the East gradually came to rest on the fusion of two identities: Roman and Christian. The first might seem a little strange, since in many ways the empire that developed in the Near East does not really fit with our conventional ideas of what it means to be Roman. As Mark Whittow says, the word 'Rome' typically puts one in mind of 'images of marching legionaries, pagan temples and the Latin language. None of these characterised the empire in 600. The striking force of its army was now cavalry; it was Christian; and the dominant language was Greek' (Whittow 1996, 96). Looking back at Byzantine culture today, we would almost certainly call it 'Greek Orthodox' rather than Roman. Nevertheless, since they called themselves Romans and thought of themselves as Roman, it is perhaps our ideas that are at fault here rather than theirs. Many other peoples in the outside world, moreover, saw them as the last of the Romans. Muslim scholars, who admittedly seldom showed much interest in the world beyond the *Dar al-Islam* (House of Islam), usually referred to the Byzantine empire as 'Rum' and, while they occasionally extended this term to Western Europe as well, they more commonly called Western Europeans *Ifranj* or *Firanj*, meaning Franks – a reference to the empire of Charlemagne (Lewis 1982, 140).

Like the Western empire, Constantinople was under serious pressure from outside in the fifth and sixth centuries, facing a threat of 'barbarian' invasion from the north and embroiled in a long-running war in the east with the Persian empire. In order to survive, it needed to create an internally cohesive entity, and succeeded in doing so by thoroughly Christianizing its population. 'By 600', Whittow says, 'the sense of being Romans and Christians was well on the way to turning the region [the Roman Near East] into a cultural bloc in its own right coinciding with the political bounds of the empire' (Whittow 1996, 46), although it should also be noted that Christianity in the Near East during this period contained a heterodox range of beliefs and cultures that is remarkable by Western standards. As the Byzantine empire came under increasing pressure from Persia and then from Islam, however, the need to consolidate these various Christian identities under a single, imperially controlled version also grew, which was gradually forged, in part through a doctrinal struggle over the religious role of icons.

In converting themselves into 'the quintessential Christian state' (Whittow 1996, 46), the Byzantines were essentially completing the process begun almost 300 years earlier by the emperor Constantine I – sometimes known as the 'thirteenth apostle' – who converted to Christianity in the early fourth century. His conversion was, of course, welcomed by most Christians, who could finally look forward to life in the empire without persecution, and Constantine made himself enormously useful to the Church. Not only did he help Christianity to become an established and protected religion, but he also resolved a serious doctrinal dispute among early Christians by summoning and presiding over the Council of Nicea to work out an agreed creed. In discharging this latter function, he founded a tradition of imperial intervention and control over affairs of the Church which was to have major resonances in Byzantium. Relations between Church leaders and emperors were subsequently quite varied: in the late fourth century, for example, St Ambrose was famously prepared to dictate to the emperor Theodosius, rather than the other way around, thus providing 'medieval churchmen in the West with an important precedent, showing the supremacy of the Church over secular rulers where their claims to power conflicted' (Myers and Wolfram 1982, 41). While that lesson may have been fully digested in the West, however, in the East Constantine's example continued to underpin a doctrine of imperial leadership in religious affairs, largely dependent for its practical realization on the prestige of individual emperors.

Conclusion

In the next chapter, the further development of Western Christendom will be compared with the other great 'community of the faithful' that developed during the Middle Ages after the division and decline of the Roman empire: the *Dar al-Islam*, or House of Islam. We will see that many Roman ideas, especially the concept of the *ius naturale*, continued to exercise a powerful role in Christian thinking, although in a significantly altered form. For now, though, it may be pertinent to conclude by reflecting on the specific kind of 'world-city' that Roman imperialism and natural law constituted. One crucial point that I have noted here is the extent to which Romans talked about the 'society of mankind' while simultaneously maintaining a civic pride in their own customs and achievements, as well as a highly pejorative attitude towards 'barbarians'. The emphasis on custom as an axis of difference between themselves and barbarians, however, provided a route through which entry into the world-city could be achieved, with such opportunities becoming more and more readily available as the empire developed. *Humanitas* and *Romanitas* were linked to one another, just as the Roman *urbis* was associated with the world as a whole, *orbis*. Entry into this world-city was undoubtedly easier than was the case with the more parochial Greek *polis*, but at the price of adopting a range of Roman customs in order to acquire the benefits of membership. The gradual expansion of the practice of granting Roman citizenship, however, meant that over time the city included more and more people who fitted this original Roman identity only loosely, if at all. This, indeed, is the essence of Roman cosmopolitanism: the city became more like the world, and the world became more like the city, with each transformed as it acquired characteristics of the other. By the time of the barbarian 'invasions', the clear distinction between Romans and barbarians had already been significantly blurred. In the Byzantine empire, the crisis was met by reconstructing a more tightly woven sense of Roman-Christian identity, which provided a vital resource in the Byzantine struggle for survival against Islam, but which inevitably limited the capacity of the Byzantines to present Constantinople as a true 'world-city' in the old Roman sense. In the West, as we will see in the next chapter, Christianity succeeded in building a wider spiritual community including both Romans and barbarians.

Further reading

The best way to carry out a more detailed analysis of ancient cosmopolitanism may well be to begin with the practice of the Roman world-city and work backwards to Stoic theory. On the former, Sherwin-White 1973 is an indispensable treatment of the institution of Roman citizenship, and the relevant sections from Kelly 1992 form a good starting-point on Roman ideas about *ius naturale* and *ius gentium*. Lintott 1993 is an excellent, compact overview of the mechanics of Roman imperialism more generally. Then, Tacitus 1920 and Cicero 1956 are vital primary texts for developing an appreciation of Roman thought about their empire and its relation to other peoples. On the Stoics, Long 1986 is an exceptionally good and clear introduction, with Moles 1996 as a useful reading on the wider philosophical background to cosmopolitan thought. Schofield 1991 is somewhat more demanding, but nevertheless very rewarding. It is worth comparing this literature with Linklater 1990 and Brown 1992, which offer interesting studies of cosmopolitan thought from a modern perspective.

3

Christendom and the House of Islam

A popular image of the medieval world in contemporary international relations theory is of 'a tangle of overlapping feudal jurisdictions, plural allegiances and asymmetrical suzerainties' that looks very different from modernity's neat consolidation of all power and authority within a relatively small number of sovereign states (Holzgrefe 1989, 11). One consequence of this view is that, unlike the ancient Greeks with their purportedly realistic analysis of war and peace between independent city-states, medieval thinkers are commonly supposed to have lacked any real awareness of international politics at all. The conventional wisdom is that their speculations about the world were dominated by a religiously inspired 'theory of the universal community' (Sabine 1961), which inevitably precluded a proper analysis of political relations between particular communities. Most textbooks on international political thought therefore give the Middle Ages the most cursory treatment, if they even discuss them at all; the reader is sometimes required to hop straight from Thucydides to Machiavelli with barely any acknowledgement of the intervening millennia (see, for example, Doyle 1997).

That is not to say that the Middle Ages have been completely ignored. The great Christian theologians Augustine and Thomas Aquinas are simply too famous to be lightly dismissed, and their theories of the 'just war' are still an important topic of discussion within the current literature on international ethics (see Ramsay 1992; Pangle and Ahrensdorf 1999). Moreover, embryonic versions of key 'modern' ideas can sometimes be found in the writings of 'medieval' thinkers. Scholars have identified, for example, a budding language of reason of state and an emerging positivist theory of law in the

Middle Ages (Post 1964; Pennington 1993), both of which are generally supposed to be key elements of modern international political thought. In a similar vein, textbooks often highlight the writings of certain thinkers, such as Marsilius of Padua and William of Ockham, who defended the rights of secular princes and thus anticipated related themes within more obviously modern ways of thinking (Boucher 1998, 119–25; see also Sabine 1961).

But there is more to the Middle Ages than theological speculation about the just war, and it does not really help us to appreciate how medieval people themselves viewed their world if we treat the period merely as a prelude to modernity, isolating those elements which resonate with modern ideas and discarding the rest. This book's decision not to treat the concept of the sovereign nation-state as *the* defining idea of international political thought as a whole is important here, because it allows us to look at the Middle Ages without immediately trying to latch on to what seem to be familar modern ideas, such as reason of state, sovereignty or positive law, in what otherwise appears as an alien environment. Indeed, if we remove the blinkers of the modern states-system for a moment, there does appear to be quite a lot of what can only be called 'international politics' going on in the Middle Ages. Within Western Christendom, just to take one example, we have the 'Hundred Years' War' between the French and English kings, occasionally mediated by members of the clergy, and perhaps with some evidence of an accepted code of chivalry, but otherwise seemingly rather uninhibited by the 'universal community' of which both are presumed to be members (see Neillands 1990). Alternatively, if we were to look at the Iberian peninsula at almost any moment during the Middle Ages, we would see an ill-defined and shifting frontier between Christians and Muslims. While relations between the two communities were often marked by conflict, they were not exclusively bloody: at various places and times we might find, as Peter Linehan remarks, a 'casual disregard for the normal indecencies of Holy War', with considerable evidence of cooperation and friendship between members of both faiths (Linehan 2001, 39). More generally speaking, war, trade and diplomacy between Christians and Muslims were commonplace features of the medieval world (see, for example, Muldoon 1979; Lewis 1982; Phillips 1998; and Cardini 2001). Since international relations theorists today evidently think that the 'clash of civilizations' (Huntington 1996) is part of their intellectual terrain, it seems odd to deny the international political character of these medieval relationships. Moreover, as we will see, scholars from both Christian and Islamic backgrounds developed a rich set of concepts in an effort to make sense of them.

There is, in short, no good reason why we should not ask the same basic questions about medieval international political thought as about the thought of any other period. How did medieval thinkers conceive of the ties that bound their own communities together? How did they differentiate their particular community from others? And how did they think that political relations between different communities should be conducted? Perhaps the most important distinguishing characteristic of medieval thought in these respects was the importance that it attached to religious faith as an element of community membership. In effect, Christians and Muslims replaced the route to 'world-citizenship' offered by the Roman empire with a different way of belonging to the wider human community, predicated more strongly on spiritual fellowship than on the linguistic and cultural dimensions of Roman civic identity (although that is not to say that non-religious forms of identity ceased to matter, as we will see in due course). After exploring the implications of this for the new communities of the faithful that emerged, I will then look at how they coped with the problems of the political division among the faithful and at the issue of how to deal with infidels.

Communities of the faithful

To begin with, we need to understand how medieval scholars, both Christian and Muslim, conceived of their own communities, and how they distinguished themselves from outsiders. Although this is by no means a straightforward question, a reasonable initial generalization would be to say that the principal axis along which they did so was in terms of the profession of religious faith. In that respect, medieval thought about international politics was built upon a fundamentally different conceptual foundation from ancient ways of thinking. As we saw in the previous chapters, religion was seldom the primary referent of concepts that were used to make distinctions between communities in the ancient world; the Graeco-Roman idea of the 'barbarian', for example, was more typically understood in linguistic or broader cultural terms than exclusively religious ones. Although ethnic, linguistic and other cultural differences remained important throughout the Middle Ages, with the rise of the new mono-theistic religions people began to treat religious belief as a much more significant component of their identity than before, and correspondingly relegated other axes of difference to a lesser role in deciding which communities people belonged to and how one should behave towards them. Thus the Middle Ages, for the most part, operated with a concept of community membership rooted in faith; its basic distinctions were between the Christian faithful and the unfaithful (*infidelis*), or between the House of Islam (*Dar al-Islam*) and the House of War (*Dar al-Harb*).

One reason for this change was bound up with the monotheistic character of Christianity and Islam. Religion certainly played a role in how ancient peoples viewed differences between communities, and they often stressed their own piety as something that made them more likely to be especially favoured by the gods. But in a world where, with a few exceptions, polytheistic beliefs typically prevailed, religious differences were much less clear-cut. Polytheistic pantheons had a lot of scope for blurring into one another, with the adoption of another people's gods and myths not an unusual occurrence. In matters of religion, sharp differences were most likely to arise from cultural practices regarding how to worship the gods, rather than from theological speculation about the nature of faith or divinity itself. Revealingly, one of the rare examples of a monotheistic faith in the ancient world – Judaism – was also associated by many classical thinkers with a relatively high level of religious and cultural exclusivity. Jews were seen as rather unusual in that they attached so much importance to their religious beliefs as part of their identity, and were unwilling to join in the 'sharing' of gods which was more common among other peoples; hence the primary importance of the First Commandment: 'You shall have no other gods before me' (Exodus 20: 3). The rise of new kinds of monotheistic faith which, in comparison with Judaism, were either less attached to a particular ethnic identity from the outset, or which were more ready to embrace other ethnic groups within their membership, therefore represented a significant change in the conceptualization of community, developing the cosmopolitan potential inherent in monotheism in a way that Judaism did not. However, we should note that, although both Christianity and Islam reflected this new estimation of the importance of religious faith to community membership, each did so in its own way; they were not identical statements of what the new kind of 'communities of the faithful' looked like. When we return to comparing their attitudes to each other at the end of this chapter, the importance of these differences will become even more apparent.

Christian fellowship and the idea of Christendom

In comparison with other monotheistic religions, the distinguishing feature of Christianity is its fundamental belief that Jesus was the son of God rather than a divinely inspired human prophet, which is how he is viewed in Islam, for example. Medieval Christians thus believed that they did not just possess the word of God through prophetic revelation but that their faith was founded on the actual presence of God on earth. They further believed that, through Holy Communion, it was possible for people to participate directly in the divine essence of Christ's body and blood, and in so doing to join within a spiritual community which transcended all boundaries of ethnicity, language, law or custom. From its origins, Christianity was seen by its followers as offering a genuinely inclusive conception of the world-city or *cosmopolis*, founded on the divinity of Jesus Christ and the possibility for individuals to participate in him. 'There is neither Jew nor Greek', said St Paul, 'there is neither slave nor free, there is neither male nor female; for you are all one in Christ Jesus' (Galatians 3: 28; see also Romans 12: 5). The only earthly apparatus which this required was the Church, whose core function was to provide the means through which the miracle of Holy Communion might repeatedly be enjoyed by the faithful.

The term 'Christendom', however, implies the existence of a political or territorial space where Christians live and where society and government is structured in accordance with the moral principles contained in Holy Scripture: to use the words which Christians began to employ in the later Middle Ages, it represents a *Respublica Christiana*, or 'Christian Commonwealth'. The use of a Latin expression to describe this spatial concept recalls the fact that Latin was the general language of revelation and scholarship within Western Christendom, and indeed the common language of the Catholic Church in the West. The concept of Christendom as a political or territorial entity, in fact, involves a fusion between Roman and Christian ideas about the nature of community, rather than simply the assertion of the Christian concept of communion, which actually requires no physical presence on earth other than the Church. Perhaps the clearest illustration of this fusion is the fact that medieval Christians in the West used a translation of the Bible into Latin known as the Vulgate, which was a part of a larger process 'not only of assimilating the pagan Roman law to Christian conceptions, but also of infusing the very language, substance and method of Roman law into Christian ideology' (Ullmann 1975, 32).

One of the most important ideas that Christians acquired from this fusion was the Roman concept of natural law, or *ius naturale*. Obedience to the law does not, in itself, play a central role in Christ's teaching: he lays down remarkably few prescriptions on the faithful, and his injunction to 'render . . . to Caesar the things that are Caesar's', to show due respect for the law and established authorities, in other words, is accompanied by the undermining counterpart to render 'to God the things that are God's' (Matthew 22: 21). Otherwise, his key command is contained in the rather broad demand to love one's neighbour, but leaves fairly open what this actually involves. The Bible does, of course, contain an elaborate legal code in the Old Testament, with a Hebraic Law which can act as an important source of prescription for Christians too, and an appreciation of the law is reflected in Paul's teaching on obedience to it (Romans). But the Roman idea of *ius naturale* might be seen as something of a later addition to Christian thought, and one which had to be accommodated by expanding the old Roman concept to include the idea of *faith* as a key source of the law, alongside the older notion of *reason* as the basis for identifying principles of natural law. Ultimately, as we will see later, this proved to be an enormously important tool that Christians could use to frame questions about the proper way of conducting their relations with one another and with outsiders as well.

The link between the Christian belief in a spiritual community and Roman political thought about the structure of legal order and the spatial exercise of power is not really surprising, when we recall that Christianity developed within the context of the Roman empire and the bond that developed especially after the conversion of the emperor Constantine, as was discussed towards the end of the previous chapter. Before Christianity became linked with Rome through Constantine, however, many adherents to the new faith came from barbarian or at least non-citizen stock, and the early Christians certainly did not discriminate against them in the way that most Romans did. Moreover, not only did many barbarians become Christians, until Constantine's conversion Christians were frequently persecuted by Romans and, even after Christianity became an accepted religion within the empire, many Romans still kept to their old pagan beliefs. The fact that someone spoke, dressed or otherwise behaved like a Roman or like a barbarian was therefore not a reliable guide to their religious commitment, and for Christians that was the most significant thing to determining who they were and how one should relate to them. Furthermore, after the fall of the Western Roman empire, the Church was not only able to survive but even succeeded in converting a number of barbarian kings and peoples to its faith. Thus, when Charlemagne, the king of the Franks, 'revived' the idea of the Western Roman empire in 800, his coronation was carried out by the pope, and his new title clearly conveys the fusion of three distinct identities: 'Charles most serene augustus, crowned by God, great, pacific emperor governing the Roman empire, and who [is] also by God's mercy king of the Franks and the Lombards' (cited in Canning 1996, 68).

The combined Christian, Roman and barbarian community that Charlemagne ruled was therefore quite different from the old Roman world-city of the ancients. It also differed from the development of Byzantine identity in the East where, as we saw in the previous chapter, the Byzantines managed to fuse Roman and Christian identities into a tightly knit unity within their diminishing empire. Facing the attack of Islam, their sense of themselves as a Roman-Christian state, a chosen people protected and occasionally punished by God, became more and more concrete, but also at the cost of becoming more and more narrow, eventually representing little more than a specifically 'Byzantine ideology focused on Constantinopolitan orthodoxy' (Whittow 1996, 164). There was, however, a quite different path of development to the establishment of Western Christendom, and one where the spiritual universalism of Christian monotheism could retain a significantly more plausible quality through its embrace of the wide diversity of different barbarian peoples (*gentes*), each with their own ethnic characteristics and customs, together with holders of the Roman citizenship, in a community which was united primarily through shared membership in the Church.

Obviously, St Paul's insistence on the literal unity of the Christian faithful within Christ Jesus bears some resemblance to the Stoic philosophy of the *cosmopolis*, but it sweeps aside the more qualified Ciceronian notion of 'degrees of closeness or remoteness in human society' through its insistence on the literal unity of humanity within the person of Christ. A key theme in Christian teaching was to love everyone as a neighbour, and that implied a radical break with the notion that one might have special obligations or duties with respect to certain people simply because they came from the same city or spoke the same language. How, then, did Christian thinkers deal with the 'differences of characters and laws among the nations', since they could no longer appeal to the Roman polytheistic pantheon of 'national gods' to explain these differences? The answer, at a theoretical level at least, was to deny the importance of the problem of ethnic, linguistic or cultural diversity by denying the existence of any significant link between religious community and ethnicity, language or custom. As an early text had it: 'Christians are distinguished from the rest of men neither by country nor by language nor by customs' (cited in Al-Tafahum 1969, 376). Instead, the Christians had a quite different way of thinking about who they were, and what rendered them different from all other peoples, such that the differences pointed to by Julian the Apostate, for example, lost their relevance as a way of framing what was really significant about who people were and how they behaved. According to St Augustine:

> notwithstanding the many great nations [*gentes*] that live throughout the world with different religious and moral practices, and are distinguished by a rich variety of languages, arms and dress, nevertheless there have arisen no more than two classes, as it were, of human society. Following our Scriptures, we may well speak of them as two cities. For there is one city of men who choose to live carnally, and another of those who choose to live spiritually. (Augustine 1957–72, 4.259–61)

The Stoic notion of a single *cosmopolis* as 'the common dwelling-place of gods and men' (Cicero 1933, 273) is turned here into the idea of *two* cities, one a heavenly 'city of God' and the other an earthly 'city of men'. It was entirely providential that Christ had come to earth at a moment when the earthly city – that is to say, the Roman empire – was itself at its peak of cosmopolitan universality, thus assisting in the spread of the Christian message, and providing two widely understood languages, Latin and Greek, in which to convey it. But this was a relatively incidental fact. The earthly city was, Augustine argued, a fundamentally unnatural institution, and its various conventions, including especially the fact of the variety of those conventions, were products more of human sin than divine goodness. To become a Christian was to make a choice to live spiritually, and thus enter the heavenly city, rendering the conventional practices of the earthly city trivial by comparison.

It was easy enough to provide within this world-view a justification for established authority and inequality, as a response to the concept of the sinfulness of all human beings. The institution of slavery, for example, could be seen as purely conventional and unnatural, but nevertheless 'the condition of slavery is justly imposed on the sinner' (Augustine 1957–72, 6.187). Indeed, to a certain extent, earthly government and law could even be seen as a divinely ordained institution for the correction of the sinful, which explained the biblical injunction to show respect for established authorities. Moreover, Augustine also maintained that it was important for Christians to observe the laws and customs of the earthly city, to the extent that these embodied 'a sort of merging of human wills in regard to the things that are useful for this mortal life' (ibid., 6.195). As A. J. and R. W. Carlyle note, this is very familiar: it 'is practically Cicero's definition, but with the elements of law and justice left out' (Carlyle and Carlyle 1962, 1.166). Augustine regarded this best possible condition of the earthly *res publica* as falling short of true justice, which was attainable only in the heavenly city, but it was nevertheless valuable because the prospective members of the city of God are confined to the mortal world themselves during their lives. Thus, while the heavenly city ultimately 'summons citizens from all peoples, and gathers an alien society of all languages, caring naught what difference may be in manners, laws and institutions', Christians are nevertheless urged to obey the laws and customs that maintain earthly peace 'provided that there is no hindrance to the religion that teaches the obligation to worship one most high and true God' (Augustine 1957–72, 6.197–9; and see 201).

In fact, one of the reasons why Christianity was able to survive after the fall of the Western empire, and even attract new converts, may have been this relative lack of concern with the ethnicity, languages or customs of its new adherents. Of course, to become a Christian meant making certain changes in one's way of life. But the demands it imposed, in terms of the time and effort required to worship and the money that the Church requested from its faithful, were not especially onerous. The injunction to love other Christians might demand that barbarians abandon their widely held ideas about seeking vengeance, often in blood, for injuries to their kin and that Romans give up their cherished sense of their unique piety as something which differentiated them from all other peoples. But, this aside, it was probably not much harder to become a Christian than it had been to become a Roman in the later period of the Western empire, when the citizenship had become little more than a reward for supporting a particular emperor. In fact, it was probably easier. Being Christian could coexist with being a Roman, but it could also coexist with being a Frank, a Dane, a German and so on; spiritual belonging did not come at the cost of giving up all of one's own national customs, and perhaps only a few of them.

Augustine and other theologians might well insist that none of this mattered very much: Christians were Christians, and, provided there was no conflict between Christian morality and the cultural practices of its converts, the fact that different Christians spoke different languages, had different physical characteristics, wore different clothes, ate different foods, acknowledged different temporal authorities, and generally lived in different ways in the earthly 'city of man' mattered not at all compared with their basic commitment to live spiritually together in the heavenly 'city of God'. Nevertheless, while the logic of this position might be impeccable, there is evidence that such material things did still matter to Christians. Even the Church itself found it hard to ignore them: as Regino of Prüm observed around 900, 'different peoples [*diversae nationes populorum*] differ between themselves in descent, manners, language, and laws', to the extent that even 'the holy and universal church throughout the world, although joined in the unity of faith, nevertheless varies its ecclesiastical customs among them' (cited in Reynolds 1997, 257). From a relatively early stage in the history of medieval Christendom, while there was plenty of talk about the unity of the 'heavenly city', there was in addition a widespread recognition not only of the continuing existence of Augustine's 'rich variety of languages, arms and dress', but also a sense that these differences mattered to how Christians conducted their relations with one another. One reason for the rapid spread of the Christian ideal of fellowship and spiritual community was its relative lack of interest in the variety of ways of life to be found in the 'earthly city'; but that variety did not go away, and it stored up problems within Christendom which call its coherence as a community into question, as we will see in a moment, after Muslim ideas about their community of the faithful have been described.

Dar al-Islam *and* Dar al-Harb

The lofty cosmopolitan disdain that many Christians displayed towards particular languages and customs was undoubtedly facilitated by their essential belief in Jesus's divinity. Although in coming to earth he assumed a specific, Semitic identity, Christ's divinity transcended any sense of ethnic or cultural particularity that this might normally imply. In this respect, Islam is a radically different faith. Muhammad was emphatically insistent that he was not himself divine, but was only God's prophet: the continuous proclamation of this point (the *Shahadah*) – that there is no God but God, and Muhammad is his prophet – is one of the basic articles of the Muslim faith, and a powerful assertion of its fundamental disagreement with Christianity. At the core of Islam, then, is the inescapable fact that Muhammad was an otherwise ordinary Arab, despite his prophetic status, and that the revelation he was moved to recite was given in Arabic and transmitted originally to Arabs alone. Islam thus contains a particular ethnic, linguistic and cultural identity from its origin, which Christianity does not. Perhaps ironically, though, from those more particularist origins, Islam has shown itself to be at least as adept as Christianity at attracting new adherents throughout the world.

Part of the answer to this puzzle is given by the fact that Islam does not portray the Arabs in the role of a 'chosen people' in the same way that Jewish monotheism does, and which was to become an important element of some kinds of Christian identity, as in Byzantium for example (see Whittow 1996, 162). Islam, by contrast, 'centres its cohesion around the dominating idea of submission and adherence, rejecting both the Hebraic notion of vocation, with its ethnic particularity, and the Christian concept of the Church' (Al-Tafahum 1969, 387). To a certain extent, membership within the Islamic community is defined by the observance of a specific legal code – the *shari'a* or Right Way – rather than a more mystical notion of participation in a divine essence, as is the case with the Christian idea of Holy Communion. This permitted Islam, despite its Arab roots, to be more inclusive than Judaism and less confined to one particular ethnicity, although it is also true that during the early years of the great conquests non-Arab converts were often regarded as 'second-class citizens' (Schacht 1970, 545). Antony Black sums the key point up rather well when he says that Muhammad 'brought into being at once a sense of Arab nationhood and a new kind of international community. For the first and only time in human history, the nation was transcended at the moment it was created' (Black 2001, 9).

The concept of 'submission' to God makes an important contribution to this flexibility because it provides a way of simultaneously abandoning narrow tribal loyalties and uniting a wider Arabic *umma* or people, while offering a model to other peoples of how to worship God through obedience to the divinely ordained code of *shari'a*. This theme is integral to early Islamic thought, where conversion to the faith was seen as involving a dramatic change in one's life in the sense of cutting oneself off from one's former community. A central moment in Islamic history, for example, was the *hijra* or migration of believers to Medina, a concept which also carries a connotation of 'breaking old ties, leaving the tribal bond' (Grunebaum 1970, 35).

The Arabic word *islam* is itself derived from the term *aslama*, which does not only mean to surrender or submit, but also includes in its original usage the sense of abandoning or deserting someone (Shaban 1979, 24). Like Christianity, then, and despite its more ethnically particularist origins, Islam contains an idea of leaving one's old community, whatever that may be, in order to participate in a new community defined in spiritual terms through submission to God and the message revealed by the prophet Muhammad.

Unlike Christianity, however, Islam places less importance on the exclusively spiritual idea of community represented by the Church, and Islamic thinkers were generally less anxious to reject the 'earthly city' than their Christian counterparts. Islamic attitudes to trade, for example, have always been more unequivocally positive than Christian ones. In part, this may reflect the stronger thread of a single, Arab cultural identity running through Islam from its inception, within which trade between tribes was exceptionally important, as opposed to the Christians' early experience of persecution at the hands of the Romans and their hostility to the barbarian practice of the blood feud. More generally, though, for medieval Christians, the unity of the community of the faithful was founded primarily on membership of the Church and especially participation in the act of communion; Islamic community is founded on practices which also have a clear spiritual quality, but a practical worldliness as well that is quite different from the miracle of Holy Communion. Perhaps because of that, these common observances in Islam provided a basis on which an especially powerful and frequently repeated sense of collective identity could be formed: the daily commitment to prayer, for example; fasting during Ramadan; or the making of a pilgrimage to Mecca, the *hajj* (see Cornell 1999, 77–95).

Building upon these ideas of a distinction between those who had submitted to God and who observed the pillars of faith and *shari'a*, and those who had not, Islamic thinkers divided the world into the *Dar al-Islam*, the House of Islam, and the *Dar al-Harb*, the House of War (although, as we will see in a moment, some of them did recognize the existence of a third, rather grey area between the two, sometimes called the *Dar al-Suhl*, or House of Truce). The *Dar al-Islam* could also be called the *umma*, an older Arabic word for a people or nation, which also signifies 'the single universal Islamic community embracing all the lands in which Muslim rule is established and the Islamic law prevails' (Lewis 1988, 32). Not all of these lands, it is important to note, would be entirely and exclusively populated by Muslims. In some respects, the Islamic sense of community differs from that we have seen operating within Christendom, by virtue of the stress that is placed on *shari'a* as defining the extent of the *Dar al-Islam*. Thanks to its extensive and rapid conquests of land from the Byzantine and Persian empires, an expansion that eventually extended much further into Asia, Islam often found itself in the position of being a faith of rulers and a minority of the local population. The new rulers would impose *shari'a*, and thus a sense emerged of the *Dar al-Islam* as a single entity, the unity of which was conceived in legal as much as, or even more than, in spiritual terms.

In their view of non-Muslims, Islamic thinkers made a key distinction between Jews and Christians, both of whom were called 'peoples of the book', and polytheists. This distinction carried significant implications for the treatment of the respective groups. As Bernard Lewis puts it, 'For atheists or for polytheists the choice was clear – Islam or death', whereas Jews and Christians were permitted to continue in their religious practices, provided that they accepted the supremacy of Muslim rule and paid tribute to Muslim authorities (Lewis 1982, 63). What is perhaps most interesting about this position is the way that, unlike the other monotheistic faiths, Muslims acknowledged the existence of, and granted some respect to, other communities of the faithful as part of its own identity; although Muslims believed that Christians were wrong to see Jesus as divine, they did acknowledge him as a prophet and therefore accorded him respect within the context of a prophetic tradition leading up to Muhammad. The Koran includes a celebrated injunction to coexistence between the monotheistic religions in Sura 109: 'To you, your religion. To me, my religion' (see Lewis 1982, 65). Lewis points out that it was unique to Islam 'to perceive and recognize two distinct predecessors to their own form of religious revelation and polity', Judaism and Christianity, since Muhammad's revelation was viewed as the 'seal' on 'a series of similar events through which God's purpose was revealed to mankind' (ibid., 64). Thus, when Islam enjoyed its extraordinary military successes and expansion in the first centuries after Muhammad's death, Jews and Christians were not expelled from the conquered territories, or required to abandon their beliefs. They were, however, reduced to a distinctly second-class status as peoples who had made a pact or covenant (*dhimma*) with their Muslim rulers, and lived under certain restrictions imposed by *shari'a* for non-Muslims living in Muslim lands. Not every non-Muslim, then, was a *harbi*, a dweller in the House of War: 'He is sharply differentiated from the *dhimmi*, the unbeliever who submits to Muslim rule, accepts Muslim protection, and pays the poll tax to the Muslim state' (Lewis 1988,

77). The implications of these two positions for the conduct of relations between Muslims and non-Muslims will be discussed later.

To sum up, the basis of both the Christian and the Islamic world-views is a concept of community founded in shared religious faith which is explicitly seen as transcending any specifically linguistic, cultural or ethnic identity and is open to all who wish to embrace it. There were, however, some important differences between the two faiths. Christianity includes an essentially spiritual conception of the 'heavenly city' of God, which allows differences in law, ethnicity, language, manners and so on to be glossed over as attributes of the 'earthly city'. In Islam, on the other hand, we find a comparatively sophisticated legal way of thinking about the continuing divisions between members of different religions and a system under *shari'a* for managing relations both within and between communities of the faithful. Christians did, to some extent, adopt a legal discourse as well, through their incorporation of the Roman idea of natural law into their belief system. Nevertheless, while the two faiths operated with broadly similar ways of conceptualizing community in terms of faith, when we get down to details, significant differences emerge in terms of attitudes towards both outsiders and the diversity inevitably found within the communities of the faithful.

Political disunity and legal unity

In the West, after the fall of the Roman empire, Christianity moved into a world which was already significantly fragmented between a number of distinct communities, each with its own laws, customs, languages and ethnic identity; above all of these, the Church succeeded in creating a sense of spiritual identity rooted in the concept of shared membership within a 'heavenly city' of God, and to some extent observance of a universal code of 'natural law'. Islam's early history was significantly different: after the death of Muhammad, it spread through a remarkably swift and extensive series of conquests, with Muhammad's successors sweeping the Persian empire aside and pushing the Byzantines out of the bulk of the old Eastern Roman empire, successfully converting large numbers of the inhabitants of the conquered territories. From these early roots, Islam developed a much stronger sense of the political unity of the community of the faithful than obtained within Christendom, built around the idea of the caliph ('deputy' or 'successor' of the prophet) as the supreme leader of all true believers: 'According to the political and constitutional provisions of the *shari'a*, there is only one Muslim community, administered by one Muslim state, and ruled by one Muslim sovereign' (Lewis 1988, 81). Nevertheless, divisions among Muslims – the early split between Sunni and Shi'a, for example, and later the decline of the caliphate and the emergence of a group of effectively independent rulers within the *Dar al-Islam* – forced Muslim thinkers to tackle the problem of political disunity as well.

Another key difference between the two faiths concerns their respective attitudes to divinely ordained law as a code linking together the spiritual community, its political divisions notwithstanding. This was an essential feature of Islamic belief. Indeed, lacking the Christian belief in the actual presence of divinity on earth, and therefore lacking the spiritual concept of 'Holy Communion' which is so important to Christians, Islam is sometimes viewed as a religion which invests a peculiar importance in obedience to the law, as opposed to spiritual faith (see Schacht 1970). The *Dar al-Islam* is thus sometimes conceived in essentially jurisprudential terms, as the place where *shari'a* is observed. The idea of natural law also played an important role in medieval Christian thought, but it was always to a certain extent an imported concept, grafted on to Christian moral and spiritual beliefs, reflecting the fusion between Christian and Roman ideas. Within medieval Christendom, this posed a persistent question about what natural law was, since, as one thirteenth-century jurist perhaps rather laconically remarked, 'Natural law can be understood in several ways' (Azo, cited in Pennington 1993, 122). Moreover, it raised questions about the enforcement and interpretation of the law, especially the respective roles of the pope, the emperor and individual kings, which went to the heart of the unity of the Christian commonwealth.

Caliphs, sultans and shari'a

Notwithstanding their spiritual or legal unity, both Christendom and the *Dar al-Islam* contained divisions between different political units. For both, this could represent something of a problem, precisely because of their posited spiritual or legal unity, and also because of an understandable analogical belief that, because the universe as a whole was ruled by one God, there should be one king for the temporal world. In its early years, Islam conformed to this image reasonably well, but after a dispute among Muhammad's followers in the late seventh century the *umma* splintered into two rival groups: 'traditional' or *Sunna* Muslims and *Shi'ite* Muslims who supported the claim of Muhammad's cousin 'Ali to the caliphate. Later, moreover, under the 'Abbasids the caliphate was essentially reduced to little more than symbolic importance, although within that context it did continue to play a role in the perception of Islamic unity, but where the *Dar al-Islam* was clearly divided among several more or less independent rulers. After the extinction of the 'Abbasid caliphate following the Mongol invasions of the thirteenth century even this was lost, and in practice several distinct Muslim rulers had to work out ways of coexisting with one another.

One interesting feature of Islamic attitudes, however, is that this political division never found complete acceptance among medieval thinkers, in view of their widespread belief in the essential unity of the *Dar al-Islam*. They gradually adopted a new language for describing political rule, developing in particular the term '*sultan*', 'the characteristic term of sovereignty in Islam', which is 'an abstract noun meaning "authority" or "government"' (Lewis 1988, 51; see also Black 2001). Its abstractness is part of its appeal, since it therefore designates one particular individual as the authority within Islam, but makes no specific territorial claims within itself, since that would actually detract from the ruler's claimed position as Lord of Islam. In this respect it differs from the European idea of kingship, which was inextricably connected with the idea of a particular community: king of the Franks, king of the English, and so on. As Lewis says,

> For each Muslim ruler, or at least for each major Muslim ruler, he himself was the Lord of Islam. . . . Territorial and ethnic titles might follow as corroborative detail in their own titulature; put in first place or alone, their purpose was to belittle a rival. The Sultan of Turkey and the Shah of Persia were titles which each used of the other and neither of himself. (Lewis 1988, 82)

Other rulers were therefore treated, inevitably, as being in a state of rebellion against the one true ruler of the faithful, and their treatment was determined by the rules provided by *shari'a* for the treatment of rebels. War against rebels was legitimate, but was not an injunction of *shari'a*, while the making of an agreement with a rival Muslim ruler could never have any kind of legal status: 'such settlements could only be seen as unilateral, since each Muslim ruler was in his own eyes the legitimate and therefore the sole ruler of Islam' (Lewis 1988, 83). Ironically, then, while treaties with non-Muslims could be seen as legal contracts and, within certain restrictions, were permissible under *shari'a*, treaties with other Muslims could not have the same status. To a certain extent, however, this lack of clarity about the locus of political authority was seen as unproblematic, provided that all rulers supported the observation of *shari'a*. Here, Muslim scholarship provided for a judicial institution, the 'judges' or *qadis*, to ensure the correct interpretation of *shari'a*, and this was a crucial element of the unity of the wider *umma*.

Islamic law is often said to derive from two sources: revelation and reason (Kamali 1999, 107). *Shari'a* is most closely connected with the first of these, and is derived primarily from Muhammad's recitation of the Koran and his other teachings and actions, which connects with a third idea – the notion of *sunna* or tradition – to give a concept of the *'sunna* of the prophet' as a part of the guidelines for right living provided by *shari'a* (Schacht 1970, 543–44; Kamali 1999, 108). The subsequent development of Islamic law took place primarily through the activities of four different legal schools, which have produced an extensive literature on *fiqh*, a product of rational speculation on practical issues. These schools are of considerable importance to the development of Islamic law, since they provide the flexibility necessary to accommodate a wide range of different circumstances, legal problems and practices. They are not distinguished from one another in terms simply of their broad ideas, although some tend to be more traditionalist and others more rationalist, but also geographically – the Hanafi school, for example, currently prevails in Turkey, while the Maliki school is much more important in North Africa – and this 'enables us to discern the contrast between the social realities in the ancient Arab . . . and the newly conquered territory of old civilization that was Iraq, as well as the various reactions of the ancient lawyers of Islam to them' (Schacht 1970, 550). *Shari'a* thus provided a reasonably flexible judicial, rather than political, way of uniting the *Dar al-Islam*.

Kingship, empire and natural law

In this respect, medieval Christianity was quite different from Islam in more fully recognizing the fact of political disunity, and developing a theory of kingship as a way of making sense of the divisions present in Christendom. Kingship was not, of course, an originally Christian institution. It was a long-standing feature of the customs of barbarian societies, combining religious and military functions, sometimes in two different persons. One of its most important traditional aspects was the significance attached to charismatic leadership. Whether as an intermediary between the people and the gods, or as a military commander, the most significant kingly attribute was *'Heil'*;

whether luck, skill or the favour of the gods, its key index was the ability to produce successful outcomes for the tribe. Kingship was thus often an elective institution, with individuals who seemed to possess *Heil* being elevated to the position of rule, but could also often metamorphose into a hereditary institution, on the assumption that the qualities associated with successful leadership were likely to be transmitted by descent (Myers and Wolfram 1982).

Kingship, in other words, was a customary barbarian political institution to which the Christian Church had to accommodate itself in Western Europe. Especially within the context of their comparatively full recognition of the existence of different kingdoms, it was vital for Christian thinkers to identify within Christendom a divinely ordained and clerically interpreted natural law to provide the more everyday glue that could hold the community together despite these political divisions. As Susan Reynolds describes the situation within Western Christendom in the early Middle Ages, one could accept the 'diversity of peoples and their customs . . . without feeling that mankind was hopelessly divided. God ruled over all, and Christian peoples with differing secular laws nevertheless shared one supreme law, God's law' (Reynolds 1997, 323). A Roman might have said much the same thing, except substituting *imperator* for God and *ius naturale* for 'God's law'. The question I want to ask now, then, is how significant a difference that change made to the way in which the uniform, unchanging law of nature was understood in the Middle Ages compared with its Roman antecedent, which we discussed in the previous chapter.

Medieval theologians retained most of the content of the older classical *ius naturale*, upon which they superimposed divine law as an additional meaning of the concept of nature; these God-given precepts were additional to, not replacements for, the classical elements of natural law. Thus, as the thirteenth-century jurist Azo put it, reflecting the complete range of medieval theological and jurisprudential thinking about nature: 'Natural law is what nature, i.e., God, teaches all animals. . . . Natural law is sometimes called the law established by the common diligence of men, and so the law of nations can be called natural law. . . . Natural law is called that which is contained in the Mosaic law and the New Testament' (cited in Pennington 1993, 122). They were adapting the older classical idea of natural law to suit their own intellectual environment and needs. As we have seen, the Stoics had proposed that man should live according to nature, in the sense of a cosmic order unified by the presence of the *pneuma*, which led them to propose the existence of a *cosmopolis* uniting all of human society on the basis of the shared capacity for reason and speech. Medieval scholars introduced two novelties into this point of view. First, they argued that natural law was not only based on the shared human capacity for reason and speech, and secondly, the cosmic order of nature was not based on the *pneuma* at all.

Natural law was equated with divine law, based on man's ability, meagre though it may be, to participate in God's plan for world; nature became God's rather than *pneuma*'s. This implied a crucial role for *faith* in addition to reason, and here Augustine's view was extremely influential, suggesting that, 'lest by his very eagerness for knowledge he should fall, through the weakness of the human mind, into some fatal infection of error, he needs divine instruction . . . [and must] show an ordered obedience in faith under the everlasting law' (Augustine 1957–72, 6.183). Reason was still seen as crucial to being human, but now with the additional proposition that rational enquiry needed to be assisted by, and obedient to, faith in the truths revealed in the Bible. Even the thirteenth-century Aristotelian theologian St Thomas Aquinas broadly agreed on this crucial point, arguing that, while human reason was essential to knowledge of the content of natural law, man's appointed end of 'eternal happiness' was 'inproportionate to his natural faculty' for reason, and needed the further direction from God that could be gained only through faith in the revealed 'eternal law' (Aquinas 1966, 17).

Thus, even before the twelfth century – which is often, with very good reason, treated as a revolutionary watershed in the intellectual world of the Middle Ages through the rediscovery of classical, especially Aristotelian, texts – there was considerable continuity between classical and medieval thought about natural law and international order. Although it is a slight exaggeration, one might say that we are not concerned with completely new ideas so much as with old ideas that were adapted by theologians and lawyers to make sense of a new context, namely Christendom's peculiar blend of Roman, barbarian and religious institutions. In fact, during the Middle Ages there was a nearly constant process of the rediscovery and reinterpretation of classical works, which continued well into the sixteenth and seventeeth centuries. The emphasis placed by classical philosophers on nature, and especially the Roman idea of natural law, exercised a particularly powerful influence, and, as Cary Nederman has argued, 'the rediscovery of Aristotle's *Politics* by the West merely confirmed the naturalism that had almost universally permeated medieval political, philosophical, legal, and theological treatises' (Nederman 1988, 3).

A further feature of the eclecticism of medieval thinking about natural law was that early medieval ideas about law stressed the naturalness of the customary practices of any given people, an idea closely bound up with the institution of kingship. This was crucial to the restriction of the powers of the ruler, which 'found in the "naturalized" feudal law a severe barrier' (Ullmann 1966, 84). In effect, a ruler could not arbitrarily enact a law that went against custom; the most that he could do was 'declare or define' the law involved in an already existing practice (Van Caenegem 1988). Of course, custom was not immutable, but it changed only through a slow and more or less invisible process of accretion, rather than being deliberately transformed through legal ordinances. For example, perhaps the most significant social change during the early Middle Ages, the evolution of the feudal system of land tenures, resulted from the conversion of 'repeated demands for new payments or services which knightly landlords made upon their peasants . . . into legal dues based on custom: the hated *consuetudines* – an old word [for custom] with a new meaning, i.e., of seignorial rights – which appear in the texts around 1000 A.D.' (Van Caenegem 1988, 182; see also Reynolds 1994). The changeability of custom, not only from time to time but also from place to place, posed problems for more theologically minded jurists, especially those with a more orthodox classical understanding of the permanence of natural law, who reasoned that this implied a distinction between natural law and custom, because the latter varied as 'different things please different people' (Gratian 1993, 4).

Three further intellectual changes had a momentous impact on the early medieval conception of natural law. The first involved the recovery of the complete texts of the most celebrated work on Roman law: the *Corpus Iuris Civilis*, a collection of legal codes produced for the Byzantine emperor Justinian in the early sixth century. The stimulus for the enthusiastic reception accorded to this text was a major crisis, often known as the 'investiture contest', that arose at the end of the eleventh century and the beginning of the twelfth. This was a bitter struggle between the imperial court and the papacy, also involving conflict over their relations with lesser nobles and churchmen. To give some idea of its seriousness, we might note that it witnessed nothing less than the excommunication of the emperor (Henry IV), who countered by deposing the pope (Gregory VII) and having a new 'anti-pope' elected (Clement III). The controversy encompassed most of the central political issues in Christendom, including 'sovereignty in the Christian community, the relationship between temporal and spiritual power, the nature of kingship, and the status of episcopal authority as regards that of the pope and secular rulers' (Canning 1996, 89).

Although the right of secular rulers to appoint ecclesiastical officers, which was one of the specific points at issue, was based on the traditional customs of barbarian societies, 'in order to parry the attack on this Germanic customary law, the royal . . . party harnessed the Roman law to their aid', since they found that it contained powerful conceptual resources regarding the rights of lay rulers and especially of the emperor himself (Ullmann 1975, 75–6; see also Jolowicz 1939; Kuttner 1982). To pursue this advantage, the *Corpus Iuris Civilis* began to be systematically studied at law schools in Bologna and Paris by the 'civilians'. These were scholars who devoted themselves to the study of Roman civil law and its application to the position of the emperor and other secular rulers. Initially, they tended to regard Roman law as a set of unquestionably right rules for the proper administration of society, and tried to understand how current medieval practices could be made consistent with them. Their focus contrasted with that of the canon lawyers, who also studied Roman law closely, but who were more concerned with the new laws that had been promulgated by popes for the administration of the Church and as norms of right living for Christians in general. After the twelfth century, many of the political controversies of Christendom were fought out between civilian lawyers, such as Baldus de Ubaldis or Bartolus of Sassoferrato, who generally inclined towards the defence of secular rulers (whether kings or the emperor), and the canonists, who tended to assert papal authority more strongly (see Pennington 1993).

A second major change in medieval thought was introduced by another act of rediscovery and enthusiastic reception, this time of Aristotle's major philosophical works, in the thirteenth century. This certainly did not introduce political naturalism into medieval thought, which had long been a staple of scholars working in the Ciceronian tradition. However, Aristotelianism did suggest an alternative way of thinking about the concept of nature itself, especially through his more empiricist attitude towards identifying the *telos* of the natural order, and his belief that individual entities might have their own purposes, rather than being wrapped up altogether in some grand cosmic destiny. This diminished the cosmopolitanism that had characterized earlier Christian and medieval thought, and, while it did not altogether erase the influence of Stoicism, it did encourage thinkers in the later Middle Ages to treat observed differences between societies as evidence of fundamental divisions in humanity, which they believed must have reflected the fact that different peoples had been given different purposes by God, rendering kingship a more 'natural' institution (Aquinas 1966). The conjunction between this revival of Aristotelianism and the increasing power of Europe relative to Islam was coincidental, but perhaps helped to inspire more aggressive attitudes towards non-Christians than might otherwise have been the case. Nevertheless, when we look more closely at the evolution of Christian thinking towards infidels we will see that the more traditional concept of natural law by no means lost its central position in framing scholarship on this topic.

Thirdly, though, while Aristotelianism came to dominate the work of scholastic philosophers and theologians, a quite different sort of classical revival was going on among medieval educators and political officials, usually known as 'humanism' (because it was rooted in the *studia humanitatis*). In essence, this was an educational movement that flourished during the later Middle Ages and the Renaissance, mainly concerned with achieving eloquence by reading and imitating the works of classical philosophers, historians and poets. Humanism is, with some justification, often associated with the Renaissance, but its practitioners were in fact 'heirs and successors of the medieval rhetoricians', only with the additional belief 'that the best way to achieve eloquence was to imitate classical models, and who were thus driven to study the classics and to found classical philology' (Kristeller 1979, 90). Most humanists were employed in similar positions to the earlier medieval rhetoricians, working either as teachers of literature, grammar and history, or as secretaries, advisers and ambassadors for rulers or civic republics. They thus offered a quite different account of how thought should be conducted compared with scholasticism, which emphasized training in Christian theology and Aristotelian philosophy; a frequent term of scholastic abuse for humanists was that they had no knowledge of theology, while humanists replied by ridiculing the awkward and highly technical style that the scholastics employed.

These three developments are all important ways in which the vocabulary of medieval Christian political thought was changing in the later Middle Ages, and to explore any of them would provide an interesting path through the transition from medieval to modern international political thought. Rather than pursue these lines of enquiry, and limited by considerations of space, I will have to leave them there, however, in order to turn to the ways in which Christians and Muslims thought about each other. Here, in fact, we can see some of the most obviously *international* features of political and legal thought during the Middle Ages (see for example Muldoon 1972), and it is therefore imperative that we look at the remarkably rich conceptual vocabulary that members of both religions possessed for understanding each other.

Relations with infidels

Once the 'barbarian' of the ancient world had mutated into the 'infidel' of the Middle Ages, outsiders were no longer simply primitives or slaves to be treated with contempt. Although they might still be seen in that role, they were now people whose everyday life could be conceived as an insult to God because of their refusal to worship in the proper manner. 'Barbarians' might be killed in war because they were 'wild' like beasts; they might be enslaved, because they were fitted by nature for no other purpose; they might be left alone after submitting to imperial authority; or they might be 'Romanized'. What was to be done with infidels? In some respects, of course, it is considerably worse to be labelled as an 'infidel' than as a 'barbarian', and certainly relations between the medieval communities of the faithful did involve a great deal of brutality, on both sides, in the context of 'holy war' between the faiths. But neither Islamic nor Christian thinkers treated unbelievers as an undifferentiated mass totally lacking in any kind of rights under the law. We have already seen that Islamic thinkers granted a considerable amount of respect to 'peoples of the book', and were prepared to tolerate their religious practices under certain constraints. Christians, too, developed ideas about the toleration of Muslims that sat alongside theories of the legitimacy of using violence against infidels. Both faiths, in other words, possessed quite a rich stock of concepts for thinking about the proper conduct of relations with non-believers.

Jihad *and the* Dar al-Suhl

The word that medieval Islamic thinkers used to describe the use of violence against the infidel was *jihad*, which is usually translated as 'holy war', but which has the literal meaning of 'striving'. Understood in this way, *jihad* is an important and versatile concept in Islamic thought. Scholars often distinguished two different kinds: 'greater *jihad*' represents an internal struggle, striving with oneself to suppress desire and to live in accordance with *shari'a*; 'lesser *jihad*' refers to the sense in which the concept has become famous, as waging war 'in the path of God'. The fact that this is the 'lesser' of the two should not be taken to mean that it is an unimportant or less commonly used meaning in medieval Islamic thought. On the contrary, 'The overwhelming majority of classical theologians, jurists and traditionists . . . understood the obligation of *jihad* in a military sense, and have examined and expounded it accordingly' (Lewis 1988, 72). Both the greater and lesser forms of *jihad*, as this last comment suggests, are conceived as an 'obligation' upon Muslims imposed by *shari'a*. Every individual male has an obligation to fight in the defence of the *Dar al-Islam*; offensively, *jihad* is the obligation of the community as a whole, and thus may be undertaken by the ruler and specialized military forces. It defines the basic policy that Islamic rulers, in classical thought at least, are supposed to adopt towards the *Dar al-Harb*, the aptly named 'House of War'. The obligation is taken to mean that no permanent peace may be established between an Islamic and a non-Islamic ruler. The most that could be agreed was a truce of no longer than ten years.

As this suggests, however, *shari'a* does at least permit truces to be made with non-Muslims, and this creates an intermediate zone between the House of Islam and the House of War, known as the *Dar al-Suhl*, or House of Truce. And, although the truces established on this basis could not be a permanent peace, as I have already mentioned, the legitimate making of truces was not seen as something that one Islamic ruler could agree with another. In this respect, relations between Islamic rulers and the rulers living in the *Dar al-Suhl* could even be said to be founded upon a more stable form of legitimacy than relations between Muslim rulers and their co-religionist 'rebel' rivals. On occasion, indeed, especially when they needed assistance in their struggles among themselves or with the Mongol invaders, Muslim rulers could show a generous attitude towards non-Muslims, while retaining a sense of their being outside the *Dar al-Islam*. Lewis, for example, quotes an Ottoman letter to Elizabeth I of England: 'Glory of the virtuous followers of Jesus, elder of the revered ladies of the Christian community, moderator of the affairs of the Nazarene sect, who draws the trains of majesty and reverence, Queen of the land of England, may her end be blissful' (cited in Lewis 1982, 205). Incidentally, as Lewis notes, Elizabeth's identity as a Christian is seen here as much more important than her status as queen: her 'Christian identity is asserted no less than three times before the writer of the document gets down to speaking of England'; moreover, the formula ends by expressing the hope that Elizabeth will convert to Islam, which is the point of wishing that her end will be blissful (ibid.).

Religion, then, was the primary axis of difference along which Islamic thinkers distinguished between themselves and other communities around the world. But, while highlighting the differences between the faithful and the unfaithful, they did not adopt an exclusively violent conception of the relations between the *Dar al-Islam* and the *Dar al-Harb*. *Jihad* was a hugely important concept in this context, and provided an ever present tool with which the use of force against non-Muslims could be legitimated. But Muslim thinkers had many other concepts available through which to make sense of non-belligerent and even, as the letter to Elizabeth I shows, quite positive relations with non-Muslim rulers and peoples. The making of truces with rulers in the *Dar al-Suhl*, and the pact with the *dhimmis* who lived within the *Dar al-Islam* but were permitted to continue observing their own religion, both reflect more peaceful and tolerant ways of conducting relations with non-Muslims which were also solidly grounded in *shari'a*.

Just war and natural law

Until the late tenth century, the question of how to deal with infidels barely arose in any significantly difficult way for Christians because Christendom, both Eastern and Western, was under more or less constant attack from outside, and little was needed other than a rationale for the use of violence in its defence, with the Roman theory of the 'just war' proving perfectly adequate for those purposes. But while Christendom remained periodically threatened after the tenth century, the losses to the Moors in Spain were recovered, and Christian rulers were increasingly on the attack in Eastern Europe and the Holy Land. The improvement in their military situation meant that Christian thinkers now faced a much wider range of questions about how infidels living under Christian rulers should be treated, and what justification there could be for engaging in war with non-Christians, other than simply in self-defence or for the purpose of the recovery of the Holy Land (which was, nevertheless, still often portrayed as an act of self-defence).

The medieval theory of the just war involved the incorporation of Christian values into the meaning of an originally Roman term, not simply replacing but rather augmenting earlier classical ideas about what the concept involved. Given the close relationship between Roman law and early Christian theology, one might think that the Roman position posed few problems in this regard. It embraced three main just causes for war: for the purposes of self-defence; to punish another city or king who failed to redeem an injury done to one's own citizens; and a murkier category of the *causa Reipublica*, which might be translated as the vital interests of Rome itself. As Frederick Russell puts it, a just war for the Romans was essentially an 'extraordinary legal procedure' (Russell 1975, 6). It followed other aspects of Roman jurisprudence, except with the admission of violence as a legitimate means of proceeding because of the absence of a competent judge, and hence the impossibility of using more normal forms of litigation.

In their use of this concept, however, medieval thinkers encountered a more substantial problem than arose with, say, their analysis of natural law. As we saw, certain common Stoic assumptions made it relatively straightforward to unify Roman law with Christian theology in general; but Christ had offered an essentially pacificist message which seemed to be unequivocally opposed to the Roman belief that one could ever have a just cause to use violence. Augustine's radical distinction between the earthly and the heavenly cities was crucial to the sustainability of the idea of the just war in early Christian theology. As we have seen, the notion that the fall of man represented a departure from man's true nature was central to this distinction, and it allowed Augustine to posit that war, like slavery, was a conventional institution designed for the correction of sin. War was, therefore, justified, provided that it was conducted with the intention of correcting the sinful in the interests of Christian love and charity. And even those theologians who departed from Augustine's extremely spiritualistic view of the city of God could maintain that war might be necessary to correct a ruler who strayed from the goals of Christian justice appointed by divine, and hence natural, law (see Russell 1975 for a detailed analysis).

The expansion of Christendom posed a number of more complex problems for the later canon lawyers, which could not be satisfactorily answered within the context of traditional just war theory alone. In the mid-thirteenth century, Pope Innocent IV, a noted expert on canon law, was one of the first to take seriously the question of whether invasions against the infidel in general might be justifiable, beyond those that could be dealt with in terms of the standard notion of defending Christendom or the Holy Land: 'What interested him was the problem of whether or not Christians could legitimately seize lands, other than the Holy Land, that the Muslims occupied. Did, in fact, Christians have a general right to dispossess infidels everywhere?' (Muldoon 1979, 7–8). This problem involved two key issues: could Christians legitimately seize the property of individual non-Christians;

and did non-Christian rulers have any right legitimately to hold political office over either members of their own faith or Christians?

Innocent IV argued that the mere fact that people were not Christians was insufficient reason either to take their property or to deny them political office. However, because he was charged with the responsibility for *all* souls, not just those of practising Christians, the pope did have a right to intervene in infidel societies, especially to 'judge infidels in cases where they violated the natural law, if their own rulers failed to punish them first' (Muldoon 1979, 10–11). This use of natural law involved a dualistic argument that clearly reflects the rather eclectic way in which medieval thinkers understood that concept. On the one hand, natural law was divine law, and in that context its primary earthly interpreter and adminstrator was the pope; for Innocent and other canon lawyers, of course, this was also conveniently part of the broader project of justifying papal authority in Christendom. On the other hand, however, the medieval concept of natural law still contained elements of the older Stoic conception of a human society founded through the shared human capacity for reason and speech, and 'infidels, like all other rational creatures, could freely select their own rulers' (ibid., 10). Innocent's position, then, allowed for a right of papal intervention because of his responsibility to ensure that divine-natural law was properly observed (a right he claimed to exercise if temporal rulers lapsed in their duty in this regard), but nevertheless reflected the classically Roman view that being an infidel, or a non-Roman, did not automatically make one irrational. Conversion to Christianity, not unlike self-Romanization, was, at least in principle, a voluntary process.

This was a potentially dangerous line of argument for infidels. What, after all, did it mean to be in breach of natural law, especially since this was such a broad and flexible concept in medieval thought? Indeed, a number of other canonists produced much more intrusive arguments regarding the status of non-Christians. Oldratus de Ponte, for example, asserted in the fourteenth century that Muslims 'are not simply members of another flock, subject to the pope; they are wild animals who should be forcibly subjected to Christian control' (Muldoon 1979, 19). As James Muldoon comments, Oldratus, echoing the Aristotelian view then coming into widespread use, 'seems to suggest that the natural violence of [Muslims] led to an uncivilised way of life that in turn caused them to violate constantly the precepts of natural law' (ibid., 21). Nevertheless, Innocent's relatively tolerant position seems to have been generally accepted among the canonists, and he has been described as 'the founder of the doctrine of the rights of infidel nations, however imperfect and incomplete this doctrine might be' (Belch 1965, 1.75).

Perhaps the major opposition against Innocent's argument that infidels had rights to property and political office, provided they were not in breach of natural law, came from temporal rulers anxious to exploit their improved fortunes to pursue a policy of territorial aggrandisement beyond Christendom. Two cases in particular stand out. First, during the fifteenth century the Spanish began a process of westward expansion, and at this early stage aimed to gain papal approval for the colonization of the Canary Islands. Their argument here closely followed Oldratus's idea of suggesting that certain infidels were inherently outside natural law, contending that the inhabitants of the islands were 'nearly wild . . . they are lacking in normal social intercourse, living in the country like animals' (Muldoon 1979, 121). We will look more closely at the evolution of this Spanish policy in the next chapter. Secondly, the Knights of the Teutonic Order were anxious to expand eastwards into Poland. Here, however, their claims were seriously complicated by the fact that the Polish kings had converted to Christianity, and therefore had come under the protection of the pope as members of Christendom. The argument about being outside the natural law was harder to sustain here, and the Poles were able to mount an effective defence at the Council of Constance. Making extensive use of both canonistic arguments about papal supremacy and the civilian arguments of Bartolus and Baldus, the Polish representative at Constance, Paulus Vladimiri, contended that religious conversion and hence entry into Christendom did not automatically imply subjection to imperial sovereignty. It was obvious to the Poles that accepting some degree of papal intervention was preferable to invasion and domination by the Teutonic Order, and Vladimiri employed Aristotelian notions about the naturalness of human society – but not the naturalness of barbarian slavery – to suggest that 'God willed all nations, whether Christian or Pagan, to be free to organize themselves politically' (Belch 1965, 1.23).

Conclusion

The shift from the Roman empire to the monotheistic communities of the faithful was thus associated with significant changes in the structure of international political thought. Many of these stemmed from the basic move from seeing community membership in terms of an eclectic and shifting mix of linguistic and customary observances to one based much more squarely on a relatively (but not, of course, completely) fixed notion of religious faith. As I have explained, this should not be taken to mean that other kinds of difference disappeared altogether, and in that sense there is indeed some justice in the conventional description of the Middle Ages in terms of a 'tangle' of overlapping jurisdictions and, especially, plural allegiances. Nevertheless, in both Christendom and the *Dar al-Islam*, sophisticated ways of handling these continuing differences emerged, most notably through the development of a legal code – *shari'a* or *ius naturale* – as a way of thinking about the unity which obtained among the faithful.

The other central point concerns relations between the communities of the faithful. Whether or not they wanted to, neither could simply ignore the existence of the other. Ideas about the legitimacy of using violence against the infidel were constant themes in both Christian and Muslim thought, but it is vital to recognize that medieval scholarship on these issues was not unnuanced and simply belligerent. Islam from its origins identified the other monotheistic faiths as predecessors to Muhammad's final revelation of God's message, and thus accorded them a special status that was reflected in diplomacy between Muslim and Christian rulers. In later Christian thinking about canon law, meanwhile, the idea that all are bound by natural law, enforced by local rulers – both Christian and pagan – but interpreted by the pope, provided a vehicle for thinking about the respective rights of different political communities. Students of the history of international political thought should therefore not be so quick to skip the Middle Ages in their headlong rush from the ancient works of Thucydides to moderns such as Machiavelli, Grotius and Hobbes. As we have seen, the Middle Ages in their own right offer a rich field for the study of different ways of thinking about how political relations between communities should be conducted.

Further reading

Black 2001 is a very good starting-point on Islamic political thought, although Lewis 1982 is a more detailed examination of key points that are directly relevant to the understanding of international political thought. Dunn 1986 is an entertaining and very readable analysis of one particular Muslim's world-view, which helps to colour in the broad themes developed by Lewis. Canning 1996 is an excellent, compact but still very general introduction to political thought in Western Christendom. Post 1964 and Pennington

1993 are good further works. But, from the perspective of international political thought, James Muldoon's work, especially 1979, but also 1972 and 2000, is of seminal importance, and I would describe it as indispensable. Belch 1965 develops some similar themes, including an extremely useful introductory discussion, and Russell 1975 is a classic study of just war theory, but both lack the range of Muldoon.

4

Reason of State, Natural Law and State of Nature

The sixteenth and seventeenth centuries, the period I will attempt to cover in this chapter, has become the heartland of the history of international political thought. It has exercised an unusually powerful influence over twentieth-century theorists, who often identify themselves with traditions rooted in this era. Certainly, no one can deny that it presents us with an impressive list of names, such as Niccolò Machiavelli, Francisco de Vitoria, Jean Bodin, Hugo Grotius, Thomas Hobbes, Samuel von Pufendorf and John Locke (see, for example, Boucher 1998, who gives all of these thinkers, except Bodin, a detailed analysis). The high level of interest in the period reflects a similar situation in the history of ideas more generally. A great deal of the most important recent work on the history of political thought has been directed towards early modern Europe: for example, Quentin Skinner, arguably the most significant exponent of the new approach to the history of ideas that I mentioned in the introduction, has concentrated his energies principally on Machiavelli, Hobbes and their contemporaries (see Skinner 2002, vols 2 and 3). Of course, the period is also famous as the home of the 'scientific revolution', an old and maybe slightly creaky idea, but one that many scholars feel is still useful for trying to convey a sense of the dramatic changes that were taking place in how people conceptualized nature and the methods they used to try to study it (Shapin 1996).

To explain the main currents of the international political thought of this important and complex period, I will begin by looking at the various concepts that early modern thinkers used to talk about the political communities in which they lived. Perhaps the most salient are the concepts of the 'state' and the 'sovereign', although not always, at this stage, linked together to give us what we would today call, almost automatically, the 'sovereign state'. I will therefore begin by reviewing the development of these two concepts, partly to trace the origins of the developing idea of the sovereign state, but also in order to see how differently many early modern thinkers understood these ideas from the way we use them now, and to highlight the continuing importance of other ideas, notably of empire and republic, to early modern political thought. Through the discussion of these concepts, I will try to convey a more general sense of how early modern thinkers conceived of the structure of their world, the nature of political authority within it, and its division into different communities.

Having given a preliminary account of some of these basic concepts, I will then look at two distinct ways in which they were employed, and here I think it is helpful to adapt an idea from Anthony Pagden (1987) and talk of the 'languages' of early modern international political thought. The first language might be called a *political* one, and because it centrally involves a concept of 'reason of state' it has become almost ineluctably – although now also somewhat controversially – associated with Machiavelli (Meinecke 1984; Viroli 1992). As well as reason of state, it gradually came to involve the ideas of the 'interests' of the state, and eventually even the idea of the 'balance of power'. By the middle of the seventeenth century, we find treatises arguing that the reason or interest of European states in general is to establish a balance of power among themselves in order to preserve their individual 'liberties' (Howell 1646; Lisola 1667; Bethel 1680; Rohan 1995). Another language existed, however, which might be described as legal or jurisprudential. Its central ideas were the old concepts of 'natural law' (*ius naturale*) and 'law of nations' (*ius gentium*), although often formulated in novel ways, which were used to think about the 'rights' (*iura*) of sovereigns and peoples (Tuck 1979, 1987, 1999). It was the province of scholars such as Vitoria, Francesco Suarez, Alberico Gentili and Grotius. The idea of two 'languages' is, of course, a device that I am imposing on the period for purposes of simplification, although it does have some literal meaning: 'reason of state' treatises, for instance, were often written in vernacular languages – such as Italian, French and English – compared with natural lawyers' general preference for Latin.

One significant point of difference between the two languages, apart from the concepts they employed, was that they involved different ways of trying to gather knowledge about their respective fields. To discern the true reason or interest of state, 'politicians' most often turned to history for hard evidence about which kinds of statecraft worked and which did not, although some felt it important to keep track of contemporary shifts in power as well. 'Lawyers', on the other hand, tended to rely more heavily on the authority of scripture, rational philosophical speculation and, increasingly, constitutions, statutes and treaties to determine who had what rights. One of the most important intellectual developments of the period was the gradual rapprochement between these two methods, especially as lawyers began to adopt a more historical framework for thinking about natural law, but without abandoning their traditional interests in theology and philosophy. Bodin was an important early exponent of this kind of approach, and that perhaps gives him an even better claim to fame than the standard view that he was the author of the modern concept of sovereignty (Bodin 1965; see also Franklin 1963; Kelley 1973). Grotius was another, but perhaps the key thinker in this story was Hobbes, who produced one of the most complete examples of what might be called a 'natural history' of legal institutions such as property and sovereignty (see Buckle 1991). A vital concept that enabled him to do so was the idea of a 'state of nature', within which natural law applied, contrasted with a civil society which came into being after the establishment of a legitimate sovereign with the authority to posit new laws for the community. After reviewing some of the main features of the two languages of politics and law in early modern international political thought, then, the chapter will conclude by looking at the development of this idea of the 'state of nature' as it was understood and used by Hobbes and his contemporaries.

States, sovereigns, empires and republics

One of the traditional beliefs of historians writing on early modern Europe was that the period was characterized by the fragmentation of medieval Christendom and the development of the modern, 'absolutist' state. This historical focus has recently been called into question, however. Nicholas Henshall, for example, has argued that the idea of 'absolutism' is a mythic product of nineteenth-century historiography, when the state's absolute dominance over society was really established, and was then projected backwards into the past (Henshall 1992; see also Oresko et al. 1997). In this respect there are two important points worth making at the beginning of our discussion. Firstly, for much of the period 'state' and 'sovereign' were not straightforwardly identified with one another: state was a political concept describing the dominion or rule of a particular prince, while sovereignty was more of a jurisprudential concept describing a particular bundle of rights and privileges which, many thought, could be distributed among several different individuals or groups.

Secondly, too strong a focus on the idea of the 'sovereign state' as it developed through the work of absolutist thinkers such as Bodin and Hobbes risks obscuring the continuing importance of other concepts for thinking about political community. Although a constant theme of conventional textbooks is the decline of the Holy Roman Empire, throughout the period the idea of 'empire' retained its importance, and might even be seen as flourishing (Muldoon 2000). The year 1525 was, indeed, the apogee of the new 'Roman' imperialism within Europe, with Charles V stimulating a new imperialist discourse which made the late medieval rhetoric of the *dominus mundi* seem a more realistic possibility than ever (Koenigsberger et al. 1989, 235), and even after the failure of that vision, empire-building remained a dominant theme of European activities beyond Europe. I do not have the scope to go into this latter concept in detail here, for reasons of space, and will focus instead on the ideas of the state and sovereignty, but that should not detract from its importance (as well as Koebner 1965, Yates 1975, Pagden 1995 and Muldoon 2000, see Armitage 1998 and 2000 for more detailed analyses). Another key idea with antique and medieval roots which retained its importance throughout the period was the idea of the *res publica*, republic or commonwealth. Some of the most successful states of the early modern period were republics – notably the Dutch United Provinces – organized on the often fragmented lines of the mixed polity (Hart 1993; see also Israel 1991), and this idea had a lingering importance for international political thought as well, especially but not exclusively through the conception of Europe as a whole as a *grande république* (Onuf 1998). Again, although I will focus here more strongly on the concepts of the state and sovereignty, it is important not to neglect these other ideas, and I will return to them briefly at the end of this discussion.

The idea of the state

In a 1589 treatise which did much to popularize the idea of 'reason of state' within Europe, Giovanni Botero began by explaining the meaning of the expression: 'State [*stato*] is a stable rule over a people and Reason of State is the knowledge of the means by which such a dominion may be founded, preserved and extended' (Botero 1956, 3). It is clear from this definition that here the concept of the 'state' does not mean the same thing as the 'people' or country as a whole; still less does it refer to the notion of a 'public' contained in the classical idea of the *res publica* and retained in early modern thought by concepts such as the 'commonwealth'. In Botero's treatise, 'state' was identified with the rule (*dominio*) that a prince exercises *over* a people; dominion, and therefore the state, is something that the prince *has*, it is not something that a particular territory, people or nation *is*. Botero's reflections on 'reason of state', and on the art of statecraft more generally, were therefore addressed to the individual prince, seeking to provide him with the means to establish, preserve and extend his rule over others, to maintain his state in other words.

This conception of the state had gradually developed during the fifteenth century, and was already well established by the time Botero was using it (see Skinner 2002, 2.376). Before that, the Latin word *status* had more often been used to describe the general condition of the commonwealth or *res publica*, a sense which was preserved into the modern era in the numerous 'statistical' studies of, among other things, the 'present state of Europe' (see, for example, Campbell 1752; Zimmerman 1787). But the volatile politics of Italy during the fifteenth and sixteenth centuries raised what Quentin Skinner describes as 'a more basic and urgent question of politics: how to advise the *signori* of Italy, often in highly unsettled circumstances, on how to hold on to their *status principe* or *stato del principe*, their state or standing as effective rulers of their existing territories' (Skinner 2002, 2.374). 'Unsettled' is putting it mildly. Machiavelli and his contemporaries, for example, witnessed numerous changes of regime in Florence alone: in 1494 a republican government was established and the Medici family driven out; the republic fell in 1512, and the Medicis returned, only for the republic to be re-established in 1527 (the year of Machiavelli's death) before it promptly collapsed yet again in 1530. To complicate matters further, many of these changes of regime involved some kind of external intervention, with the rulers of other cities and principalities – the pope, the Holy Roman emperor and the king of France, for example – all taking a hand in the politics of northern Italy, to Machiavelli's dismay at the involvement of these 'barbarians' in Italian politics (Machiavelli 1988, 91). In these circumstances, and they were not untypical, the question of how the prince could best maintain his state was a pressing one, as was the related question of how a republic might endure, one which Machiavelli, for example, took up in his *Discourses on Livy* (Machiavelli 1996). Gradually, the idea of the prince's state which we later find in Botero's work grew in importance, in response to the increasing demand for advice on how to protect one's dominions.

To the extent that it has a territorial connotation, and it definitely does, this conception of 'state' might best be understood as an 'estate', comprising the lands which belong to the ruler as his personal property, a concept which most early modern lawyers would have described as *dominium*, clearly related to the term *dominio* Botero uses to describe the state. This is sometimes seen as closely linked to the modern idea of 'sovereignty' as well, implying rule or domination (Kratochwil 1995), but, as we will see in a moment, the word that most lawyers used to talk about political authority in that sense, implying *rights* to rulership over a people, was still *imperium*: by contrast, the prince's state, many scholars believed, originated in violence and was therefore maintained by force (this was an integral feature of the Italian discourse on 'reason of state').

Nor does 'state' in this early context often have the sense of an entire political community, comprising territory, population and government, that we would give it today. Such a community would probably be more likely to be described as a 'republic' or 'commonwealth', using the standard expression *res publica*. Gradually, however, the word state – or *stato*, *état* or *Staat* – did come to be used in that sense, a not dissimilar development to the way in which, as we saw in chapter 2, the Roman idea of *imperium* added the notion of a concrete territorial space over which rule was exercised to its original meaning of a right of command within the Roman *res publica*. By the mid-seventeenth century, the concept of the state was unquestionably used in this more abstract way to describe an entire political community, and was becoming distinct from the idea of the prince and his personal standing to become a personification of the political community as a whole. In this respect, as in many others, Hobbes is often seen as marking the completion of this process through which the idea of the state reached its ultimate referent as encompassing the entire commonwealth or body politic (see Skinner 2002, 2.402–4, 3., ch. 6).

Summum imperium *and* souveraineté

The word 'sovereignty' derives largely from Jean Bodin's attempt to depict the Latin expression *summum imperium* in his French treatise *Six livres de la republique*. Bodin described *souveraineté* as 'the absolute and perpetual power of a commonwealth' (Bodin 1992, 1), justifying its absolute character on the grounds that 'persons who are sovereign must not be subject in any way to the commands of some-one else and must be able to give the law to subjects' (ibid., 11). The distinction between sovereign and subjects was thus central to his understanding of the indivisible nature of sovereignty: if sovereignty means not being subjected to any other human authority, he reasoned, it must be impossible to be a subject and sovereign simultaneously. Therefore, 'the prerogatives of sovereignty have to be of such a sort that they apply only to a sovereign prince. If, on the contrary, they can be shared with subjects, one cannot say that they are marks of sovereignty' (ibid., 49). Bodin did not treat this entirely as a question of logic, however, but also justified it on practical grounds with the argument that if the rights contained in *imperium* were to be divided it would result in an illogical and dangerously unstable situation: 'Sovereignty will ... be tossed up and back between two parties, and sometimes the people, sometimes the prince will be the master – which are egregious absurdities and utterly incompatible with absolute sovereignty, as well as contrary to the laws and to natural reason' (ibid., 27). His view was that the 'power of making and repealing law includes all the other rights and prerogatives of sovereignty, so that strictly speaking we can say that there is only one prerogative of sovereignty, inasmuch as all the other rights are comprehended in it' (ibid., 58; see also Franklin 1973).

This conception of sovereignty represented a rejection of the then widely held idea of the 'mixed polity', which figured prominently in thought on reason of state, and helped to underpin early modern ideas about the importance of balancing forces within and between societies (see Fukuda 1997). It also involved an attack on the then more conventional way of conceiving of sovereignty still in terms of a bundle of different prerogatives contained in the classic idea of *summum imperium*, and which was often seen as divisible. Nevertheless, before we look more closely at that point of view, it is worth noting that some of the most important critics of Bodin's attempt to mount a defence of princely absolutism, such as Johannes Althusius, did accept his conception of sovereignty as absolute, perpetual and indivisible, questioning instead the locus of this ultimate political authority. The crucial move that Althusius made, and which was subsequently taken up by a range of different political theorists, was to deny that the sovereign power always resided in a prince, and to argue for popular sovereignty, if only as a residual form (Althusius 1964; see also Gierke 1966). In the case of the French Huguenots, the populist implications of this argument were refracted through the institution of 'inferior magistrates' (i.e., public officials), in whom was vested the right to resist a tyrannical prince or government, 'a right which is founded on the prior and natural right of the sovereign people to treat the commonwealth as a means for security and improving their own welfare' (Skinner 1978, 2.376–7). Thus, following Bodin's justification of princely absolutism, a debate emerged which put the location of the sovereign power at issue, but which left the principle of the indivisibility of the sovereign power unquestioned.

Other participants in the debate about sovereignty did not leave this important component of Bodin's theory unchallenged, however (Franklin 1991; Borschberg 1994, 106–35; Oresko et al. 1997, 3–4). It is noteworthy, for example, that, about one hundred years after Bodin wrote the *Six Books of the Republic*, Hobbes still had to fight much the same battle, confronting 'an opinion received of the greatest part of England' that sovereignty could be divided (Hobbes 1996, 127). This is confirmed by Julian Franklin's analysis of the way in which the 'confusion' created by Bodin's theory of indivisible sovereignty was 'cleared up in the course of the debate on the locus of sovereignty in the German Empire' (Franklin 1991, 299). Bodin's doctrine was enormously difficult to apply to this situation, since either it would have meant denying the constitutionally guaranteed prerogatives of the German princes, or it would have implied that the empire was not a monarchy at all. Ironically, the Peace of Westphalia exacerbated this problem: it simultaneously affirmed the territorial rights (*Landeshoheit*) of the German princes while endorsing the international personality of the emperor, who was one of the most important signatories of the treaties (see Pütter 1790). What status, then, would the treaties have had if Bodin's theory was to be accepted?

As historians of international thought are well aware, there were efforts to solve this problem, most notably in Pufendorf's description of the empire as a special kind of constitutional arrangement – which he called a 'states-system', *systema civitatum* (Pufendorf 1991, 144; see also Wight 1977, ch. 1; Robertson 1998, 34) – within which sovereignty was indivisibly held by the states, all of which were bound together by special ties of comity. However, while 'there were some who followed Pufendorf', there was also an 'unbroken succession' of theorists who adopted the contrary, and in some ways much more straightforward, line that Bodin had simply been wrong, and that 'the sharing of sovereignty as well as the distribution of its parts are ... modes of mixture that are ultimately consistent with the co-ordination of governmental functions' (Franklin 1991, 328). In his survey of the debate on sovereignty in the empire, Franklin identifies Christoph Besold as the originator of 'a theoretically decisive account of the divisibility of sovereignty in a mixed constitution' (ibid.). While this was a conceptual device used to prop up the constitution of the Holy Roman Empire, elsewhere it could be used for the opposite purpose. In the context of the Dutch revolt against Spanish imperialism, for example, ideas about *summum imperium* were developed which stressed its divisible character as the basis for the legitimacy of the Dutch States-General waging war against the Spanish, and which were 'specifically directed against and conceived as a superior alternative to the Bodinian notions' (Borschberg 1994, 135).

The chief lesson that should be drawn from this brief overview of the development of the concepts of the state and sovereignty is that early modern political thought was extremely complex and cannot be reduced to a single logic. The link between the increasingly abstract concept of the state-as-commonwealth and the judicial concept of the rights of *souveraineté* relied upon the kind of absolutist fusion developed by Bodin and Hobbes (see Skinner 2002, 2.398–404), but the persistence of the language of the divisibility of sovereignty points towards the continuing importance of other ways of thinking about the nature of political community than the idea of the 'sovereign state'. The more one delves into the conceptual vocabulary of the early modern period for thinking about the nature of political community, the more it resembles the 'tangle' of different and overlapping forms of community that so many commentators observe in the Middle Ages. The idea of the sovereign state was one way of thinking about this, and doubtless an important one, but the persistence of the conception of sovereignty as divisible, especially in the form of continuing reflections on *summum imperium*, suggests that one should not be too hasty in reducing all of early modern international political thought to speculation about this idea (see Keene 2002 for a more detailed discussion of where this might lead). Nevertheless, that is not to say that the idea of the state was completely unimportant; nothing could be further from the truth. The state, and in due course the idea of the sovereign state, anxious to protect its liberties, was one of the more prominent themes within early modern political discourse, and it is to this that I will now turn in more detail.

Reason of state, interests and balance of power

'Princes rule people, and interest rules princes' (Rohan 1995, 161). Thus begins a short tract on *The Interest of the Princes and States of Christendom* written by Henri de Rohan, the military leader of the

Protestant Huguenot faction during the religious wars in France (the treatise was actually published posthumously in 1638 – after the French religious wars were over – and was dedicated to Louis XIII's Catholic master-statesman Cardinal Richelieu). In this pithy aphorism, Rohan captured the central thrust of a new way of thinking about international politics which took the 'interest' or 'reason' of states as its central concept and promised to use that idea to tell the ruler how best to maintain his position in a turbulent and violent world. I will begin by taking this treatise as an exemplar of what was of course in fact a large and complex literature on these political themes, and use it to try to identify certain key ideas in this way of thinking about international politics, the origins and development of which we can then trace.

The state's interests in early modern Europe

In the fiercely competitive environment that Rohan described, understanding one's interest correctly was literally a 'matter of life and death for states' (Rohan 1995, 161). But it was not a straightforward task. It was not something that could be done through the time-honoured method of abstract philosophical and theological speculation about the eternal, divinely sanctioned laws of nature, or even through the historical study of examples of statesmanship from the past: 'one cannot establish an immutable rule for the government of states, because revolutions in world affairs change the fundamental maxims of policy' (ibid., 159). According to Rohan, the only way to survive was to pay constant attention to one's immediate political environment, and above all keep track of the activities and interests of other powers (*puissances*).

   In the particular context of the late sixteenth and early seventeenth centuries, it was especially important to keep an eye on the two mighty states of Spain and France, which dominated Christendom 'like two poles, from which warlike or peaceful influences are passed down to the other states' (Rohan 1995, 161–2). Rohan concluded that the true interest of France lay in thwarting Spanish ambitions. The French should expose the self-interested reasons behind Spanish efforts to present themselves as the protectors of Catholic Europe; should attempt to match Spain's formidable network of spies and its diplomatic service; and, when necessary, should be prepared to 'meet force with force, because neither persuasion nor justice can lay down the law to one who is armed' (ibid., 172). If France could match Spanish military power in this way, it would not only serve its own interests, but it stood to win the gratitude of all the other princes and states of Christendom by preserving a balance (*contrepoids*) that was essential to the continuing survival of the lesser powers (ibid., 173; see also 171 and 173n.).

Rohan's treatise contains two noteworthy themes that distinguish it from the medieval speculations about natural law and kingship that we examined in the previous chapter. The first difference is that Rohan deals entirely and exclusively with the interests of states, which he conceives most consistently in terms of gaining and maintaining power, rather than other possible policy goals, such as upholding true religion, promoting a moral purpose or even simply providing for the general welfare of the realm. Even though religion is the foundation of the first 'interest' of Spain, for instance, Rohan suggests that the main reason why the Spanish make a great show of their Catholicism is because this is useful to the state's other goals, which ultimately involve increasing its power: thus, for example, while zealously inciting the French king to exterminate the Protestants in his own country, at the same time the Spanish 'give under-hand encouragement and assistance to those same Protestants' in order to foment a civil war to weaken France (Rohan 1995, 164–5). The other three 'interests' which Rohan attributes to Spain are even more clearly oriented to the pursuit and maintenance of power: Spain should pay proper attention to gathering intelligence about other states, which includes 'winning over the principal ministers of other states' to their own cause; it should build up a skilful diplomatic corps which must always be preparing for war, but which should 'always display a desire for peace, in order to put other states to sleep'; and, finally, it should 'always be powerfully armed, an assured method of keeping one's subjects obedient, one's neighbours respectful, and thwarting the designs of one's enemies' (ibid., 165). Traditional beliefs in the defence of the Christian faith and the need to wage war against the Turk, staples of medieval international political thought, appear as little more than platitudes that wily statesmen use to extend or maintain their power (ibid., 166). Religion was still an integral feature of Rohan's world – most of his life had been spent fighting for the Protestant cause, after all – but in statecraft it becomes little more than a cloak for the state's real purposes, used by the wise to hoodwink the gullible.

The second notable feature of Rohan's treatise is the emphasis it places on the fluidity and turbulence of politics within Christendom. There is little room here for the medieval belief in an orderly, providential universe designed and functioning according to God's plan; on the contrary, Rohan's world is a violent place that is prone to revolutionary changes in its organization which do not seem to have any discernible purpose. This is hardly surprising, given that his life had been dominated by the many twists and turns of the French civil wars. One of Rohan's contemporaries, Michel de Montaigne, remarked that the tendency of both sides in the religious wars to claim divine approval for their cause, and the constant ups and downs with which both sides had to contend, merely showed that 'it is hard to bring matters divine down to human scales without their being trivialized' (Montaigne 1991, 243). In Montaigne's work and more widely across Europe, the idea that the world danced to the tune of 'fickle Fortune' rather than divine Providence was a commonplace, and what people prized above all was *constancy* in the face of sudden changes in fortune. This is the context in which Rohan appealed to the concept of reason, which he described as the only true guide to one's self-interest and therefore to the conduct of state policy, contrasting *la raison* with 'unregulated desires', 'violent passions' and 'superstitious opinion' (Rohan 1995, 187).

Reason of state, in other words, should replace passion, superstition and even, one might add, religious faith as a guide to policy, because reason provided the only reliable way of charting one's course in a world that was continuously being 'agitated' – another favourite term of Rohan's – in unpredictable ways, and where piety merely left one vulnerable to *puissance*. The emphasis on the fluid nature of politics also explains the appeal of the idea of a balance or equilibrium which Rohan presents as a central goal of statecraft: it appears in his work as a stabilizing principle, the purpose of which is to reassure states that they are unlikely to be extinguished in the near future (Rohan 1995, 173). In brief, while one has to accept the turns of fortune with stoic constancy and equanimity, if one can through rational policy establish a balance there is at least a possibility of minimizing those fluctuations for a while, thus carving out a space where the state will be secure and life within it bearable. As Richard Tuck comments, 'from the 1590s *balance* becomes the key term, for it is an appropriate description for such a state once politics is seen in terms of interests' (Tuck 1993, 96; see also Pocock 1972, 129).

The development of reason of state

It is evident from the way that Rohan took these ideas for granted in his treatise without feeling any particular need to justify them as maxims of policy that they were already part of the common currency of international political thought by the mid-seventeenth century (Howell 1646 and Lisola 1667 are similar examples). In fact, some of the concepts he used, such as the idea that the state has its own 'reason' which should guide its policy, were of very long-standing and even of ancient origin. As I mentioned in chapter 2, the Romans had regarded otherwise illegitimate actions as potentially justifiable on the grounds that they were in the public interest (*rei publicae causa*), and even Cicero 'referred to "reason of state" in a modern way when he said that utility was often an excuse for evil in the republic, and mentioned a *ratio reipublicae*, or *ratio et utilitas reipublicae*' (Post 1964, 255; and see Lintott 1993, 24, 27). Medieval authors were also prepared to accept that the divine natural law did not have a monopoly on human reason, and that the concept of *ratio* could be applied to the business of the king's or prince's government. It was widely accepted during the Middle Ages that 'necessity' could justify temporary suspensions of the law, and that it could be permissible, Christian pacifism notwithstanding, to fight for one's country (Post 1964, 263, 284).

Nevertheless, 'necessity' was hardly seen by classical and medieval thinkers as a normal condition of politics, and throughout the Middle Ages there remained a persistent belief that the interests of the ruler were 'subordinate to . . . the reason of the community as a naturally existing entity that was approved by God and the law of nature for the social and political end of man on earth' (Post 1964, 303). Both of these assumptions were challenged in the new way of thinking about reason of state exemplified by Rohan. The interests of the prince were no longer subordinated to any other considerations: Rohan's aphorism asserts that 'princes rule people, and interest rules princes'; it does not go on to say that God, natural law, justice or anything else rules the state's interest. And in Rohan's world necessity and the struggle for survival is a constant theme of policy. The fickleness of fortune is an everyday problem, not merely something which occasionally intervenes to provide a justification for actions that would normally be unconscionable.

The movement from classical and medieval ideas about the *ratio et utilitas reipublicae* to Rohan's notion of *la raison* or *l'intérêt d'état* therefore represents a major change in the way that people thought about international politics, and the purpose of this section is to explain how this transformation happened. The story begins in the turbulent world of Renaissance Italy, where thinkers such as Niccolò Machiavelli and Francesco Guicciardini began during the early sixteenth century to develop a new appreciation of the importance of violence and the use of force to statecraft and – in a phrase that

Guicciardini coined – began to describe this theme in terms of a *ragion di stato* distinct from more conventional Ciceronian ideas of moral reason (Viroli 1992). The new idea was not always welcomed, but it quickly entered the language people used to talk about international politics. In 1547, for example, a prominent Italian humanist and cleric, Giovanni della Casa, found it necessary to criticize people who were speaking of a 'reason of state' in contrast with more conventionally moralistic ideas of the 'reason of the city': 'Vainly . . . do they affirm these things who make two reasons – the one unjust, false, dissolute, disposed to thievery, and to make evil; and to this they have put the name "reason of state"' (cited in Schellhase 1976, 124).

Despite these objections, Guicciardini's term was picked up by other writers, such as Botero, who used *Ragion di stato* as the title for a treatise on statecraft that employed a number of Machiavellian and Guicciardinian ideas, while trying at the same time to make the concept rather more respectable. Thanks to the efforts of authors such as Botero, the concept and the new way of thinking about international politics associated with it quickly spread across Europe (see Burke 1991). It had, for example, become a core principle of French diplomatic policy by the time of the Thirty Years' War and guided their activities during the lengthy negotiations for the Peace of Westphalia (Osiander 1991, 28; see also Church 1972). It gained numerous adherents in England, in part because it provided an 'uninhibited and non-legalist' rationale for colonial expansion (Tuck 1999, 109). By the mid-seventeenth century, looking in particular at French policy but providing recommendations for his own state as well, one British author felt able to comment that 'pure reason of state . . . is now grown to the highest point of subtlety, and sways the world more than ever' (Howell 1646, 148).

Although the content of Machiavelli's, Guicciardini's and Botero's advice to princes on how to maintain their rule contained many novel elements, scandalously so in Machiavelli's case, there was nothing particularly new about the idea that scholars should write books advising princes how to rule. On the contrary, this was a well-established genre which had flourished during the Middle Ages (see Gilbert 1938). The usual point of medieval treatises on the theme was that the prince should strive to be a good Christian: thanks in part to the working of providence, this would secure his reputation and his rule, and thus would bring honour and glory to his kingdom. Medieval thinkers therefore tended to stress the importance of piety and other Christian qualities such as benevolence and mercy as central features of good princely rule.

Many Italian humanists before Machiavelli had already expanded this way of thinking by adding to it a recovered awareness of the classical Ciceronian conception of the virtues. This was gained from the classical texts that they were busily finding and reading, which placed great importance on the need to study rhetoric and history in order to become a truly virtuous man, and thereby added some further virtues to the medieval list: eloquence, prudence, temperance and courage, for example, now sat alongside Christian ideas of piety, faith and honesty (see Skinner 1978, 1.126–8). Furthermore, in harking back to these classical principles, Italian authors also adopted the Ciceronian idea that the prince's virtue should be understood as opposed not to sin or impiety, as a Christian world-view might suggest, but rather to the Roman goddess of Fortune (*fortuna*): 'They always conceded her [Fortune] a great power over human affairs, portraying her with a wheel on which the fates of men are kept turning by her sheer caprice. They insisted, however, that her sway is not inexorable, since she can always be wooed and even subdued by a man of true *virtus*' (ibid., 1.95). In other words, while they still agreed with medieval Christian thinkers that to be a good ruler the prince needed to cultivate his virtues, they now understood that requirement not as a part of God's plan for the world, but rather as something that was required in order to overcome the twists of fortune. Already, before Machiavelli, a key element of later reason of state thinking about international politics had been established.

But the Christian–Ciceronian mix of ideal princely virtues and the resulting recommendations about statecraft were still a long way from Rohan's notion of interest as the ruling theme of policy and his conceptualization of interest in terms of the augmentation of the state's power. The emergence of the modern doctrine of reason of state also involved a shift in how Italian thinkers viewed the challenge of subduing *fortuna*, and hence the specific character of the virtues that the prince needed to cultivate. This development can in large part be explained by a change in the way that Renaissance authors borrowed from their classical predecessors, and in particular a turn from Cicero to the work of the Roman historian Cornelius Tacitus (see Schellhase 1976). For defenders of the Florentine republic, such as Machiavelli, Tacitus' own republicanism appealed. But above all it was Tacitus' subject-matter that recommended him ahead of Cicero. He provided a graphic account of the collapse of the Roman republic and the maintenance of the principate, neatly paralleling the events that the late fifteenth- and early sixteenth-century Italians were themselves living through. Tacitus' was a history that suited the times, describing as it did 'a period rich in disasters, frightful in its wars, torn by civil strife, and even in peace full of horrors' (cited in ibid., 71; and see 70).

The significance of this shift is obvious if we compare Guicciardini's and Machiavelli's advice with that given by more orthodox early sixteenth-century humanists, steeped both in Christian morality and classical Ciceronianism, who continued to recommend that the prince should concentrate on cultivating benign virtues such as eloquence and piety. The famous humanist scholar Desiderius Erasmus, for example, argued along precisely these lines in a treatise written just three years after Machiavelli's, insisting that 'our first and foremost concern must be for training the prince in the skills relevant to wise administration in time of peace, because with them he must strive to his utmost for this end: that the devices of war may never be needed' (Erasmus 1997, 65). Erasmus laid a particular emphasis on the point that war-making was contrary to Christian values, and more pragmatically noted the enormous costs that war necessarily imposed: 'A prince', he concluded, 'cannot revenge himself on his enemy without first opening hostilities against his own subjects' (ibid., 107). And in that context, it might be better, Erasmus argued, to accept defeat rather than wage war: 'Wise men prefer sometimes to lose a case rather than pursue it, because they see it will cost less to do so' (ibid., 106).

Machiavelli was vigorously opposed to this point of view. He unequivocally stated that a ruler 'should have no other objective and no other concern, nor occupy himself with anything else except war and its methods and practices' (Machiavelli 1988, 52). Rather than cultivate the arts of peace, the primary consideration of the prince, Machiavelli insisted, should be to maintain his military strength, and this implied the importance of a quite different set of virtues as appropriate to successful rule. 'The main foundations of all states', he said, 'are good laws and good armies', and it was the latter which occupied the bulk of his attention because 'it is impossible to have good laws if good arms are lacking, and if there are good arms there must also be good laws' (Machiavelli 1988, 42–3). This is the ultimate consideration for any prince for a very simple reason: 'a ruler is capable of defending himself if he can put together an army that is good enough to fight a battle against any power that attacks it', and 'states that have the capacity to maintain an army in the field are not lost' (ibid., 38, 83). Although Machiavelli's ideas about the need for this army to be composed of a citizen militia have not stood the test of time so well, this core insight into the centrality of military power to statecraft is the key element of Machiavelli's art of the state that persists into Guicciardini's idea of reason of state, and from there on into more modern speculations such as Rohan's. As regards the princely virtues, this remained a core concept in Machiavelli's thought, and as in the more conventional literature was frequently juxtaposed by him against the fickle currents of fortune that the ruler had to overcome. In this endeavour, however, he saw little use for Erasmus's Christian virtues of piety and honesty, other than as a cloak behind which to hide the reality of a ruthless policy. This pointed towards a rather different idea of virtue: 'one must', Machiavelli argued, 'be sufficiently prudent to know how to avoid becoming notorious' (ibid., 55).

The expression '*ragion di stato*' which Botero used for the title of his treatise had been coined by Guicciardini in his *Dialogue on the Government of Florence*, written in the early 1520s (Guicciardini 1994). As the title of this treatise suggests, it offers two different points of view on Florentine politics at a pivotal moment in the fortunes of both princely and republican government in the city. On the one hand, the *Dialogue* presents a defence of the Medici regime which preceded the republic of 1494; on the other, it offers a blueprint for a stable republican government dominated by a virtuous aristocracy who 'devote themselves to attaining glory and true honour, which consists entirely in doing generous and praiseworthy deeds to benefit and exalt their native city and be useful to other citizens' (ibid., 91). Towards the end of this debate, however, one of the participants, Bernardo del Nero, comments that it is impossible to maintain *any* regime without the use of force and that this necessarily entails ignoring the dictates of one's conscience on occasion. Instead of acting like a good Christian, then, the ruler must look to 'the reason and practice of states' (ibid., 159). This, the argument goes, was the only realistic thing to do if one wanted to 'live in the world'; 'it is impossible to control governments and states, if one wants to hold them as they are held today, according to the precepts of the Christian law' (ibid., 159, 158). In talking, of course, not just about the 'practice' but also the '*reason*' of states, Guicciardini was appropriating one of the most valued terms of the old way of thinking about politics. As Viroli puts it, 'Guicciardini takes the trouble to explain to the late pupils of Cicero that, besides moral reason, there is another reason, the reason of the states, that must at times guide the actions of the political man' (Viroli 1992, 194).

Reason of state originally expressed, then, a specific position with respect to what the prince needed to do in order to keep a grip on his dominions, and one that struck a clear contrast with more conventional Ciceronian – or Aristotelian, for that matter – ways of thinking about politics in early modern Europe. Previous writing on this topic, believing that the proper end of a *res publica* should be to promote the freedom of its members and their ability to pursue a good life, had stressed the need for the prince to live and rule in a virtuous manner, linking together classical virtues such as prudence, temperance, courage and justice with Christian ideas about piety, faith and honesty; this, it was thought, would be sufficient to ensure the prince's, and also his city's, glory and honour (Skinner 1978, 1.126–8). By contrast, the reason of state theorists insisted on the importance of the use of force to maintaining the state. This idea features prominently in Guicciardini's analysis. Just before making the contrast between moral conscience and reason of state outlined above, Bernardo del Nero had remarked that 'all states are illegitimate; and excepting republics, inside their own city walls and not beyond them, there is no power whatsoever that is legitimate' (Guicciardini 1994, 158–9). This was clearly Guicciardini's own belief, since an almost identical statement appears in his *Maxims*: 'You cannot hold states according to conscience. For if you consider their origin, they are all illegitimate [*tutti sono violenti*], with the exception only of republics ruling their own cities, and nowhere else' (ibid., 172; and see also Guicciardini 1949, 164–5).

The actual words that Guicciardini uses here to describe an 'illegitimate' regime are '*governo violento*': a government or state, in other words, established through violence, rather than one which emerges 'naturally', as the Ciceronians and Aristotelians would have it. And it is important to note that this principle, as Guicciardini understood it, did not apply just to princes, but extended to a republican regime as well. The power of a republic is only 'legitimate' *within* its territory (*patria*). Beyond the city walls, republics find themselves in exactly the same situation as princes, needing to maintain their grip over their lands through the use of force, and therefore subordinate to the identical 'reason of states' that princes need to follow. Indeed, even when Florence was under a republican government, del Nero observed, its military leadership was entrusted to 'people who loved their country more than their soul', and were therefore prepared to violate God's commands if necessary (Guicciardini 1994, 158). In terms of their international relations, in other words, the difference between the republic and the prince's *stato* was beginning to break down. Both relied on force to maintain their position; both were subject to reason of state.

The pivotal argument in early Italian thinking about reason of state, then, began from the proposition that all princely regimes originate in violence, and that *all* regimes need to be prepared to use violence, rather than pursue more traditional ideas of princely virtue, to maintain themselves in a world that is presumed to be conflictual and competitive. Failure to do so will simply result in loss of the state. Where did this belief come from? Of course, we have already seen that the turbulent politics of the Italian Renaissance made the fragility of the state painfully evident, but it is also worth noting that both Machiavelli and Guicciardini saw this as something more than just a contingent feature of their own particular time; historians both, they were determined to take the longer view, and both grounded their position in a claim about the negative features of human character and behaviour. In Machiavelli's assessment, 'this may be said of men generally: they are ungrateful, fickle, feigners and dissemblers, avoiders of danger, eager for gain' (Machiavelli 1988, 59). To discharge the vital task of keeping an army in the field, then, the ruler needed to keep a firm grip on his soldiers, 'because armies are never kept united and prepared for military action unless their leader is thought to be harsh' (ibid., 60). Guicciardini's views were somewhat less clearly stated but point in a similar direction. Sometimes, he took the fairly conventional view that 'men are naturally inclined to good', but that, 'because their nature is frail, and the occasions inviting to evil infinite, they are readily turned from their natural bent by self interest [*interesse proprio*]' (Guicciardini 1949, 5). Elsewhere, though, he argued that 'men are not ruled by reason', and suggested that it was foolish to base one's expectations of others on what it was reasonable for them to do, but rather to expect them to behave in accordance with what their 'nature' inclined them towards, and in this he came very close indeed to the more dismal Machiavellian view (ibid., 53, 61). This comes through most clearly in another of his maxims: 'To speak of the people [*uno popolo*] is in truth to speak of a beast, mad, mistaken, perplexed, without taste, discernment, or stability' (ibid., 227).

Reason of state beyond the Renaissance

Machiavelli's negative view of man and his conclusions about the need for the ruler to be feared rather than loved went so much against the grain of conventional thinking about the princely virtues that it earned him a positively satanic reputation. Later reason of state theorists, fearful of being too closely linked to this reputation, tended to be rather more circumspect. Botero, for example, began his treatise with a rehearsal of the core virtues of the prince that looks quite traditional, and he insists in an almost Erasmian way that the 'disagreeable possibilities' of both civil and foreign war 'may be avoided by the exercise of the arts which win for a ruler the love and admiration of his people' (Botero 1956, 12). His reasoning here reinforces the sense that this is a departure from Machiavelli's and Guicciardini's idea of reason of state: Botero goes on to explain that – in contrast to the idea that all states originate in violence and must survive in a violent world – 'in the earliest times men were moved to create kings and to place themselves under the rule and leadership of others by the affection they felt for them and high regard (which we call admiration) for their valour, and we may deduce that these are the feelings which keep the subjects obedient and peaceful' (ibid.).

Nevertheless, despite these conventional themes, Botero's discussion of reason of state does draw upon his predecessors to a significant extent. Reminiscent of Machiavelli's idea of their fickleness, 'the common people', we are told by Botero, 'are by nature unstable', implying that the prince must constantly be seeking diversions to prevent them from pursuing a change of regime, and apparently 'military enterprises are the most effective means of keeping a people occupied, for nothing arouses their interest so much as an important war' (Botero 1956, 74, 76). More substantively, as Skinner points out, Botero's attitude towards the prince's cultivation of virtues is underpinned by a calculating disposition which is distinctively Machiavellian. When, for example, he identifies prudence and valour as two crucial elements of government, he notes that 'in the decisions made by princes interest will always override every other argument; and therefore he who treats with princes should put no trust in friendship, kinship, treaty nor any other tie which has no basis in interest' (ibid., 41). Botero is, as Skinner puts it, 'recognisably an inhabitant of Machiavelli's moral universe' (Skinner 1978, 1.249), and his critics seized on this, accusing him in turn of Machiavellianism (see Viroli 1992, 273). Nevertheless, the debate about the merits or otherwise of this position was now carried on largely in terms of the new vocabulary that Machiavelli and Guicciardini had created: it was about 'good' reason of state and 'bad' reason of state, but it was still about reason of state, rather than the older Ciceronian vocabulary of the moral reason of the city or *res publica* (Burke 1991). Botero's was only one illustration of the widening currency of the idea, and by the end of the sixteenth century 'we find the same phrase [*ragion di stato*] being used as the title of dozens of political treatises in which a Machiavellian conception of prudence is elevated to a high place among the political virtues' (Skinner 2002, 2.158).

We have seen that the core doctrine of sixteenth-century Italian thinking about *ragion di stato* was that, in order to maintain his state despite the fickleness of fortune, the prince needed to cultivate the art of war because his rule, like others, was founded on violence rather than law. One way in which this doctrine found a broader appeal was through the idea of fortune's inconstancy becoming a widespread theme in European thought, notably in the work of Montaigne and a Dutch scholar called Justus Lipsius, whose writings *On Constancy* became an international bestseller, helping to spark a general European philosophical movement that is often called 'neostoicism' (Oestreich 1982). This wider philosophical argument about fortune and the role of reason in coping with its fickleness provided the crucial foundation for seventeenth-century treatises such as Rohan's, which broadened out Machiavellian and Guicciardinian prescriptions about what the prince needed to do to maintain his state, or rule, into a thesis about the interests of states in preventing the rise of any one prince to a position of 'universal monarchy' (Lisola 1667). 'Reason of state' became less of a striking contrast with the Ciceronian moral 'reason of the city', and more a rational attempt to protect the interests and preserve the liberties of European commonwealths in general. It was still beyond the normal bounds of jurisprudential ideas about rights and legitimacy, and for the most part would remain so until the eighteenth century. But it was an increasingly accepted part of the everyday discourse of European statecraft and diplomacy.

Natural law and the law of nations

'Natural law' was, of course, always a more respectable concept than 'reason of state' for thinking about politics, and its analysts never had to endure the infamy that attached to Machiavelli's name. That does not imply, however, that the concept was a settled or uncontroversial one in early modern international political thought. On the contrary, its very importance to speculation about legal rights meant that how one defined natural law was always of the first importance to political debates. In this context, the discovery of the Americas brought many of these debates into sharp focus. Of course, the discovery had such a profound impact on sixteenth-century geography and natural science that it is easy to overestimate the extent to which, in itself, it posed a novel problem for theologians and political theorists. In fact, the immediate issues it raised were essentially similar to those that we discussed earlier in the work of medieval canon lawyers. The real impact of the discovery – and, even more importantly, the conquest and colonization – of the Americas was to force this long-standing issue about how to conduct relations with non-Christians into the foreground of theological and political debate, especially in Spain, where it very quickly became apparent that there were numerous contradictions and unanswered questions in the work of the canonists. Attempts to solve these problems in the sixteenth century led to significant further developments in European thinking about the rights possessed by non-Christians, and ultimately helped to generate an essentially new account of natural law.

Spanish theories of the law of nations after the conquest

To understand why this was the case, we first need to appreciate one of the ironies of Spanish expansion during the sixteenth century. Although the huge technological edge that they enjoyed over the American Indians ensured an astonishingly quick military victory for the Spanish, they found it much more difficult to justify their conquest and treatment of the Indians. Indeed, as Anthony Pagden observes, after some fifty years of fiercely contested debates about the Indies, Spanish thinkers were confronted with a conclusion that they found logically valid, but recognized was practically unacceptable: namely that 'the Spaniards had to withdraw from America and return to the Indians all that they had taken from them' (Pagden 1990, 32). Here, I want to focus on the intellectual difficulties presented by Spanish activities in the New World, and the work of scholastic and humanist thinkers that led to this rather surprising conclusion. I will begin by explaining some of the reasons why Spanish thinkers encountered such intractable problems in trying to justify the conquest. Then, I will examine early scholastic responses, discussing the revival and rejection of the Aristotelian theory of 'natural slavery'. Finally, I will look at the further development of the debate about the Indies between scholars firmly entrenched in the scholastic tradition (Bartholome de Las Casas) and others more strongly influenced by humanism (Juan Gines de Sepulveda).

Let us begin by asking why sixteenth-century Spanish theologians found it so difficult to justify the conquest of the Indies. There are two interesting points about the specific circumstances in which these thinkers operated here. First, earlier accounts of how to treat non-Christians in medieval canon and Roman law had tended to focus on the authority of the pope or the Holy Roman emperor. Hostiensis, for example, had presented his theory of the direct authority of the pope over all members of his flock, including people who were not yet confirmed in the Christian faith, as part of his broader argument justifying the position of the pope with respect to the emperor (Muldoon 1979). Alternatively, many Romanists had tried to bolster the position of the emperor by proclaiming him *dominus mundi*, or lord of the world. In either case, this presented a straightforward justification for Spanish activities in the New World, provided that they could persuade either the pope or the emperor to grant them rights to territories, or to govern peoples, which these authorities were in a position to do by virtue of their supposed universality.

Certainly, the Spanish had close connections with the pope at the time (Alexander VI), and were able to secure a series of bulls from him, one of which, *Inter caetera*, 'was regarded as the juridical charter of Spanish imperialism, and its chief theoretical defence against intruders from abroad and against interfering humanitarians at home' (Parry 1940, 4). These papal bulls were, however, less secure a justification than they might at first glance appear. The Hostiensian theory on which the pope's right to dispose of infidel lands rested was not without its critics, and (as we saw in the previous chapter) the more widely held position was that associated with Innocent IV, which allowed the pope only limited, indirect rights of intervention that certainly did not extend to overthrowing non-Christian rulers or depriving non-Christians of their property. For most scholastic theologians and lawyers, the Hostiensian argument was too extreme a statement of papal authority to be acceptable, and this seriously undermined the usefulness of papal donation as a tool for justifying the conquest, still less the seizure of lands and other property from the Indians (see Vitoria 1991, 258–64).

The idea that the Spanish king might claim his lands in the New World under the aegis of the Holy Roman emperor as *dominus mundi* was potentially rather more fruitful, especially because of the fact that the Spanish king who presided over the most dramatic period of the conquest, Charles V, happened to be the emperor as well. Indeed, his reign and his phenomenal acquisitions in the New World seemed to many contemporaries precisely to signal 'the revival of the medieval conception of universal empire' (Muldoon 2000, 116). However, this convenient fact became less useful when Charles's possessions were split between the Spanish and Austrian branches of his dynasty (the Habsburgs), with the former retaining control over the Indies and the latter over the Holy Roman Empire. Moreover, for the Spanish scholastics who debated the question of the Indies, even under Charles V, an exaggerated account of the emperor's importance was hard to maintain in the face of developments in legal scholarship since the twelfth century. One of the leading scholastics, Francisco de Vitoria, argued that there was nothing in either natural, divine or human law to confirm that the emperor truly was the lord of the whole world, with genuinely universal jurisdiction, and that, even if Charles was *dominus mundi*, this did not necessarily give him the right to 'occupy the lands of the barbarians, or depose their masters', since he had only a limited form of jurisdiction (Vitoria 1991, 258). The simple assertion of either papal or imperial authority was not much of a foundation, in other words, for the justification of Spanish conquests in the Americas.

The second major problem that confronted the Spanish thinkers was the need to respond to the Reformation. As Pagden puts it, it was central to their 'whole project to refute the claim of these "modern heretics" [the Reformers] that the authority of a prince depended not upon God's laws but upon God's grace' (Pagden 1990, 18). The Reformers had argued that anyone who fell from God's grace – who lapsed into sin, in other words – lost his authority and might be deposed by the true faithful. This argument could act as a perfectly good justification for the conquest of the Indies, since it would allow Christians to depose any non-Christian ruler and deprive his pagan or infidel subjects of their property. Later, indeed, some Protestant groups in North America had few qualms about applying its logic to their dealings with native tribes there, although it was always a rather extreme position that was frowned upon by most established political authorities. In any case, it was clearly not available to the Spanish scholastics of the sixteenth century, since they were equally, or even more, interested in promoting the counter-Reformation within Europe as they were in justifying the conquest of the Indies; not to mention the fact that on the whole they subscribed to Innocent IV's earlier refutation of this 'heresy' in its medieval form. The scholastics' need to refute the Lutheran position consequently limited their ability to use the fact that the Indians were not Christians to claim that they had no rights, and Vitoria concluded quite simply 'that the barbarians are not impeded from being true masters [i.e., having *dominium*], publicly and privately, either by mortal sin in general or by the particular sin of unbelief' (Vitoria 1991, 246). Vitoria certainly thought that the Spanish had a right to preach the Christian religion to the

Indians, and he saw that this could provide a justification for war against the Indians if this right was not respected. But the Indians' lack of God's grace by itself was not sufficient reason to depose their rulers or seize their property, and in any event efforts at their conversion had to be peacefully conducted, since only voluntary adoption of the faith could have any value.

These two problems indicate the severe nature of the difficulties that the Spanish theologians and jurists confronted as they attempted to justify the conquest of the Indies, the deposition of Indian rulers and the seizure of Indians' property. On the one hand, claims based on papal or imperial donation, which were an important part of the initial ideological armoury with which Spanish rulers made their case for the New World, proved on close examination to have serious problems from the point of view of orthodox theological and jurisprudential scholarship of the sixteenth century; few of the scholastics were prepared to invest much weight in them. Secondly, it was insufficient, and indeed positively dangerous, to ground claims to the New World merely on the fact that the Indians were unbelievers, since this could potentially undermine the defence of Catholic orthodoxy in Europe. Because these potential lines of argument were closed to them, the scholastics were forced back on natural law itself as the only reliable basis upon which any account of the Spanish and Indian rights in the New World could be established. However, as we have seen, the medieval conception of natural law was extremely eclectic. In the early Middle Ages, it already included not only elements of the classical Roman *ius naturale* – involving both Stoic ideas about human reason and Roman legal theories about the law of nations or *ius gentium* – but was also treated as synonymous with divine law as laid down in the Bible. After the thirteenth century, this was overlaid by yet another ingredient: the Aristotelian conception of nature and natural law, as interpreted by Thomas Aquinas. In working out precisely what were the implications of natural law for the problem of the Indies, then, Spanish thinkers such as Vitoria were primarily engaged in clarifying this confused combination of numerous distinct elements, in order to bring them to bear on the particular case in hand.

One of the first attempts to apply medieval ideas about natural law to the Indies made use of Aristotle's convenient theory of natural slavery. This line of argument, for example, was developed by John Major, a Scottish theologian, who contended that the Indians qualified as natural slaves according to Aristotle's formulation because they were destitute of reason in the way the philosopher had described (see Pagden 1990, 20). This position, however, was rejected by Vitoria, and others, because, even though they continued to regard the Indians as 'barbarians', they nevertheless accepted that 'they have some order in their affairs: they have properly organized cities, proper marriages, magistrates and overlords, laws, industries and commerce, all of which require the use of reason' (Vitoria 1991, 250). Indeed, some scholastics – notably Melchor Cano – went even further to suggest that the whole Aristotelian idea of 'natural slavery' was misconceived. As Pagden comments, they argued that 'slavery could, by definition only be a category in law', and since Roman law, betraying its Stoic roots, defined a slave as ' "someone who has been deprived of his liberty contrary to nature", there could evidently be no such creature as a *natural* slave' (Pagden 1990, 23; emphasis original). Here we can clearly see one of the central tensions in the eclectic medieval conception of natural law being played out, in this case with Stoic egalitarianism triumphing over the more hierarchical Aristotelian conception of nature, to the advantage of the American Indians.

The idea that the Indians were irrational, and hence destined for the function of bodily service appropriate to a natural slave, was discarded in favour of the contention that they were akin to children, and hence that there was a justification for taking them under tutelage. It is easy to see how radical this is as a departure from the Aristotelian theory that the *telos* of a barbarian is slavery. In the view worked out by the scholastics, the Indians might indeed 'be handed over to wiser men to govern', and might even 'be governed partly as slaves' (Vitoria 1991, 291). But, this was to be conducted out of charitable motives and, crucially, the Indians could own property for themselves in the meantime, as a child could do (see ibid., 249); one day, they could be expected to mature into fully rational, and hence naturally free, human beings. This position, it is worth noting, is much closer to the Roman attitude towards barbarians than the Aristotelian position. It goes beyond Innocent IV's more reticent position that Christians might intervene in the affairs of a non-Christian society in order either to protect Christians or to punish a breach in the natural law that the infidel rulers had ignored. However, it does not go so far as to assert a natural condition of enmity between Europeans and barbarians, or the naturalness of enslaving the latter. Vitoria's position is more activist than Innocent's, in the sense that Spanish rulers are now entitled to step in as guardians of a people that have not yet reached the 'age of reason', as a consequence of the Indians' barbarism rather than their infidelity; but it admits that, on the crucial question of owning property, the Indians have rights under the natural law and that the rule of the Spanish does not confer a permanent slave status on the Indians as a realization of the latters' natural purpose or essence.

We must be careful not to exaggerate the significance of this argument at the time. Vitoria also suggested seven other just titles under which the conquest and Spanish rule might be justified. The 'mental incapacity' of the Indians is actually the last he mentions, and it is given one of the shortest treatments, which rather suggests that he felt that a stronger case for Spanish activities in the Indies could be mounted on different foundations. In these alternative justifications, however, Vitoria's position is often still strongly reminiscent of Roman practices. In one case, for example, he refers to the Spanish king's right to protect those Indians who are his 'friends and allies', and asserts that the justice of such a policy is confirmed by the Romans, 'who extended their empire in just this way, by coming to the aid of their friends and allies and profiting from the opportunity to declare just wars' (Vitoria 1991, 289). Of course, as a scholastic theologian, Vitoria buttressed this appeal with reference to Augustine and Aquinas, but the essentially Roman (albeit, in this instance, hardly Stoic) character of his account of the proper way of dealing with barbarians is nevertheless clear.

The arguments of Vitoria and the other scholastics had a remarkable impact on Spanish policy, helping to produce the 'New Laws' of 1542, in which serious restrictions were placed on some of the practices that they had held as violations of the natural rights of the Indians. These laws provoked a furious reaction from the colonists, as well as a celebrated debate in 1550 between two of the leading lawyers concerned with the problem of the Indies: Bartholome de Las Casas, a Dominican priest who had spent a considerable part of his career ministering to the Indians and defending their rights; and Juan Gines de Sepulveda, a lawyer and historian with marked humanist sympathies, who had recently produced a treatise (the *Second Democrates*) in which he vigorously attacked the Vitorian notion that the Indians could have legitimately owned property or been politically organized before the arrival of the Spanish. In this debate, which to some extent can be seen as a clash between scholastic and humanist thinking on the question of barbarians, we can detect numerous themes that continued to concern theorists through the seventeenth century.

Let us look in particular at Sepulveda's position, since Las Casas's *In Defense of the Indians* was mainly a response to the *Second*

Democrates, and was in fact an explanation of the reasons why it should not be published (although the Spanish did not treat the Indians with quite the magnanimity that Las Casas hoped, he did have the minor triumph that Sepulveda's treatise was indeed proscribed). The most significant feature of Sepulveda's argument, and the most objectionable from the scholastic point of view, was that 'all property relations are the product of civil society'; at a stroke this 'recast the whole issue of the legitimacy of the Conquest in the language of humanist jurisprudence' (Pagden 1990, 28). This key humanist idea – that property should be seen as an institution of the civil law rather than natural law – inevitably granted an enormous amount of power to the sovereign, who was responsible for making civil law, with potentially disastrous consequences for the natural law rights of the American Indians. Against him, then, Las Casas developed an even more forceful version of Vitoria's natural law position, seeking to limit as much as possible the idea that the pope or any Christian ruler might even have a right of punishing other peoples who were in breach of natural law (Las Casas 1974). The force of naturalist jurisprudence meant that Sepulveda lost this particular argument, but he showed the importance of developing an idea of property within natural law that would permit the occupation of the Americas, and there we find the key intellectual developments in the work of Hugo Grotius. We will return to this rich vein of speculation about property in a moment.

The mechanical philosophy of nature

First, though, I want to look briefly at another important change in speculation about natural law which took place at about the same time as the discovery of the Americas, but in this case through the discovery of what Robert Hooke called a 'new visible world' thanks to instruments like the microscope and the telescope (Shapin and Schaffer 1985, 37). Ultimately this led to the emergence of a new way of thinking about nature, associated with what is commonly called the 'scientific revolution', but which its main exponents would probably have described as 'natural' or 'mechanical' philosophy (Shapin 1996). We saw in the previous chapter that some medieval scholars had employed a conception of nature that initially married Christian beliefs about God's role in the world with the Platonic theory of the separation between form and matter, coupled to a Stoic conception of the cohesion and universalism of the natural order, whereas others always maintained a more basically Ciceronian conception of nature and natural law. During the thirteenth century, this had been revised under the influence of the rediscovery of Aristotelian physics, which made the problem of motion – or, to put it another way, the fact of change – central to late medieval natural philosophy. Nevertheless, even after Aristotelian thinking became dominant, the later medieval conception of nature remained consistent with the earlier belief that changes in nature were fundamentally *purposive*, whether this was understood in terms of the specific functions that all natural things were striving to realize or in terms of some broader cosmic purpose possessed by nature understood as a whole. To understand change or motion was to understand its purpose or *telos*.

The first major breach in this way of thinking was made by Nicolaus Copernicus, a Polish astronomer, whose major work (*De revolutionibus orbium coelestium*) was posthumously published in 1543. The 'Copernican revolution' is typically associated with the idea that a heliocentric model of the universe, with the sun at its centre, should replace the geocentric model of medieval Ptolemaic astronomy. However, the most radical element of Copernicus's challenge to medieval orthodoxy was not to change the model of the universe in this way, but rather the suggestion that there was no objective 'centre' to the universe at all; his position was that it was simply more convenient for scientific purposes to assume that the sun was the central point rather than the earth because this allowed better sense to be made of planetary movements. As R. G. Collingwood observes, Copernicus's system 'destroyed the entire theory of the natural world as an organism', and thus as something that could be seen as growing towards an ultimate purpose: 'An organism implies differentiated organs . . . [but] if the world has no centre, the very basis of these differentiations disappears' (Collingwood 1945, 97).

This revolutionary line of argument gradually gave rise to the idea that one should think of the natural world not as an assembly of 'qualities', in the sense of the forms possessed by different entities, but rather in material or quantitative terms. Of course, the chief claim of the Aristotelian conception of nature had been its ability to explain the phenomenon of change: every natural thing changes as a result of its effort to actualize its potential being, to realize its function as defined by its own inherent form. Sixteenth-century rationalists had demolished this with biting scepticism directed against ungrounded Aristotelian claims to know the true qualitative essences of things, and with the new empirical scientific discoveries produced by astronomers such as Copernicus and Galileo Galilei (see Brundell 1987, chs 1 and 2). This left them, however, with an important constructive task still to be performed: to give an alternative account of the natural world, and particularly of the problems of change and motion within nature. One of the central questions for the new philosophy of nature was how change could be explained, once the qualitative idea of a *telos* had been removed from the concept of nature.

The first step was to redefine the problem in the quantitative terms of the new physics, rejecting the qualitative vocabulary of Aristotelian natural philosophy. Thus, as René Descartes put it, the concept of motion means nothing more than 'the translation of a piece of matter or a body from the neighbourhood of the bodies immediately touching it, these being regarded as at rest, to the neighbourhood of others' (Descartes 1983, 51). The new philosophy asserted that the Aristotelian notion that things have 'natures' in the sense of qualities or essences that they are trying to realize is merely an invention of the human mind, superimposed on a purposeless material universe that consists entirely of materials undergoing quantitative changes in terms of their location in space and time. Moreover, in a radical move that parted company with virtually all post-Socratic philosophies of nature – including the Stoics, with whom their idea of the materiality of the universe otherwise had considerable affinities – the new natural philosophers posited the existence of a general principle of attraction between material objects that explained their observed motions. Initially, this was associated with work on magnetism, but it was eventually given its fullest expression in Isaac Newton's work on the laws of gravitational attraction. Even before Newton, though, this implied a radical change in the meaning of the concept of a 'natural law'. Previously, medieval scholars had understood this in terms of a set of general *moral* prescriptions, consistent with the teleological conception of nature as a divinely created order. During the sixteenth and seventeenth centuries, however, natural philosophers began to see the 'law of nature' in terms of the regular *physical* laws that governed the action and interaction of material objects in accordance with the principle of attraction, possessing little or no ethical content of its own.

The idea of a state of nature

Having briefly looked at this new way of thinking about nature, let us return to the debate about the Indies and the possibilities of the colonial appropriation of land. We left this discussion in the hands of Sepulveda and his humanist conception of property rights as an institution of civil society, rather than as something governed by natural law – understood in scriptural terms. The continuing force of naturalist jurisprudence undermined Sepulveda's position, and indeed his idea of property, with all its implications for colonialism, required the incorporation of natural law to its defence before it could become an integral feature of a defence of the *legitimacy* of colonial appropriation. This move was made by thinkers such as Grotius and Hobbes (but see Jahn 1999 for a fuller discussion of the evolution of the idea of a state of nature in its application to the Americas). The former developed a coherent scheme of the relationship between a natural right of appropriation and a civil law of property, which did much to weave together the humanist and scholastic threads emerging from the Spanish debate about the conquest. Hobbes's contribution, however, was in some ways even more wide-ranging, offering an even broader synthesis that drew into the jurisprudential language of natural rights many of the political ideas of Machiavelli and the reason of state theorists. In his conception of the state of nature, then, the different elements of the conceptual vocabulary of international political thought that I have discussed thus far come together, making Hobbes's work a fitting conclusion to this chapter. As we will see in the next, for many eighteenth-century theorists it proved to be an important jumping-off point, and critical foil, for their contrasting ideas about international politics.

Grotius on property

In developing his analysis of private property rights, Grotius drew heavily on classical Roman law to identify two different kinds of ownership in the law of nations, each of which was acquired in its own way. His account rested on a distinction between the original acquisition of property, before the establishment of civil societies, and the institution of private property within civil society, founded on the consent of its members. According to Grotius, the first of these operated according to the principle of *occupatio*, which can be understood as appropriation; in the second context, property is called *dominium*, which is probably nearest to what we would call ownership today. The key to *occupatio* is the proposition, which Grotius had first advanced in *De jure praedae*, that everyone has a natural right to self-preservation. He began from an idea of individual self-ownership, observing that individuals already hold some rights even before the creation of the civil societal institution of *dominium*, because 'life, limbs and liberty would in that case be the possessions belonging to each, and no attack could be made upon these by another without injustice' (Grotius 1925, 2.54). He also claimed that at this early stage in human history all property in the world was held in common, with no individual ownership of land or things. And, since individuals were entitled to do what they must for survival, their rights to life, limbs and liberty were therefore extendable in this natural state through appropriation, such that 'each man could at once take whatever he wished for his own needs, and could consume whatever was capable of being consumed' (ibid., 2.186).

The right to appropriate through occupation, however, exists only as a natural right. Grotius argued that at some point in human history, as population levels increased and people began to form themselves into social associations, they transformed their naturally acquired possessions into a publicly recognized institution, *dominium*, regulated by laws made by the appropriate public authority. This fundamental change in the character of property had to come from 'a kind of agreement', and he supposed that, once the idea of community ownership had been abandoned and further unilateral appropriation was no longer allowed, the members of society simply decided to confirm each other in their ownership of what they had already occupied (Grotius 1925, 2.189–90). This idea of a pre-social condition of natural liberty was already well established in early modern thought, and was closely associated with the belief that it endowed everyone with rights which they retained into political society (Skinner 1978, vol. 2). Grotius broadly agreed with this description of the state of nature, but his disagreement with the justification of resistance on these grounds sprang from his view that they were wrong to regard the rights associated with natural liberty as inalienable. Depending on the circumstances under which people agreed to join together in a civil society, translating their property rights into *dominium*, they might even give up their rights over their persons in such a way as to deprive themselves of any justification for resistance against the holder or holders of the sovereign power.

In that respect, and in comparison with later Lockean theories of appropriation as the basis for enduring political rights, Grotius's theory appears highly conservative. In Karl Olivecrona's view, for example, the central difference between Grotius and Locke is that the former 'allowed appropriation without the consent of others only in the earliest stage of the world and presumably for very limited purposes; it lost its importance with the introduction of *dominium* by way of convention' (Olivecrona 1974, 223). It does seem likely that Grotius saw the idea that individuals have a natural right to acquire property as defunct in the context of the societies he lived in, where ownership was presumably to be understood in terms of *dominium*. But in a different way, Grotius anticipated an element of the more radical theory of appropriation that was later to be at the heart of the Lockean account. Grotius's distinction between *occupatio* and *dominium* rests, as we have seen, on the fact that the associated rights belong to very different situations: the state of nature and civil society. Olivecrona is correct to observe that one way in which Grotius understood this distinction was temporal, in the sense that the state of nature was part of the early history of mankind that preceded the formation of civil societies. At the same time, however, Grotius also took a *geographical* view of the distinction, observing that the natural right to *occupatio* might still be exercised and defended 'if one finds himself in places without inhabitants, as on the sea, in a wilderness, or on vacant islands' (Grotius 1925, 2.92). And one would be justified in supposing that the main example he had in mind here was not so much the high seas, where the Dutch were defending their rights to free navigation on the basis of the argument that the seas could never be made subject to *dominium*, but rather that *locus classicus* of the Lockean theory of appropriation, America, where, according to Grotius, 'the community of property, arising from extreme simplicity', could still be observed even in his era (ibid., 2.187; on Locke and America, see Lebovics 1986; Tully 1993; and Arneil 1996).

Hobbes on the state of nature

In at least one crucial respect Hobbes's account was even more all-encompassing than Grotius's. In his description of the state of nature Grotius stressed human instincts towards both self-preservation and sociability. Hobbes took the vital further step of introducing the bleaker Machiavellian conception of human behaviour into his analysis of the state of nature. Rather than emphasizing the positive instinct towards sociability alone, Hobbes's moral psychology was more detailed and more complex. He did note the importance of positive or benign human passions, such as benevolence, good will and charity, but he also noted the importance of desire for glory as a key passion that animated human behaviour (Hobbes 1996, 41–2). Indeed, animation is precisely the role of the passions.

Hobbes developed this point of view within the context of a mechanistic conception of nature, and consistently likened human action to matter in motion. The driving force in his scheme, however, was not the attractive force of sociability, with nature drawing people into social association, so much as the more disintegrative force of individual selfishness, with actions caused by a mixture of desires and aversions (Hobbes 1996, 38). The importance of a passion such as the desire for glory, then, was its role in causing people to act in a certain way, and some countervailing force, the introduction of a different desire or something to cause an aversion, would be required in order to move people to act differently. The central problem that Hobbes identified within the Grotian scheme was the lack of any such countervailing force in the state of nature, without which Grotius's faith in our instinct for sociability was in vain. 'For the Laws of Nature', as Hobbes said, 'without the terror of some Power, to cause them to be observed, are contrary to our natural Passions, that carry us to Partiality, Pride, Revenge and the like. And Covenants, without the Sword, are but Words, and of no strength to secure a man at all' (ibid., 117).

This is where Hobbes's image of the sovereign as 'Leviathan' becomes important. Picking up themes from Bodin's conception of indivisible sovereignty, and from the Machiavellian appraisal of human behaviour, Hobbes concluded that the only way of ensuring the force of law in controlling the human passions was to invest the sovereign with an overwhelming force that could be deployed to keep order. It is noteworthy that, in many ways, this represents an advance on Machiavelli's assessment of the prospects for political community. The latter had merely sought to advise the individual prince on how to maintain or enlarge his state, given a world in which ordinary people were motivated more by selfishness than piety. Hobbes, on the other hand, believed that he had found a more generalizable way in which social order, and all the fruits that grew therefrom, could be maintained, given a similar problem. The difference between the two was that Hobbes, with a mechanical conception of nature powerfully informing his political theory (see Shapin and Schaffer 1985; Meyer 2001, ch. 4), was able to think more systematically about the problem than Machiavelli, and with this perspective on the problem was able to contemplate the possibility of *changing* the balance of forces between the individual and the sovereign in such a way as to ensure the triumph of the latter in the project of keeping order. His solution, especially his idea of the Leviathan, was unpalatable to many in terms of its implications for the political organization of domestic societies. Nor, internationally, did it promise much beyond the maintenance of the individual's security in what Hobbes saw would remain a periodically violent, and always militarized, state of war.

Conclusion

The idea of a state of nature was not, then, widely accepted as a perfect resolution of the tensions between the political language of reason of state and the jurisprudential language of natural law. In the hands of Hobbes it had done an excellent job of using the jurisprudential language of natural rights to address the kinds of questions and problems which had previously been the preserve of reason of state treatises. And it is significant that this was achieved through the partial adoption of a more 'historical' conception of natural law. Both Grotius and Hobbes turned the idea of natural law into something with a chronological, and possibly geographical, application, confined to a specific state of nature which was, by definition, distinct from civil society. It was not, however, a particularly sophisticated historical concept, and its exponents generally fell back on the idea that it had a *normative* purpose, rather than being a genuine attempt at the historical description of the development of mankind, although they often tried to cling on to the latter idea as well (see Ashcraft 1968). To make it properly historical, however, and therefore *really* engage with the historically based account of the turbulence of human affairs stressed by the reason of state theorists would have undermined the philosophical cohesion of the natural law framework. Therein lay the key conundrum for the state of nature theorists of the seventeenth century. The solution to the problem, as we will see in the next chapter, lay in the development of the concept of *human* nature, building on the moral psychology already provided by Grotius, Hobbes and Locke, but freeing it from what was increasingly seen as the sociological absurdity of their idea of a 'state of nature'.

Further reading

Tuck 1999 is probably the best work currently available on early modern international political thought, albeit with somewhat more of a focus on the jurisprudential language of rights than the discourse of reason of state. Viroli 1992 is an excellent complementary reading on Italian reason of state thought, but Meinecke 1984, despite now being somewhat dated, is still worth reading for its broader coverage of the field. Burke 1991 is an excellent chapter-length survey and, although in French, the introductory discussion to Rohan 1995 is also very useful. On international political thought, many other textbooks offer more detailed studies of individual thinkers such as Machiavelli, Grotius and Hobbes: Boucher 1998 and Pangle and Ahrensdorf 1999 are especially good, with the latter in particular developing an extremely interesting interpretation of 'post-Machiavellian' thought. On Bodin, Franklin 1963, 1973 and 1991 are essential reading. On Grotius, see Bull, Kingsbury and Roberts 1992, Borschberg 1994 and Keene 2002. Overall, Skinner 1978 is still an excellent starting-point for further work on early modern political thought, rich in as yet often unrealized possibilities for scholarship on international relations.

5

Human Nature, Civilization and Culture

The period between the Peace of Westphalia and the French Revolution is often seen as a time when the new principles of the 'Westphalian system' were becoming more widely understood and accepted in the everyday conduct of international affairs, and when the balance of power was being manipulated by diplomats with growing confidence and sophistication (see Morgenthau 1949, 150; also Osiander 1991; Sheehan 1994). In political philosophy more generally, though, the same period is often labelled as the age of 'Enlightenment', and commentators have frequently remarked on the apparent contrast between the optimistic intellectual aspirations of the Enlightened *philosophes* and *Aufklärers*, on the one hand, and, on the other hand, the increasingly realistic practice of power politics that seems to characterize eighteenth-century diplomacy. In one of the earliest textbooks on the history of international political thought, for example, while stressing the importance of the 'struggle for power and wealth' to the actual conduct of international relations during the period, Frank Russell described the Enlightenment as an intellectual movement that was 'entirely favourable to the acceptance and propagation of new ideas of cosmopolitanism, internationalism, and pacifism' (Russell 1936, 179, 181). That view is still widely held today. As Chris Brown, for example, has recently put it, while international lawyers were gradually reconciling themselves to the new forms of balance of power diplomacy, 'With the thinkers of the Enlightenment and their successors, this rather self-satisfied acceptance of the status quo disappeared, and a critical edge was restored to international thought' (Brown 2002, 38; see also Thompson 1994, 84).

The interpretation of Enlightened international political thought as a critical reaction to the growing acceptance of the balance of power by diplomats and lawyers within the Westphalian system is coloured by the thinkers and texts that commentators today take as characteristic of the movement in its international political aspects. By far the most attention is paid to the German philosopher Immanuel Kant, described elsewhere by Brown as 'the greatest of all theorists of international relations' (Brown 1992, 14). The literature on Kant's international political thought is immense (see, for example, Doyle 1983; Hurrell 1990; Franceschet 2002), and because much of it is dominated by the study of his essay 'Perpetual Peace' it helps to fuel the popular impression that the intellectual movement of the Enlightenment adopted a critical attitude towards the current practice of international affairs and was generally favourable to projects of international federation of the kind that Kant proposed. Second in importance, judging by the volume of interpretive studies in international relations theory today, is Jean-Jacques Rousseau, and through him the Abbé de Saint-Pierre, author of another project for 'perpetual peace' that Rousseau edited and criticized (Rousseau 1991; see for example Waltz 1959; Williams 1989). Although Rousseau's status as a member of the Enlightenment is, to say the least, ambiguous, his fiery denunciation of the international state of war, and the celebrity his work attaches to the perhaps otherwise rather obscure Saint-Pierre, helps to reinforce the conventional wisdom that the main intellectual themes of eighteenth-century international political thought revolved around cosmopolitan and pacificist ideals, bolstering a critical stance against the prevailing practices of international affairs. Only a few commentators on international politics (such as Knutsen 1992, 105–27) look in any serious way at the wider currents of eighteenth-century thought within which Kant's and Rousseau's arguments were crafted, or seek to explain why some Enlightened *philosophes* actually approved of the balance of power as an instrument of policy (see Hinsley 1963, 163).

To get at these wider currents of international political thought during the Enlightenment, and to limit the pervasive influence of Kant's essay 'Perpetual Peace', we need to bear the complexity of this intellectual movement in mind: 'A loose, informal, wholly unorganized coalition of cultural critics, religious skeptics, and political reformers from Edinburgh to Naples, Paris to Berlin, Boston to Philadelphia' (Gay 1966, 3; see also Porter and Teich 1981). Different 'Enlightenments' within this broad 'family' – such as the Scottish, for example – might provide a wholly different perspective on the *philosophes'* attitude to international politics from the predominant focus on Kant's version of the German *Aufklärung*. Bearing this in mind, my plan here is to look more closely at the conceptual vocabulary that the *philosophes* employed, with a particular focus on Scotland as well as France and Germany. It is arguable whether or not the Scottish Enlightenment had a greater impact on the subsequent development of international political thought than Kantian philosophy, although it is certainly not a straightforward task to separate them and measure their respective importance. However, with regard to the conceptual focus adopted in this book, the Scottish Enlightenment is an especially interesting field of enquiry because it helped to drive a significant change in the concepts that scholars used to talk about their world.

Despite a few notable exceptions – particularly in France, such as Rousseau himself and Charles de Montesquieu – many of the *philosophes* virtually stopped using the concept of a 'state of nature', which had become, as we saw in the previous chapter, an extremely important part of the vocabulary of seventeenth-century theorists. Several of the Scots decided that these earlier exercises in imagining the state of nature, despite their claim to be historical, were in fact unscientific and hypothetical metaphysical speculations, and therefore a waste of time. As Adam Ferguson put it, in his influential *Essay on the History of Civil Society*: 'whatever may have been the original state of our species, it is of more importance to know the condition to which we ourselves should aspire, than that which our ancestors may be supposed to have left' (Ferguson 1995, 16). Instead, they began to focus on the concept of 'human nature' because this was something that could be studied empirically by observing how people actually behaved in society. By examining the history of human society, one could uncover the characteristic features of human nature, and thus reveal the 'regular springs of human action and behaviour' (Hume 1902, 83). Here, then, I will begin by looking at this important idea of human nature, before examining the various ways in which eighteenth-century thinkers coped with the increasing volume of evidence they possessed about the diversity of human societies, largely through the ideas of different 'national characters' contributing to different degrees of progress towards a uniform goal of civilization, or through the concept of more radically incommensurable national 'cultures'. The chapter concludes on a rather different note by returning to the central problem discussed in the previous chapter, concerning the relationship between the legal basis of international order and the practice of statecraft, particularly the balance of power: under the pressure of the French Revolution, conservative reactionaries developed a historical narrative linking the balance of power and European public law together which enjoys considerable influence in international political thought and therefore deserves at least brief consideration here.

Human nature and the science of man

By the middle of the eighteenth century, political theorists were beginning to entertain serious doubts about the usefulness of the idea of the state of nature as an analytical tool. Ferguson, for instance, argued that there was nothing particularly 'natural', or even particularly interesting, about the aberrant case of 'a wild man ... caught in the woods, where he had always lived apart from his species'; on the contrary, 'we are to take the history of every active being from his conduct in the situation to which he is formed', and, in that respect, 'Mankind are to be taken in groups, as they have always subsisted' (Ferguson 1995, 9–10). His point, in other words, was that man's nature was to be social, and so one should study human nature only in society, not in some artificial pre-social construct of the so-called state of nature.

> If we are asked, Where the state of nature is to be found? we may answer, It is here; and it matters not whether we are understood to speak in the island of Great Britain, at the Cape of Good Hope, or the Straits of Magellan. While this active being is in the train of employing his talents, and of operating on the subjects around him, all situations are equally natural. (Ferguson 1995, 14)

Although they certainly did not simply abandon the old jurisprudential language of natural law (see Haakonssen 1985, 1990), this point of view was widely shared among Ferguson's Scottish colleagues (Berry 1997), and it was by no means exclusive to them. Others, indeed, were sometimes even more brutal in their criticisms. Jeremy Bentham, for example, attacked the idea of a state of nature as 'too wild to be seriously admitted' since 'it is plainly contradictory to the revealed accounts of the primitive origin of mankind', and he lampooned ideas about natural law and natural rights even more viciously when they were adopted by the French revolutionaries (Bentham 1960, 34; 1843). It was, however, less consistently rejected in France. Montesquieu, for example, took the more conventional line that, to understand natural law, 'one must consider a man before the establishment of societies' (Montesquieu 1989, 6). In the great project of the French Enlightenment, the *Encyclopédie*, 'one looks in vain for any attacks on natural law and the state of nature', and the various entries there reflect a basically conventional understanding of the idea (Vyverberg 1989, 26). Nevertheless, even in France the ideas of Ferguson, Hume and the rest of the Scots definitely did have an impact and led some scholars to question the idea of a state of nature on similar grounds, and to begin adopting the new vocabulary around the idea of '*civilisation*' (Gusdorf 1971, 334).

The gradual decline in the popularity of the concept of the 'state of nature' did not entail a drop in eighteenth-century thinkers' estimation of the importance of speculation about nature as such. On the contrary, as one naturalist concept slowly vanished, another appeared in its place. The study of 'human nature' quickly became such a hallmark of eighteenth-century thinking about politics and society that it almost seems to have been impossible for a scholar in that period to try and analyse anything without first saying what 'human nature' was and how it mattered to the particular topic under investigation. The reason for this was succinctly explained by David Hume in the introduction to his *Treatise of Human Nature*: in order to emulate and extend Isaac Newton's tremendous success at explaining the motion of matter in the physical world, Hume argued, scholarship should now move on to a similarly scientific approach to the study of human nature, a 'science of man' that Hume believed to be the true foundation of *all* proper enquiry into any subject: physics, morality, politics, and so on (Hume 1967, xix).

The idea that the analysis of human nature should form a key part of any science of politics or morals was not, of course, entirely novel. We have already seen that seventeenth-century theorists such as Hobbes and Locke had also tried to base their analysis of the natural condition of mankind upon a kind of psychological theory of human behaviour (see Hirschman 1977; Holmes 1995). Hobbes's *Leviathan*, for example, began with a series of reflections, 'On Man', the main purpose of which was to identify the various passions which moved people to behave in certain ways. His description of these is very similar to the way in which many Enlightened *philosophes* conceived of their task in constructing a new science of man: like Hume, for example, Hobbes also talks about the heart as a 'spring'. But the 'moral psychology' that Hobbes and Locke and the rest developed was deployed within the context of a *jurisprudential* vocabulary in which the concepts of natural law and the state of nature were the principal vehicles for contemplating the political consequences of human nature. By contrast, the new science of man was couched in a more *sociological* vocabulary, where human moral psychology was analysed by the study of man in society, and where the implications for politics and society were most often (but not always: see Muthu 1999) developed through a contrast between civilized and barbaric peoples rather than through speculation about natural law and natural rights.

Reason, passion and biology

If human nature was such a pivotal concept for the new science of man, how then did the *philosophes* conceive it? Generally speaking, they identified three elements to human nature. First, echoing a line of argument stretching back to ancient thought, they said that all people have the capacity of *reason*, so that politics and society should be organized in accordance with the dictates of reason. Of course, this position was hardly novel, but we have to acknowledge that it still commanded enormous influence throughout the eighteenth century: one of the cardinal themes in Enlightened thought was that reason provided an infallible guide to how people might live together in peace, prosperity and order. This was not the full extent of the *philosophes'* moral psychology, however. The second point they made, drawing in part on ideas from Hobbes, and in turn from the older sources on which Hobbes had drawn, both Stoic and 'neostoic', was that human beings are also animated by certain *passions* or *sentiments*, often clashing with the faculty of reason. The resulting antithesis between reasoned action and passionate impulse was fundamental to most Enlightened thought about how to construct a lasting pattern of social order. It is important to note here that not everyone took an entirely negative view of the passions in this context, or that the project of the Enlightenment was in some way to eliminate the passionate side of our nature in favour of a cold and calculating reason. In the first place, some sentiments were admitted to be morally desirable: as Rousseau famously commented, 'men would never have been anything but monsters if Nature had not given them pity in support of reason' (Rousseau 1997, 153). Moreover, the *philosophes* generally appreciated that, although reason might be necessary to determine what was good or useful for society, only passion could make a person *feel* committed enough to the pursuit of rationally desirable ends to choose to act in accordance with them. A political theory that failed to engage the passions would ultimately fail to move anyone to act on its behalf, and its impact on everyday life would be correspondingly negligible (Hume 1902, app. I). Another of the cardinal themes of Enlightened political thought was that, while reason might provide an infallible guide to how one should live, a system that did not account for human passions, especially in their darkest manifestations, would be doomed.

The dualism of human nature between its reasonable and passionate dimensions was such a central preoccupation of Enlightened thought that it played a defining role with respect to the views of the *philosophes* on the project of building a more peaceful international order, as we will see in just a moment. The third aspect of human nature is somewhat less important in this immediate context, but nevertheless deserves a brief mention here since it was to have a profound importance in the late nineteenth and early twentieth centuries. The key point here is that human beings do not just share reason and a set of passions; they share certain biological or physiological similarites as well. Thus some of the *philosophes*, notably Denis Diderot, sought to develop a theory of 'universal morality' out of the basic physical aspects of human nature, arguing that society should be organized in accordance with fundamental and universal needs of subsistence, recreation, procreation and so on (Strugnell 1973, 18–20; Diderot 1992). Human nature in this most physical sense thus provided a further way in which the project of building a peaceful order could be understood: satisfy everyone's needs, and the problem of war would vanish. War was, in effect, a result of the perversely *un*natural character of most European societies, a position developed to its fullest extent by Rousseau, albeit from a rather different starting-point. Many of the *philosophes* agreed, up to a point, with Rousseau, though, that the key problem with modern civil society was that it failed to satisfy basic needs in everyone's human nature, sometimes scandalizing polite society with their frankness. Of course, Diderot's universal morality notwithstanding, humans also exhibit certain physiological *differences* from one another, the elaboration of which point into racial theories gave this alternative line of thought about human nature, or natures, much of its subsequent popularity, as I will explain in due course. Race figured sometimes in the Enlightenment, but it was only one among several ways in which peoples were distinguished from one another, and it was seldom accorded a leading explanatory role.

The uniformity of human nature

Although they had developed a complex moral psychology of human nature based on the tense relationship between reason and passion, the *philosophes* all broadly agreed with David Hume's famous assertion that

> Mankind are so much the same, in all times and places, that history informs us of nothing new or strange in this particular. Its chief use is only to discover the constant and universal principles of human nature, by showing men in all varieties of circumstances and situations, and furnishing us with materials from which we may form our observations and become acquainted with the regular springs of human action and behaviour. (Hume 1902, 83)

Irrespective of the specific psychological conception they adopted, this was one of the few propositions on which all the *philosophes* could agree. Refined, urbane critics of absurd conventional mores, such as Voltaire; fiery advocates of natural virtue against the corruption of civil society, such as Rousseau or Diderot; Kantian believers in the ultimate progression of humanity through reason and the rule of law towards the civil perfection of human capabilities; the pragmatically sceptical 'natural historians' of human society from Scotland, Hume, Smith and Ferguson: all agreed that there was an essential, uniform and unchanging core to human nature, which could somehow be isolated from the various customs and manners that coloured actual human behaviour in so many different shades around the world (see Berry 1982, ch. 1; Vyverberg 1989, ch. 2).

Human reason, of course, was relatively easy to universalize: Stoics had been doing so for hundreds of years, and to established arguments on this issue all the *philosophes* really added were a few elegant turns of phrase. The *philosophes* also insisted, again not entirely originally, that people everywhere exhibited similar *passions*. Hume's own version of the uniformity thesis, for instance, made considerable use of this argument: 'Ambition, avarice, self-love, vanity, friendship, generosity, public spirit: these passions, mixed in various degrees, and distributed throughout society, have been, from the beginning of the world, and still are, the source of all actions and enterprises, which have ever been observed among mankind' (Hume 1902, 83). Something similar operated for Kant, who famously invoked the 'unsocial sociability' of human nature as the basis for an apparently instinctive 'tendency to come together in society, coupled, however, with a continual resistance which constantly threatens to break this society up' (Kant 1991, 44). The physiological argument made famous by Diderot leant heavily for its moral universalism on the evidence of similarities between human beings that was beginning to emerge from works such as George-Louis Buffon's influential *Natural History*. The argument was not yet developed into an explicit theory of ethnically defined racial differences, even though hints of such an outlook may be detected in some of Buffon's comments on negroes, alongside his general insistence on the uniformity of humanity and criticism of the treatment of Africans in the slave trade (Popkin 1973).

As an aside, it is worth noting here that some of the most notorious comments on the subject of race come from unlikely places. Even as moderate and Enlightened a philosopher as David Hume, in his essay 'Of National Characters', declared that he was 'apt to suspect the negroes, and in general all the other species of men (for there are four or five different kinds) to be naturally inferior to whites' (Hume 1994, 86n.). Immanuel Kant, whose essay on 'perpetual peace' is so often chosen as *the* textbook example of eighteenth-century cosmopolitanism, agreed with Hume. In one of his early pre-critical works, Kant more or less repeated Hume's view, adding the comment that 'the Negroes of Africa have by nature no feeling that rises above the trifling', and were 'so talkative that they must be driven apart from each other with thrashings' (Kant 1960, 110–11). His more mature *Anthropology* also betrayed racist opinions (see Berlin 1992, 163). These views were not universally shared among the *philosophes*, and certainly not by Diderot, but it is telling and interesting that such generally cosmopolitan thinkers could still see such radical differences within human nature.

To return to the uniformity thesis, there were two main reasons why it was so important to the Enlightenment, and why theorists working from so many different perspectives all came to uphold it. In the first place, the thesis was integral to their *scientific* project. For all its brilliance, Newtonian physics had only had to deal with matter in motion, and the new students of human nature realized that they were operating on a vastly more difficult terrain. Having begun his influential study *The Spirit of the Laws* with a quick sketch of the new natural science, for example, Montesquieu ruefully observed that 'the intelligent world is far from being as well governed as the physical' (Montesquieu 1989, 4). The problem was that human beings did not follow their laws so consistently as the inanimate entities with which Newton had been concerned. An enquiry into the laws governing human action and behaviour was complicated by the fact that these laws were of many different kinds, and some of them were variable and violable, unlike the physical laws identified by the

Newtonians. But, if they were to deliver on their scientific promise, the *philosophes* needed to imitate the success of the Newtonians in finding general laws governing the physical world. Despite the greater complexity of human action, they still wanted to locate 'consequences almost as general and certain ... as any which the mathematical sciences afford us' (Hume 1994, 5). There had to be 'regular springs of human action and behaviour', otherwise this task would be an impossible one, and the only basis on which human action could be said to operate in this way would be if 'constant and universal principles of human nature' did indeed exist. The uniformity thesis had to be upheld, or else the science of man would fail to be properly scientific.

The second point is that the science of man was, above all, a *moral* science. The *philosophes* were looking for 'universal principles, from which all censure or approbation is ultimately derived' (Hume 1902, 174). They hoped to find normative standards on the basis of which to judge existing political and social orders, and to furnish them with the material out of which to sketch a vision of how things should be. The force of such arguments would inevitably be lessened if no universal standard could be located in nature, since that would potentially open the door to relativism and deprive moral science of its special status. The idea of the uniformity of human nature was, then, as integral to the Enlightenment's normative project as to its scientific one (Berry 1982, 20–3). At this point it is perhaps worth noting a common criticism that the *philosophes* were inconsistent here, mixing up an empirical account of nature as it is with a normative account of nature as an ideal standard against which existing human societies could be compared (see, for example, Sampson 1956). This slippage persisted despite Hume's insistence that the confusion of the real with the ideal had been one of the cardinal errors of traditional natural law thinking, and his vigorous argument for maintaining a separation between factual and normative statements.

Tellingly, in view of his increasingly rare use of the concept of a state of nature in the context of the Enlightenment, Rousseau is perhaps the exemplar of this position, with his adoption of an idea of the 'natural state' of mankind as the basis for a scathing attack on the inequalities and corruptions of civil society. He argued that the character of man had changed 'by imperceptible adulterations' with the development from one to the other, so that civil society consists of 'an assemblage of artificial men and factitious passions which are the product of all these new relationships, and have no true foundation in nature' (Rousseau 1997, 186); as we have seen, this was very much the position that Ferguson was attacking. Nevertheless, it is clear that Rousseau saw the differences one observes between men in different political communities not as differences in human nature, but as the result of the degree to which these 'adulterations' have progressed under their various governments. Each instance of 'civilized man' represented a departure from a single, general idea of 'natural' or 'savage' man. Kant's sketch of a cosmopolitan universal history might be taken as another example of a reliance on the uniformity thesis for normative reasons. He was committed to the forward-looking proposition that 'the history of the human race as a whole' was 'the realisation of a hidden plan of nature' to develop to perfection the 'natural capacities of mankind', and this would be nonsensical if there were no such thing as a universal human nature (Kant 1991, 50). The concept of human nature provided Rousseau and Kant with the template against which to measure the imperfections of existing civil societies, and to perform this role it had to possess a discernible uniformity.

Human nature at work: war and peace

The study of human nature would, the *philosophes* hoped, provide the key to understanding how governments and society as a whole should be organized. In that regard, they applied themselves to a question which was at the forefront of diplomats' minds: how to build a lasting peace among European states. With the devastating wars of religion a recent memory, with the traditional pillars of the order of Christendom an increasingly distant one, and with a growing fear of the destructive capacity of new military technologies, the great European treaties of the late seventeenth and the eighteenth century shared a common aspiration to build a new kind of peace or friendship between nations that would be 'Christian', 'universal' and 'perpetual'; the exact phrasing varies from treaty to treaty, but the same three adjectives are nearly always there. (They typically appear in the preambles to treaties: see Grewe 1988, 184, 205, 231, 240 and 259; also Parry 1969, 42.322.) 'Perpetual peace' was one of the standard diplomatic formulae of the time: a little hollow – as Leibniz, Rousseau and Kant all pointed out – but not without meaning or significance. Although it is a simplification, it is not unfair to represent the dominant issue in international political thought during most of the eighteenth century – until the French Revolution, at least – in terms of this larger diplomatic effort to establish a perpetual peace in, and sometimes even beyond, Europe.

In this context we should realize that the balance of power was not just a pragmatic tool for statesmen acting in isolation from scholars and political philosophers. Along with cognate notions such as the 'balance of property', it provided a crucial part of the intellectual solution to the Hobbesian problem of how to maintain order given the unruly and unsociable character of some human passions, but without vesting power in an authoritarian Leviathan. The attractions of the idea for Enlightened scholars, indeed, partly explain the alacrity with which diplomats turned to it at Utrecht, as well as the enduring popularity of the idea of balancing as a maxim for foreign policy. The beauty of the balance as an alternative to the Leviathan was that, as Hume later remarked, it represented a way in which 'human nature checks itself' (Hume 1994, 160). Hobbes's solution had placed the control of human passions in the hands of an absolute monarch, but the more liberal and republican-minded *philosophes* were just as worried about the danger that monarchs' passions would lead them to rule in an arbitrary way, and many were equally worried about the danger of despotism if all power was left in the hands of the people, as in a democracy (Kant 1991). They wanted a political *system* – again, note the analogy with Newton's systematic approach to the study of nature – that would control *rulers* as well as their subjects. Domestically, that implied constitutional arrangements that would divide powers between different branches of the government, so that each would check the other: republicanism, in other words. Internationally, it required rulers to follow a policy of balancing power against each other, and this was a policy that they would want to pursue anyway, since it was consistent with their chief reason of state: the preservation of their own 'liberties'. Both in theory and in practice, then, the balance of power was the fundamental institution of European political order. To the extent that there was any need left for the law of nations, it was often merely as a kind of afterthought, covering the few remaining issues that would be left over as possible reasons for dispute once the important business had been settled (see Hume 1902, 205–6).

There is another, slightly more subtle, point in this argument about the desirability of the balance of power in comparison with other ways of organizing international affairs (meaning, in practice, the pre-Utrecht and even pre-Westphalia patterns of international order). The idea that rulers would pursue their own interests did not only offer a powerful reason for using the balance of power as an ordering mechanism, as outlined above, but was also one of the *purposes* of this kind of order. If not reason of state, one might ask, what motives would a ruler feel, and what goals would he or she be likely to pursue? The old order had been built on the hope – rather naive and unsupported by proper empirical evidence, the *philosophes* thought – that rulers would behave as good, law-abiding Christians. But the old way of conducting international politics had also prominently featured the pursuit of glory, territorial aggrandizement for its own sake, religious crusading (or persecution) and a host of other motivations of dubious moral standing which the *philosophes* persistently highlighted. Encouraging rulers to pursue their reasons of state was, in the first place, to encourage them to conduct their affairs in a more *reasonable* way, allowing qualities such as prudence and moderation to stand forth in a more positive light. Moreover, it directed rulers' attention away from extravagant goals such as glory towards more prosaic calculations of interest. Indeed, once the balancing idea was widely understood, it allowed for the possibility of conceptualizing a 'general interest' of Europe as a whole, where one sought to improve one's position but without disrupting the wider equilibrium, an idea that was quite well established by the Congress of Vienna at the end of the wars of the French Revolution, and added greatly to the sense that the balance of power was a legitimate basis for policy. An important illustration of this line of thinking is the flowering of ideas about the beneficial effect of *commerce* on international relations in the eighteenth century (for example, Campbell 1752). In general terms, the very notion that encouraging commerce was part of any sensible ruler's reason of state in itself reflected the rise of a less glorious, more bourgeois, conception of the goals that the state should set for itself in international affairs, corresponding with a broader political movement – of which Hobbes himself may be seen as an important spokesman – to establish the pursuit of self-interest as a benign alternative to more violent and arbitrary passions such as the pursuit of glory (Hirschman 1977). We will return to this notion in a moment, because it helped to inform the development of eighteenth-century thinking about human progress as well.

Virtually all diplomats and most of the *philosophes* were therefore in agreement on what Voltaire called 'the wise policy of maintaining . . . an equal balance of power' (cited in Hinsley 1963, 163), and that conjunction is sufficient to explain the increasingly dominant role that the balance played in the general project of building a 'perpetual peace'. Not all of the *philosophes* came to this conclusion in precisely the same way, however, and it is important to get a sense of the range of their thinking about the concept of human nature. Once again, Rousseau followed his own path, especially the way in which he constructed a quite different account of human nature and its relation to the problem of war. Like most other *philosophes*, Rousseau stressed the passionate dimension of human nature as well as the capacity for reason. He thought, however, that in the state of nature these passions were generally morally benign, or even positive, and certainly did not lead to the warlike natural man as so many imagined. Rousseau's 'natural man' not only felt pity for other human beings in suffering, but was also characterized by great timidity. By themselves, as all people were in the state of nature, people were simply too weak and isolated to indulge in violence. The aggressive and competitive behaviour that people witnessed in everyday life was not, Rousseau argued, evidence of what man was like by nature; on the contrary, it showed how the establishment of civil society had corrupted man. Civil society itself was not necessarily at fault here, but certain key institutions of modern European societies – most notably that of private property – which had produced this unhappy situation.

The corruption of natural man within civil society was bad enough, but the consequences for international politics were even worse. Within civil society, people at least had the institution of law to govern them, even if that institution was only necessary because man could no longer live according to his nature. In relations between nations, however, there was nothing of the kind; institutionally, at least, international politics were still in the same ungoverned, anarchic condition as the original state of nature:

> as man with man, we live in the civil state and subject to laws; as people with people, each one enjoys natural liberty: and our situation is far worse than if these distinctions were unknown. For living at the same time in the social order and in the state of nature, we are subject to the inconveniences of both, without finding the security of either.
> (cited in Tuck 1999, 203)

Thus, as Richard Tuck puts it, Rousseau's theory of international politics added a 'sceptical twist' to the original Hobbesian problem that vexed so many eighteenth-century philosophers: even the Hobbesian Leviathan could no longer be seen as an adequate solution to the problem of war. The best that could be hoped for under these circumstances was something akin to the balance of power, for want of anything better; schemes for international federation were attractive, but hopelessly idealistic.

To escape this pessimistic conclusion one needed to see human nature as holding within itself the possibilities for the solution of the problem of 'perpetual peace'. That, certainly, was the point of Hume's

urbane defence of the balance of power, but in a quite different form
it was also the central thrust of Immanuel Kant's argument that
'nature guarantees perpetual peace by the actual mechanism of human
inclinations' (Kant 1991, 114), a view which, as Martha Nussbaum
has observed, effectively exhibits a return to the teleological conception of nature we witnessed in Stoic and Ciceronian thinking
(Nussbaum 1997, 41), especially in the role it vests in Providence.
Kant's reinterpretation of nature, particularly his identification of a
'natural' process of human historical development, allowed a way of
pushing beyond the balance of power as a solution to the problem of
peace, a solution which might instead be achieved, Kant thought, by
a federation of free republics (Kant 1991). Far from being a purely
speculative idea, with no grounding in the contemporary practice of
international politics, this was actually one of the routes that statesmen pursued in their efforts to maintain order and build peace. In
North America, for example, a federation of republics was precisely
the solution that was adopted to prevent war between the thirteen
former colonies after they had won their independence from Britain
(Onuf and Onuf 1983; Deudney 1995). In Europe too, as we will see
in a moment, it was an important theme in debates about the true
character of international order following the French Revolution and
the establishment of what, French apologists claimed, was a federal
system (Hauterive 1800).

Diversity, progress and national character

An especially difficult problem for the new concept of human nature
– indeed, the whole 'science of man' – manifested itself most strongly
outside Europe, however. If the principal development in European
politics before the French Revolution was the establishment of a balance between powers, beyond Europe the most important development was the origin of European *dominance* in Asia, a quite novel
state of international affairs. One result of their new imperial role
in Asia was that Europeans were now in possession of vastly more
information about these peoples than they had ever had before (see
Marshall and Williams 1982). The evidence of striking differences
between European and Asian ways of life was unavoidable, and as
some European states began to become entangled in the government
of Asian peoples, especially the British in India, the questions this
raised could not be avoided. How could such great diversity be
explained? What implications did it have for relations between

European and non-European peoples? How and why had Europeans come to enjoy a position of dominance over Asians, and did this have any connection with the differences between their respective societies' ways of life? How should European governments act towards their new subjects, particularly if the latter followed customs which the former found distasteful?

Progress and the uniformity of human nature

As we have seen, the *philosophes* were committed to the uniformity thesis as a necessary condition for the science of man, but they were equally committed to an empirical approach to that science, deducing general principles from the careful accumulation of observations about how people actually live in the world. They flatly rejected the abstract, metaphysical speculations of theologians and earlier natural lawyers as a starting-point. This kind of *a priori* thinking, Hume argued, led to all sorts of bizarre and unsubstantiated hypotheses: 'only experience, which teaches us the nature and bounds of cause and effect, and enables us to infer the existence of one object from that of another . . . is the foundation for moral reasoning, and is the source of all human action and behaviour' (Hume 1902, 164). He therefore insisted that the student of morals and politics should begin by observing 'human life . . . in the common course of the world' and experimentally work out 'general maxims from a comparison of particular instances', rather than dream up systems composed of logical inferences from 'a general abstract principle' divorced from experience of the real world (Hume 1967, xxiii, and 1902, 174). Etienne Condillac, another of the leading methodologists of the Enlightenment, took a similar view in his *Treatise on Systems* (Gay 1969, 165).

Although everyone agreed on the importance of empirical observation, there was some disagreement among the *philosophes* as to how best to proceed. Hume, for example, criticized his French colleague Montesquieu for proposing an 'abstract theory of morals', based on the rationalist proposition that laws 'are the necessary relations deriving from the nature of things' (Hume 1902, 197n.; Montesquieu 1989, 3). Rousseau advocated an experimental method, but he was wary of 'the uncertain testimonies of History', and admitted the importance of 'conjecture' to his method (Rousseau 1997, 125, 142, 159). Nevertheless, one thing was clear: the available evidence of human life 'in the common course of the world' that the eighteenth century presented could be said to have pointed towards the uniformity of human nature only with the utmost indirection, if it did so at all. To be frank, there was more than a hint of *a priori* reasoning in Hume's insistence that 'history informs us of nothing new or strange' about human nature. Nor was Hume alone in that regard. One of the early works of the French Enlightenment, Voltaire's *Essay on the Customs and Spirit of Nations*, acknowledged that 'Custom spreads variety over the universal scene, while nature spreads unity', and admitted that 'The empire of custom is much more vast than that of nature', yet still offered a vigorous assertion of the uniformity of human nature on the basis of the universality of reason (cited in Vyverberg 1989, 59). Moreover, the *philosophes* were now confronted with ever greater quantities of evidence attesting to the fact of human diversity, as reports on non-European ways of life flooded in from travellers, merchants, explorers, soldiers and diplomats. They were fascinated by this burgeoning literature, and recognized that it seemed to point towards the fact of human diversity, but they still could not afford to abandon their belief in the uniformity of human nature, since that was the principal foundation for their new science. It was vital, then, to explain the diversity of human political and social organization around the world in a way that would be consistent with the uniformity thesis.

The concept of *progress* proved to be an extremely useful tool for the job. Its beauty was that it allowed the evident diversity of human societies around the world to be identified with the historical changes that one would expect – *ex hypothesis* – any single human society to undergo as it progressed along the long road from barbarism to civilization. In 1773, Edmund Burke captured the general thrust of the approach and its implications for diversity very neatly in a letter to the Scottish historian William Robertson:

> we possess at this time very great advantages towards the knowledge of human nature. We need no longer go to history to trace it in all its stages and periods. . . . now the great map of mankind is unrolled at once; and there is no state or gradation of barbarism, and no mode of refinement which we have not at the same instant under view. (cited in Marshall and Williams 1982, 93; see also Robertson 1972)

The diversity of societies in the eighteenth century could thus be explained in terms of a *uniform* process of transition, conducted at varying paces, from one *universal* condition (the state of nature, or, increasingly, barbarism) to another *universal* goal (the perfection of civil society). Even those *philosophes* who wished to criticize European manners found the conceptual framework of this argument congenial to their purposes, since all they had to do was replace 'progress' with 'degeneration', and then much the same argument could work in reverse: different societies had degenerated to different degrees from the universal starting-point of the state of nature; instead of, say, Tahiti becoming more like Europe, Europe should become more like Tahiti. This kind of critical argument was more exceptional than ordinary, however, and most of the *philosophes* happily accepted the progressivist interpretation of history.

The roots of the specifically eighteenth-century idea of progress lay partly in a seventeenth-century debate about the merits of the 'ancients' and the 'moderns' in literature, the arts and the sciences. By the beginning of the eighteenth century, there was no clear winner in this dispute, and one might even have said that the defenders of the 'ancients' were marginally ahead, thanks to the success of Jonathan Swift's satire of modernist pretensions in *The Battle of the Books* (see Nisbet 1980, 151–6; Marshall and Williams 1982, 132). Even during the Enlightenment, the ancient way of life had its defenders. While vaunting the importance of nature, however, the *philosophes* overwhelmingly came to the view that their contemporary European societies represented a decisive advance on anything that had gone before, and by the end of the eighteenth century this position was widely accepted. Anne Robert Turgot, one of the leading economists of the eighteenth century and later to become controller-general under Louis XVI, is often credited with the first comprehensive statement of this view of the concept of progress. The essence of his position was that what were normally supposed to be the negative passions of man – 'self-interest, ambition, vainglory' – had led to an astonishingly positive result: 'manners are softened, the human mind enlightened, isolated nations brought together; commercial and political ties finally unite all parts of the globe; and the total mass of human kind, through alternations of calm and upheaval, good fortune and bad, advances ever, though slowly towards greater perfection' (in Nisbet 1980, 180). Turgot's eulogy to progress happily coincided with his belief that the society which had advanced furthest in this upward direction was his own France; the advancement of Turgot's career soon followed. His ideas were picked up and expanded by other *philosophes*, notably the Marquis de Condorcet, Ferguson and, of course, Kant (Condorcet 1795; Ferguson 1995; Kant 1991).

Explaining diverse national characters

The use of the concept of progress to cope with the observed fact of diversity without abandoning the uniformity thesis left the *philosophes* with one remaining task: to explain why societies progressed at such varying rates, and why some – China, for example – had apparently ceased to make any progress, or had even slipped back a bit, after initially advancing further and faster than European societies. Explanations of this point typically made use of a more general kind of argument about diversity which was contained in the idea of distinct 'national characters' (see Vyverberg 1989, ch. 4). The position was something like this: individual human beings everywhere have the same nature, but when living under different political systems, or when inhabiting different geographical environments and climates, their behavioural tendencies, their shared customs, religious and moral beliefs, and thus the 'spirit' of the nation to which they belong, will vary accordingly. Moreover, because of the constancy of human nature, peoples' responses to their environments are predictable, hence permitting the scientific explanation of even the most glaring differences between societies as a whole.

The degree of progress a society has achieved, then, will be correlated with its type of government and geographical circumstances. The seminal example of this argument about different national characters, albeit with less of a focus on the concept of progress, is Montesquieu's *Spirit of the Laws*, which seeks at length to demonstrate that legal systems differ from one place to another because of 'the nature and the principle of government that is established' and the 'physical aspect of the country' (Montesquieu 1989, 8–9). Hume adopted a similar formulation, labelling governmental and geographical factors respectively as 'moral' and 'physical' causes of national character, although, unlike Montesquieu, he much preferred the 'moral' factor as an explanation, doubting that explanations based on physical causes made any sense at all (Hume 1994, 78–92). Nevertheless, even Hume managed to find a use for geographical differences in the context of political economy: 'Nature, by giving a diversity of geniuses, climates, and soils, to different nations, has secured their mutual intercourse and commerce, so long as they all remain industrious and civilized' (ibid., 151). Through these and similar arguments, the *philosophes* could not only rescue their thesis of the uniformity of human nature from the problem of the observed diversity of human societies, they actually turned the latter problem to their advantage, using it to add a crucial element to their theorization of the development of civil society. The 'great map of mankind' thus provided them with the directions they needed not just to explain but even to direct the progress of civil society. The world beyond Europe was to become one of the major sites where Europeans could develop and refine their ideas about controlling these processes of social development.

Diversity and *Kultur*

Not everyone in the eighteenth century came to the conclusion that differences between European and Asian societies were evidence of the relative progress of the former. Even within the Enlightenment, as I said earlier, the argument from progress could quite easily be turned on its head, using more 'natural' societies to criticize the degeneracy of European civil society, an attitude made famous by Diderot's praise of Tahitian society as more in tune with human nature than France, but occasionally expressed by others, including Voltaire and Montesquieu. In principle, moreover, the use of environmental 'moral' and 'physical' causes to explain observed differences between 'national characters' did not require a further step into theories of relative 'progress', or even the making of moral comparisons between societies, as shown by both Montesquieu and Hume at their judicious best, the latter's views on 'negroes' notwithstanding. But if one wanted to retain the thesis that human nature was the same everywhere, diversity was always going to be a *problem* to be explained away. Any other view required the Enlightenment's crucial uniformity thesis to be abandoned, or at least revised to such a significant extent that it would become something else entirely. The principal eighteenth-century philosopher to argue in that way was Johann Gottfried Herder.

Herderian anthropology

Herder was originally Kant's pupil at Königsberg (they later fell out bitterly), and has been hailed as the father of modern anthropology, literary criticism, linguistics and linguistic philosophy. He has also been condemned as the author of the uniquely German conception of the *Volk* that is hard to separate from its more sinister manifestation under the Nazis, although that latter view – of Herder as the architect of an aggressive and destructive German nationalism – has been the subject of serious criticism over the last few decades and is no longer so widely held (Barnard 1965, 71; Berlin 1992). Herder certainly believed in the uniqueness of different nations, but he was a ferocious critic of the militarization of their relations with one another, and savaged the notion that one could identify a 'master-race' that should hold all others in subjection (see, for instance, Herder 2002, 377–9).

Herder is interesting to us at the moment because of his vigorous assault on the uniformity thesis: 'human nature', he said, 'is not identical in different parts of the world' (cited in Berlin 1992, 180). Most importantly, while it was a universal attribute of human nature to possess 'culture', each particular national culture was unique and could only properly be understood by entering into its own language and spirit: to depict the 'living painting' of a culture, 'one would first have to *sympathize* with the nation' (Herder 2002, 291–2). 'Enlightened' attempts to develop a science of man built on a few generalizations about human nature were therefore profoundly mistaken. What they produced was only the abstraction and extrapolation of one's own world-view at the expense of others', rather than any useful knowledge. As Herder put it,

> To apply such a criterion or standard is not just misleading, it is meaningless. For 'European culture' is a mere abstraction, an empty category. Where does, or did, it actually exist in its entirety? In which nation? In which period? . . . Only a misanthrope could regard European culture as the universal condition of our species. The culture of *man* is not the culture of the *European*; it manifests itself according to place and time in *every* people. (cited in Barnard 2003, 135; emphases original)

Moreover, the mistaken belief that a particular culture represented a uniform and universal human nature led, Herder argued, to imperialism: the 'crime of abusing humanity' (Herder 2002, 381). Nor did he accept the Enlightenment claim that this was justified because it would spread the benefits of civilization. All it produced, according to Herder, was 'a foisted foreign culture, a formation [*Bildung*] that does not develop out of [a people's] own dispositions', which 'oppresses and deforms, or else it plunges straight into the abyss' (ibid., 382).

It is important to note Herder's appeal to 'the culture of man'. As this suggests, notwithstanding his insistence on the uniqueness of each national culture, he still held to a cosmopolitan belief in the underlying unity of humanity, or *Humanität* (see, for example, Herder 2002, 342; Humboldt 1963, 266; see also Meinecke 1970). His argument for particularism was essentially an epistemological thesis; it was concerned with the kind of knowledge we can possibly have about humanity. We cannot, as the *philosophes* supposed, know humanity by building up putatively universal categories, because those will inevitably fail to capture its richness. The 'culture of man' will always remain somewhat mysterious and unknowable, but we can participate in it through immersion in particular cultures, which give us a glimpse of what humanity is, but only ever a partial sense of the whole.

Because of his rejection of the abstraction of universal categories, Herder might appear to be a critic of modern science cast in a Newtonian mould. That is true, but it is important to note that he was not rejecting 'science' as such. On the contrary, his approach was closely related to what Peter Reill describes as a 'new language of nature' which had arisen to occupy an influential position in eighteenth-century thought, through which 'Nature was reanimated' (Reill 1996, 14, 18). This was not dissimilar to the pre-Newtonian, Stoic conception of a harmonious universe filled with 'hidden sympathies' and 'active forces', which could be known through empirical observation mixed with intuitive insight, rather than the mathematical formulae of the Newtonians. Nature, on this view, was an *organism* rather than a mechanism, and this organic image was one that Herder adopted and adapted to his understanding of the culture of man and the individual cultures of different nations (Barnard 1965; Schick 1971).

The political implications of Kultur

Herder's epistemology pointed towards an aesthetic world-view rather than a political theory as such. His organicist conception of nature did, however, carry obvious political implications which he developed through the idea of the nation or *Volk* – a 'family writ large' – which he saw as the natural organ of political association (Barnard 1965, 54–5). The nation was linguistically defined, since language was, in Herder's view, the primary human attribute that permitted the development of culture. (In this respect his theory reflects the development of the other theme from Enlightenment reason in the Ciceronian Stoic conception of man as distinguished from animals by the capacities for reason *and speech*.) Just like an organism, the nation had to 'grow' in a way consistent with its original make-up. Herder's politics was, in this context, rather conservative, rejecting revolutionary changes introduced on the basis of what reason directed. Despite that, he was not a supporter of monarchical absolutism. The idea of the *Volk* implied a role for the people in politics, albeit not in a Rousseauian direct democracy so much as in something resembling Kantian republicanism, where political culture would be reflected in 'participation within a diffuse framework of diverse bases of activity and power' (Barnard 2003, 157).

The people, when properly educated, would be able to understand the cultural framework of their nation and develop their political institutions accordingly; prior to that moment, however, something more patriarchal was required, with popular leadership provided by an intellectual elite. The main concepts Herder used to describe this political process of the development of the nation were of *Bildung* (building up) and *Tradition* (passing on). *Bildung* was to become especially pivotal to German thinking about cultural progress. It is sometimes translated as 'civilized', but perhaps 'cultivated' would be nearer the mark. Certainly, while Herder's organicist conception of politics allowed him to describe social development in terms of maturation, his theory had fewer of the strongly evaluative judgements made by the political economists and historians of civil society. On the contrary, 'Herder refused to view stages of development in an outright dichotomous manner. One reason for his refusal to apply such dichotomies as traditional and modern, primitive and civilized, static and dynamic, sacred and secular was his cultural relativism' (Barnard 2003, 147).

The world-view developed by Herder enjoyed enormous popularity in Germany, where it connected with – indeed, helped to shape – the '*Sturm und Drang*' literary movement driven by 'romantic' thinkers. His ideas of the *Volk*, *Bildung* and *Kultur* appealed both politically and spiritually, the latter especially as an alternative to what was already widely perceived in Germany as the excessively materialistic conception of civil society favoured by the British and the political economists. In the wider romantic movement, however, the political themes of Herder's nationalism increasingly became associated with the idea of the state as the true representative of the nation: in the work, for example, of Adam Müller there was an almost mystical conception of the state as the embodiment of the organic wholeness and spiritual essence of the national culture (Barnard 2003, 59). The romantics also vigorously insisted that Herder's philosophy showed that the *philosophes'* vision of perpetual peace had to come to terms with the historicist approach that he developed: 'The (postulated) *purposiveness of nature* (however beautiful, and indeed necessary this view might be in other respects) is here completely beside the point; only the (actual) *necessary laws of experience* can provide a guarantee for future success. *The laws of political history*, and the *principles of political culture*, are the only basis from which we can show "that eternal peace is no empty idea"' (Schlegel 1996, 109).

Conclusion: the impact of the French Revolution

The Enlightenment should not be understood, then, as making a single contribution to international political thought, not least because 'the' Enlightenment was really an amorphous collection of loosely related intellectual movements. Here, I have highlighted two key conceptual developments which carry, as we will see in the next chapter, significant implications for the further development of international political thought in the nineteenth century. On the one hand, especially but not exclusively from the 'Scottish Enlightenment', comes an idea of human history as progress towards 'civilization', where different levels of development along that path are explicable in terms of the physical and moral causes that have shaped particular 'national characters'. By contrast, from Herder, but also with touches of Rousseau and Diderot, we have an idea of distinct national 'cultures' as intrinsic elements of humanity, which it would be dangerous to try to push towards a singular, homogeneous conception of civilized society. We will see in a moment that both of these ideas were pregnant with possibilities for further development.

Before we leave the eighteenth century, though, it is important to add one final note to our discussion. The Enlightenment, important though it unquestionably was for the future development of international political thought, was by no means as dominant within the period as a whole as I have suggested here. In particular, I have thus far failed to consider the less philosophical, but in some ways more practically important, literatures on the law of nations and European statecraft, each building from the natural law and the reason of state traditions that we discussed in the previous chapter. I have space to make only a couple of brief points about these ways of thinking, but that should not detract from their significance.

First, the literature on the law of nations was gradually becoming oriented more and more towards the historical analysis of treaties. With the exception of a few more philosophically inclined lawyers (Vattel 1916), an increasing amount of legal scholarship was beginning to concentrate on turning out compendia of treaties, with a commentary on their essential features. Gradually, a sense was developing that legitimacy in European public law depended on a complicated web of treaty obligations that sovereigns had assumed – now meticulously recorded and well understood by all diplomats – rather than any real basis in some more abstract rationalistic scheme of natural law, however philosophically sophisticated. For most of the eighteenth century, this literature did not attempt to offer a synoptic overview of European public order as a whole; the focus was usually on the obligations of individual states, rather than identifying general principles on which the order as a whole was based (Dumont 1726 is a good example).

The pivotal development which transformed this legal literature was the French Revolution and, more particularly, the remarkable expansion of French military power under Napoleon Bonaparte and his deposition of many of the old dynastic families in the countries he conquered. The French, rather disingenuously perhaps, argued that they were trying to restore the core principles of the European 'federal' system, which they said had originally been created by the Peace of Westphalia through its confirmation of the 'reserved rights' of the Holy Roman emperor, but which had been destroyed *before* the revolution by the rising power of Russia, Prussia and especially Britain (Hauterive 1800). To this, conservatives responded by invoking the classic argument which we saw in the previous chapter had been developed in the seventeenth century to resist overly aggressive imperial powers within Europe: the idea of the balance of power. They married this together with the legitimist discourse on the law of nations, to argue that European peace treaties had been systematically working towards the principle of the balance because the core normative principles of what they christened the European 'states-system', *Staatensystem*, were the protection of the liberties and sovereign rights of established governments: two key works in this respect were by the French historians Christophe-Guillaume de Koch and Maximilien Frédéric Schoell and by the German historian Arnold Heeren (Koch and Schoell 1817; Heeren 1834; see also Keene 2002, 14–22). The balance of power ceased to be merely a *political* convenience, but now became a vital part of the 'common law' of Europe (Welsh 1995, 34).

The defence of the 'old regime' thus came to be presented as a struggle for the fundamental legal principle of European public order: mutual respect for state sovereignty, operating through the maintenance of a balance of power. In a way, this weaving together of the political and legal languages of seventeenth-century international political thought represented an alternative fusion of the two from that which had been achieved by Hobbes and other 'state of nature' theorists. Here, by contrast, the political and jurisprudential languages came together in an essentially conservative historical political discourse, dedicated to the principle that monarchical dynasticism was right because it was sanctioned by custom, rather than any reliance on philosophical ideas about 'natural law' or 'social contract'. The whole discourse was therefore insulated, so to speak, from the conceptual changes that the Enlightened *philosophes* had been introducing into the old state of nature argument, and at the beginning of the nineteenth century, as we will see in the next chapter, it posed one of the key challenges for liberal inheritors of the new idea of 'civilization' that the Enlightenment had developed.

Further reading

Berry 1997 and Vyverberg 1989 are two works that develop key themes from this chapter, but Gay's two volumes (1966 and 1969) still provide one of the best introductions to the wider Enlightenment. A good set of recent essays on Kant's Perpetual Peace can be found in Bohman and Lutz-Bachmann 1997, although Linklater 1990 or Brown 1992 might be better starting-points for a study of Kant, while Hurrell 1990 is an excellent article-length discussion. Notable works dealing with related themes in international political thought include Hinsley 1963, Hurrell 1990, Welsh 1995 and Onuf 1998; Rousseau 1991 also contains valuable interpretive insights. Barnard 1965 and 2003 are both excellent studies of Herder, with considerable significance for students of international politics. While Zammito 2002 is a more recent, although not exactly introductory, analysis of Kant and Herder's studies of anthropology – a topic with a decisive, but neglected, relevance to theories of international politics and the concepts discussed in this chapter – Muthu 1999 covers some similar themes but perhaps in a rather more digestible fashion, and would be worth reading first. Among the *philosophes*, Ferguson 1980 and Hume 1994 certainly repay reading, alongside the more obvious texts from Kant and Rousseau. Herder 2002 is a valuable new collection and translation of Herder's philosophical writings.

6

The Liberal Idea of Civilization and its Critics

'It is a curious feature of international relations theory', says Justin Rosenberg, 'that the nineteenth century seems largely to have dropped out of view' (Rosenberg 1994, 162). Astonishingly enough, there is some truth to this claim even for a subject with such an obligation to the past as the history of international political thought. It was not always thus. Back in 1936, the nineteenth century was still, so to speak, news: Frank Russell's *Theories of International Relations* devotes about twice as much time to the nineteenth century as it does to the seventeenth, roughly the reverse of what would probably be the case in textbooks today (Russell 1936). Arnold Wolfers's early study *The Anglo-American Tradition* is somewhat more evenly balanced, but still includes several studies of prominent ninteenth-century thinkers, such as Richard Cobden, John Stuart Mill, Herbert Spencer and Alfred Thayer Mahan (Wolfers 1956). In more recent textbooks, however, these and many other thinkers from the nineteenth century – especially American, British and French liberals – do indeed seem to have 'dropped out of view'. As Rosenberg points out, Martin Wight's 'academy of "international thought" is fully staffed by the end of the eighteenth century' (Rosenberg 1994, 162), and, with the exception of G. W. F. Hegel and Karl Marx, the nineteenth century makes the most fleeting appearances in even some of the best recent textbooks (see, for example, Doyle 1997; Boucher 1998; Pangle and Ahrensdorf 1999; Knutsen 1992 is, yet again, a notable exception).

Some omissions are particularly noteworthy. Nietzsche apparently does not belong in the canon of 'great thinkers' about international politics (Doyle 1997, Boucher 1998, and Brown et al. 2002 do not mention him), while the only reference that Thomas Pangle and Peter Ahrensdorf make to John Stuart Mill is to chide him in a footnote for the 'not uncharacteristic fatuity' of his belief that commerce would render war obsolete among civilized countries (Pangle and Ahrensdorf 1999, 306n.). And that is to mention only a couple of those thinkers whose reputation remains strong enough in contemporary political theory that their absence from textbooks on the history of international political thought is immediately obvious. There are plenty of thinkers who enjoyed immense prominence during the nineteenth century itself, but whose current neglect is not the fault of international relations theorists alone: François Guizot and Benjamin Kidd are just two examples demonstrating the ephemeral nature of academic fame, both of whom, as it happens, made interesting and important contributions to international political thought (Guizot 1878; Kidd 1898 and 1902: on Guizot see Siedentop's remarks in Guizot 1997; on Kidd, see Crook 1984).

It is beyond the scope of an introductory textbook such as this to venture a detailed explanation for this blind spot. Indeed, it is quite possible that it is simply a matter of intellectual fashion, and that the wheel will turn again in due course; moreover, it is inherent in the construction of any 'canon' of 'great thinkers' that there will be some notable casualties who are not included, and that by itself does not invalidate such an approach. One point that is worth noting, though, is that some nineteenth-century thinkers seem to have lasted better in terms of their current popularity than others: Hegel is perhaps most likely to get sustained attention nowadays, with Marx close behind; it is the nineteenth-century liberals such as Mill who have probably suffered most. The fact that it is the liberals who are now most likely to be neglected is rather ironic in view of the intellectual and political ascendancy that they enjoyed for much of the nineteenth and early twentieth centuries. As I will explain in a moment, their idea of 'civilization' helped to set the tone for many of the most important debates of the period. Pick up virtually any nineteenth-century treatise on international politics and international law and one will find it packed with references to 'civilization', the 'family of civilized nations' and 'uncivilized peoples'. But, despite its importance, the liberal idea of civilization has never had the stage entirely to itself, and, having set up the core liberal conception of civilization and its implications for international order, I will turn to the various critics of this idea, especially in the context of the turbulent intellectual and political environment of the period from the middle of the nineteenth to the middle of the twentieth century.

The liberal idea of civilization

What does 'civilization' mean? Virtually everyone in the nineteenth century used the term, even if only to refer to it scathingly (see, for example, Woodward 1929, 30; Marx 1996, 5), but few ever defined it properly. One problem, of course, is that 'civilization' is an extremely vague idea, and one moreover to which even individual thinkers will sometimes attach several different meanings at once. However, one of the most influential formulations was given by Guizot, in a series of works on the history of civilization in Europe and France that was widely admired by his contemporaries; Mill, for instance, described them as 'models of the manner in which history should be studied' (Mill 1985, 370). Taking Mill at his word, I will begin by looking at Guizot's model account and will then move on to discuss how some of the most important nineteenth-century liberal thinkers, like Mill himself, developed it as a way of thinking about their international political environment.

Guizot's idea of modern European civilization

Guizot, incidentally, was not only a historian with an international reputation, but also a successful politician: he served as foreign and prime minister for several years in France under the 'July Monarchy', his career ended by Napoleon III's *coup d'état*. As a politican, he had a reputation for moderate conservatism; as a historian, he straddled the line between liberalism and conservatism in much the same way that a similar scholar-politician, Edmund Burke, had done during the late eighteenth century (see Guizot 1864; O'Connor 1955). It is not for his political career that he is interesting to us right now, however, but rather for his celebrated series of lectures *The History of Civilization*, which he delivered at the Sorbonne between 1828 and 1830 (Mill 1985, 262).

The lectures commence with a general account of the meaning of the word 'civilization'. To begin by identifying what does *not* belong to the concept, Guizot gave examples of four conditions which he thought one could not call 'civilized': a people 'whose outward circumstances are easy and agreeable', but whose 'moral and intellectual energies [are] ... in a state of torpor'; a people who have their basic material and moral needs satisfied, but where 'a certain portion of truth is doled out to each, but no one is permitted to help himself' (this is supposed to represent Asia); a people who enjoy a high degree of individual liberty, 'but among whom also disorder and inequality almost everywhere abound', which approximates more closely to Europe in the perhaps not-too-distant past; and, last of all, a world of absolute liberty, and considerable equality, but where 'scarcely such a thing is known as a general interest . . . few public ideas . . . hardly any public feeling . . . but little society' (Guizot 1878, 21–2). Although none of these counts as 'civilized', according to Guizot's understanding of the term, the third is closest, since at least it 'may contain germs of civilization which may progressively shoot up' (ibid., 22), but that is all.

From this exercise in negativity, Guizot felt that he could positively conclude that 'civilization' must comprise two elements which are 'intimately connected, and . . . reciprocally produce one another' (Guizot 1878, 27). First, 'the notion of progress, of development . . . of a people advancing, of a people in the course of improvement and melioration' (ibid., 23). Civilization, in other words, requires a condition of social progress, very often conceived in material terms: Guizot talks of 'an increase of national prosperity' and 'a manifest increase in the power and well-being of society at large', as well as the sense that society is better organized, and there exists 'a more equitable distribution of this power and this well-being' (ibid.). Prosperity, power and good government, one might say, are the hallmarks of a civilized people. But, as we have seen, even a people who were well-off, but who suffered from moral and intellectual 'torpor', would not be called civilized: 'man', Guizot says, 'is formed for a higher destiny than this' (ibid.). Secondly, then, civilization must include 'the development of individual life, the development of the human mind and its faculties' (ibid., 24).

The concept of civilization, as understood in the nineteenth century, therefore refers to progress at both the social and the individual levels; it exists when the former 'becomes enlarged, quickened and improved' and the latter 'distinguishes itself by its energy, brilliancy, and its grandeur' (Guizot 1878, 25). Mill, for example, thought that civilization implied: 'a dense population . . . dwelling in fixed habitations, and largely collected together in towns and villages'; a highly developed level of agriculture, commerce and manufacturing industry; 'human beings acting together for common purposes in large bodies, and enjoying the pleasures of social intercourse'; and a state of affairs 'where the arrangements of society, for protecting the persons and property of its members, are sufficiently perfect to maintain peace among them' (Mill 1882, 1.187–8). Density and urbanization, prosperity and technological advancement, social coordination and good government, in other words, are the essence of Mill's definition of the concept, and, while they do not simply repeat Guizot, they exhibit a fairly close fit. His definition perhaps stresses more strongly the broader social aspects of civilization, but he unquestionably believed that it also involved an individual moral dimension, like virtually all other nineteenth-century thinkers (Robson 1998, 347; and see for instance Arnold 1993). We have, then, a definition 'of civilization in general' (Guizot 1878, 35).

As Mill pointed out, though, we cannot leave it there: 'like many other terms of the philosophy of human nature, [civilization] is a word of double meaning. It sometimes stands for *human improvement* in general, and sometimes for *certain kinds* of improvement in particular' (Mill 1882, 1.186). Having set out the broad characteristics of civilization as a general concept, Guizot then proceeded to lay out 'the peculiar character of this [i.e., modern European] civilization', in contrast with others, especially 'ancient civilizations' such as 'Egyptian civilization', civilization in India, ancient Greece, and so on (Guizot 1878, 35–6). In making this comparison, Guizot noticed a striking difference between 'modern' (or European, he uses the terms more or less interchangeably) and 'ancient' civilization: the *internal variety* of the former. All ancient civilizations possess a 'unity of character . . . as though it had emanated from a single fact, from a single idea' (ibid., 35).

> How different to all this is the case as respects the civilization of modern Europe! Take ever so rapid a glance at this, and it strikes you at once as diversified, confused and stormy. All the principles of social organization are found existing together within it; powers temporal, powers spiritual, the theocratic, monarchic, aristocratic, and democratic elements, all classes of society, all the social situations, are jumbled together . . . as well as infinite gradations of liberty, of wealth, and of influence. (Guizot 1878, 37)

This has not, he admits, always been a happy state of affairs, but its lasting benefit, according to Guizot, is that the experience of coping with variety has contributed to a general sense of liberty and toleration within European countries and the European political order as a whole: 'The inability of the various principles to exterminate one another compelled each to endure the others, made it necessary for them to live in common, for them to enter into a sort of mutual understanding' (Guizot 1878, 39). While all ancient civilizations therefore tend towards tyranny, only in Europe, due to 'the constant warfare in which they [the various elements of European civilization] have been engaged', has liberty been attained (ibid.).

In Guizot's history, then, the word 'civilization' not only has a dual meaning, it has a dual, and perhaps even a triple, application. Firstly, in general, it refers to the mutual progress of social welfare and individual moral or intellectual development. Secondly, in its specific context, it refers to the way in which different peoples have achieved, or sought to achieve, this general condition: thus, 'European civilization', 'Greek civilization', 'Egyptian civilization', and so on. This latter usage is something which Guizot never precisely defines; here he describes civilization as an 'event' or 'fact', which, rather unhelpfully, 'is so general in its nature that it can scarcely be seized' (Guizot 1878, 17). Terms he uses which capture at least part of the meaning of the word in this context, though, are 'social order', 'the political organization of society' and 'the grand emporium of a people, in which all its wealth – all the elements of its life – all the powers of its existence are stored up' (ibid., 18n., 19).

The third application is more shadowy still. It is patently clear that Guizot thinks the specifically European civilization preferable to any other 'social order' that exists in the world. Only European civilization, with its great internal diversity, offers 'the reflected image of the world' (Guizot 1878, 39). As Guizot put it, in one of the slightly mystical outbursts which he sometimes permitted himself: 'European civilization has ... penetrated into the ways of eternal truth – into the scheme of Providence – it moves in the ways which God has prescribed. This is the rational principle of its superiority' (ibid., 40). Here, and this is a point on which Guizot is, perhaps deliberately, vague, there are grounds for believing that the specifically European form of civilization more closely approximates to Guizot's general definition of the concept than any other kind of social order, and that it will be the history of European civilization – which Guizot, of course, was writing at that moment – that will inevitably play a central role in what he hoped would one day constitute 'a universal history' of the 'general civilization [which] pervades the human race' (ibid., 19, 18). European civilization is, in a sense which no other civilization captures, the civilization of the world or of humanity as a whole.

Liberal views of civilization and its problems

This line of argument is so familiar nowadays, and perhaps will appear so obviously riddled with prejudices, that it may be necessary to ask why his contemporaries thought so highly of Guizot and his lectures. To answer that question, we need to recall first that French historians enjoyed considerable prominence within Europe as a whole, a prominence which has now largely been forgotten, notwithstanding the exception of Alexis de Toqueville (see Mill 1985). As we saw at the end of the previous chapter, for example, French historians such as Koch and Schoell had played a vital role in helping to construct the conservative image of European public order as founded on the principle of the balance of power during the French revolutionary wars. In his review of Guizot's work, which appeared in one of the most prominent British journals of liberal opinion, Mill juxtaposed his new account of civilization with this older conservative history of the European political system, suggesting that one of its most useful functions in England would be to 'help to correct the false and mischievous views' which Schoell had imposed on Koch's work, as 'one of the conservative sages . . . of the restored Bourbons' (Mill 1985, 372).

Guizot's history of civilization, in other words, could be read by British liberals such as Mill as a kind of antidote to the conservative conception of European public order that had developed during and after the revolution. That image, as we have seen, presented the balance of power and dynastic territorial sovereignty as the key institutionalized principles of European public order, both of which Napoleon had violated with calamitous effect, but which had been triumphantly restored by conservatives after the Napoleonic wars. The importance and value of Guizot's history to liberals such as Mill was that it stressed, by contrast, that the principles of progress and liberty were the fruits of the turbulent history of European civilization. European civilization's essence did not lie in preserving the past simply for its own sake; it lay in the glorious future towards which, Guizot insisted, mankind was slowly and painfully moving. Thus, the two great warring discourses of the late eighteenth and early nineteenth centuries had effectively been united in a potent synthesis. The French revolutionaries had claimed to be struggling for the improvement and rationalization of society, the enlightenment of the individual, and liberty and equality for all; the conservatives responded that they were fighting for the time-honoured values of European public law and political order; Guizot, Mill saw, had demonstrated that they were essentially the same things, so long as one adopted the right kind of historical perspective.

Thus largely purged of its conservative associations with the balance of power and monarchical dynasticism, the pursuit of 'civilization' could easily become a fundamental goal of liberal international political thought. The famous liberal theory that free trade would bring about a more peaceful world hinged on it: as Cobden remarked, for example, commerce was the 'grand panacea' not simply because of its intrinsic benefits, important though those were, but because the extension of free trade would 'like a beneficient medical discovery . . . serve to innoculate with the healthy and saving taste for civilization all the nations of the world' (Cobden 1995, 1.45). Constant offered the similarly optimistic prospect that the 'age of war' had given way to the 'age of commerce', on the grounds that, 'While in the past each nation formed an isolated family, the born enemy of other families, a great mass of human beings now exist that, despite the different names under which they live and their different forms of social organization, are essentially homogenous in their nature' (Constant 1988, 52–3). What commerce did was spread civilization, and it was this that would bring about peace by providing this basic homogeneity or, as Guizot had put it, uniformity (*unité*) in international affairs that could also herald a new age of peace and 'civilized calculation' to replace savage warfare (see Guizot 1864, 8–9).

It would be quite wrong, however, to suggest that the optimistic view of civilization's progress described above was unqualified. Liberals recognized that real difficulties could lie ahead. Mill noted one particular development that especially worried him:

> The most remarkable of those consequences of advancing civilization, which the state of the world is now forcing upon the attention of thinking minds, is this – that power passes more and more from individuals, and small knots of individuals, to masses; that the importance of the masses becomes constantly greater, that of individuals less. (Mill 1882, 1.189)

The move from an individual to a mass society was not, Mill noted, an incidental by-product of the advance of civilization. It was integral to the whole process: 'What makes all savage communities poor and feeble? The same cause which prevented the lions and tigers from long ago extirpating the race of men – incapacity of cooperation. It is only civilized beings who can combine' (Mill 1882, 1.191). The increasing combination of individuals into larger and larger masses was thus a necessary result of the advance of civilization. Although they acknowledged its inevitability, however, liberals had grave worries about this development. First, as Constant noted, it changed the way in which politics worked, transforming the relationship between the individual and the state (see Holmes 1984). The extensive participation and face-to-face debate which had marked politics in ancient societies was no longer available to moderns: 'Lost in the multitude, the individual can almost never perceive the influence he exercises. Never does his will impress itself upon the whole; nothing confirms in his eyes his own cooperation' (Constant 1988, 316). Civilization to some extent made up for this by having 'infinitely multiplied and varied the means of personal happiness', but it nevertheless meant that freedom now consisted 'of peaceful enjoyment and private independence' to reap the benefits of this new material prosperity, rather than active participation in politics (ibid.).

A potentially disastrous problem could arise here from the fact that civilization had not only multiplied 'the means of personal happiness'; it had also, as liberals fully realized, especially in the aftermath of the Napoleonic wars, multiplied the means of destruction. The greatest danger to civilization, then, came not from savage peoples, whose inability to combine effectively meant they could easily be brushed aside by the vastly greater power of a civilized state, but from a civilized state in the hands of an uncivilized, warlike leader, for which Napoleon was the obvious model. The need, then, was to ensure, through an appropriate system of 'representative government' – perfected, many believed, in Great Britain's constitutional monarchy – that a country's rulers would reflect the character of the society itself (Mill 1946). Savage peoples could be ruled by savages, and it would harm no one but themselves; civilized peoples needed civilized rulers, or else they could pose a threat to all of humanity. Great men with a despotic will such as Napoleon; radical fanatics with a vision for society; arbitrary and belligerent, or just plain incompetent, dynasts; all were equally dangerous.

Another liberal worry about the implications of the new mass politics of civilization was that it would lead to the worsening of individual moral and intellectual character, especially when coupled with the degenerative effects of too much 'peaceful enjoyment' of 'personal happiness'. As Mill warned, 'There has crept over the refined classes . . . a moral effeminacy, an inaptitude for every kind of struggle' (Mill 1882, 1.206). The problem was further compounded by the shift to mass politics, where 'The individual becomes so lost in the crowd, that, though he depends more and more upon opinion, he is apt to depend less and less upon well-grounded opinion' (ibid., 1.208). The solution to both of these problems, most liberals believed, was to be found in something very similar to the 'moral causes' of national character which their eighteenth-century predecessors had identified; as Mill put it, 'national institutions of education and forms of polity calculated to invigorate the individual character' (ibid., 1.214). Civilization was not, as Guizot's history might possibly lead one to think, either an automatic process or one over which sensible liberal policies could have no effect. Liberals definitely believed that they were moving with the broad upward flow of human history, but they also believed that the stream could be, and sometimes needed to be, diverted to prevent it from running down undesirable channels.

National self-determination and the spread of civilization

Looking at the various ways in which liberals developed their idea of civilization, one of Guizot's main points about the specifically European form of civilization may seem to have been lost. Guizot's central argument, as we saw a moment ago, was that European civilization's most distinctive feature was its internal variety, and especially that its different elements were able to tolerate the others, thus enjoying the stimulation of conflict and change without being utterly torn apart. The liberals, however, talk about, to repeat Constant's words, 'a great mass of human beings ... that, despite the different names under which they live and their different forms of social organization, are essentially homogenous in their nature'. Mill's prescription that educational and political institutions should be 'calculated to invigorate the individual character' similarly seems to suggest a certain liberal template of society or government that appears to work against Guizot's idea of European civilization, where 'All the principles of social organization are found existing together.'

How did liberals square this circle? How did they combine the element of social or political homogeneity, which they believed was implied or required by civilization, with the element of variety which they believed was its driving force? This was an extremely difficult question for the nineteenth-century liberals to answer satisfactorily, and it is certainly arguable that they never succeeded in solving the problem. Here, though, it is worth noting that all liberals were strongly committed to the principle of national self-determination. The reason why they could so enthusiastically embrace this principle was that they believed that civilization was something that could be universalized without challenging – indeed, could positively embrace – the peculiarities of individual nations as they struggled to pursue their own path towards social development, although this would, liberals supposed, require them to liberate themselves from monarchical or foreign rule. That different national characters existed was a point that all liberals accepted, adding little to the earlier remarks of Hume and others on the subject that we reviewed in the previous chapter. Free trade, though, was something that worked through connections between individual people; it left, liberals claimed, the political relations between states – specifically their mutual independence from one another – unaltered. It did not even, on some views, require any governmental action at all – merely that government keep out of the way. Cobden, one of the leading advocates of this point of view, still felt that it would be desirable for liberals to intervene to assist movements of national liberation, while he felt they should eschew imperialism, positions with which Mill disagreed. But the crucial point was that both felt that, once free, nations should be permitted to determine their future for themselves. Civilization was merely the broad parameter within which this freedom operated.

There was one notable exception to this general rule of non-intervention for Mill, however. The right to have one's private independence respected and protected only applied, Mill argued, 'to human beings in the maturity of their faculties' (Mill 1946, 9). Civilized government was a benign affair that took a due account of the wishes of the people expressed through their representatives, and was limited by the need to ensure that people were interfered with only in so far as that was necessary to protect the liberties of others. But these benefits of civilized government were extended exclusively to civilized peoples. In considering the people to whom liberals owed the duty of non-interference, Mill argued that:

> we may leave out of consideration those backward states of society in which the race itself may be considered in its nonage. The early difficulties in the way of spontaneous progress are so great, that there is seldom any choice of means for overcoming them; and a ruler full of the spirit of improvement is warranted in the use of any expedients that will attain an end, perhaps otherwise unattainable. Despotism is a legitimate mode of government in dealing with barbarians, provided the end be their improvement, and the means justified by actually effecting that end. (Mill 1946, 9)

Thus we come to another of the dominant ideas of nineteenth-century liberal international political thought: the contrast between a 'family of civilized nations', among whom an international order built around the principle of non-intervention was appropriate, and a world of 'backward' or 'barbaric' peoples beyond, who needed to be administered despotically through imperial mechanisms in order to bring them up to a level where they would be capable of 'standing by themselves in the conditions of the modern world'. One rule of international relations applied within the family of civilized nations and another outside it. It was a grave error, Mill contended (into which some liberals – such as Cobden – fell), to think that 'the same international customs, and the same rules of international morality, can obtain between one civilized nation and another, and between civilized nations and barbarians' (Mill 1882, 3.252).

Although this casual denial of the international personality of barbarian peoples would probably be the most objectionable element of nineteenth-century liberal thought today, it was not so in the context of the nineteenth century. Cobden's position was the more unusual one, and many liberals viewed European empires as a providential opportunity to spread the blessings of civilization to the less fortunate peoples of Asia and Africa. These were also places, one might add, where they had few qualms about experimenting with their projects for educational and political reform to invigorate individual character (Stokes 1959). Nevertheless, the main objections to the liberal idea of civilization made little of this. It was the liberal attitude towards other Europeans which generally attracted more criticism, as we will see now when we turn to conservative and historicist thought.

The social question, the state and the world-spirit

As outlined above, the basic liberal response to the transformed character of modern society in the nineteenth century – its size, its complexity, its transformed social and economic character – was to embrace those changes by channelling them through the concept of modern European civilization produced by French historians such as Guizot. They saw the growth of commerce as essentially benign, and as positively increasing the 'means of personal happiness' and prospects for international peace. They did recognize, though, that it could be destabilizing unless it was accompanied by the right form of government: an essentially *laissez-faire* system, which would not harness the new wealth and power that commerce brought to projects of war or authoritarian despotism, but would voluntarily limit itself to ensuring that each individual had the right to pursue his or her own personal happiness without interfering with others engaged in the same pursuit. Within those parameters, which liberals believed to be extremely broad and flexible, different nations must freely determine their own national characters and governments in whatever way they saw fit.

This was a powerful thesis; it probably deserves to be labelled the dominant theme of nineteenth-century international political thought. Nevertheless, throughout the century, liberals faced continuous intellectual challenges from people who questioned the merits of their idea of civilization. Conservatives feared the prospect because they disagreed with the materialism, nationalism and constitutionalism that liberals presented as the solution to the social problems which had caused the French Revolution and which, everyone knew, still lurked beneath the surface of the restored dynasties after 1815. The conservatives were quite happy with the notion that international society should take an interest in how domestic societies and political systems were organized; they just had an illiberal view of what the outcome of that process should be. On the other hand, and rather more importantly, many thinkers were sceptical of the liberal promise that civilization could be combined with national culture, and that a harmony of nations would develop in some Cobdenite or Mazzinian scheme of cosmopolitan brotherhood. They felt that the tentacles of liberal civilization reached deeper than that; they worried that its materialistic and scientific rationality threatened to extinguish human diversity altogether; and, most importantly, they were beginning to develop the historical and philosophical apparatus to construct an alternative synthetic world-view to rival that developed by Guizot and Mill.

The social question and European public order

Let us begin, though, with the conservative alternative to liberalism. We should note from the outset that, despite liberals' growing antipathy towards the concept, in the immediate aftermath of the Napoleonic wars, the balance of power was still the official operating principle of the European political system, and even in Britain it remained the guiding idea behind foreign policy in the hands of Castlereagh, Canning and later Palmerston (see Sheehan 1994). Especially in the period from 1815 to 1848, liberal criticisms of the balance of power could hardly be said to have been dominant, and within diplomatic circles their influence was extremely limited. We should also note, however, that conservatism itself had undergone profound, one might almost say revolutionary, changes since the eighteenth century. For a start, the mechanics of the balance of power had been transformed by the Napoleonic wars. Power was no longer concentrated in the heart of the continent, but had shifted away decisively from France and the Austrian empire to the geographical margins of the system (something that was also to happen, but even more decisively, after the world wars of the twentieth century). Britain and Russia had emerged as the leading military and economic powers in the victorious coalition against Napoleon, and it was effectively thanks to Russian manpower and British money that the defeat of France was finally secured.

Moreover, the balance of power was now looked on more as an object of policy than an article of faith. Optimistic eighteenth-century hopes for a self-sustaining mechanism on a Newtonian model where human nature might 'check itself' were increasingly discarded in favour of the idea that this delicate equipoise needed constant care through carefully managed diplomatic negotiation within an appropriate diplomatic culture. The European balance was therefore now embedded in a wider 'concert' of the European great powers, founded on their shared willingness to engage in systematic consultation and cooperation (Holbraad 1970, 2–4). The concert was intended as the continuation during the peace of the wartime 'Quadruple Alliance', now extended to include France, the alliance's former enemy.

Alongside the concert, and of greater significance for European conservatives, was another alliance, between Austria, Prussia and Russia, which was known as the 'Holy Alliance', and its explicit purpose was to suppress revolutionary movements and nationalist uprisings across Europe. The Holy Alliance reflected the conservatives' perception that social problems within states lay at the root of problems in international society; their conclusion was that the solution to social problems lay in coordinated international action. This was the chief lesson that they drew from the French Revolution and its attendant wars: an individual ruler acting on his own resources, even in as powerful a nation as France, might prove to be incapable of maintaining domestic order. Moreover, if insurrection in one country could not be contained, it would spread – medical images of germs, disease and infection within the 'body politic' or the 'political organism' were popular among the conservatives – to others (see de Maistre 1977). For Metternich, then, as for other leading conservatives, 'the social conflict in Europe transcended the political issues between states' (Holbraad 1970, 30; see also Woodward 1929, 5–6).

Metternich's doctrine of intervention clearly departs from earlier conservative ideas about international order. It might even be said to represent a transformation in the understanding of the concept of the balance of power and its role in preserving the sovereign 'liberties' of different states. All conservatives still accepted the balance of power as the basis of international order; they all subscribed to Burke's view that it was accepted as 'the known common law of Europe at all times, and by all powers' (cited in Welsh 1995, 34). The institution had done sterling service in reactionary treatises against Napoleon, especially when his conquests threatened to establish him as a European hegemon. In the previous chapter, we saw that historians such as Koch, Schoell and Arnold Heeren had been quick to point to its importance as a traditional principle of European public law, connecting it to the idea of the importance of maintaining the 'internal freedom' of all the members of international society – an idea which they rapidly associated with the principle of 'territorial sovereignty' derived from the constitution of the Holy Roman Empire.

During the revolution, however, particularly at times when the reactionary powers seemed to be in the ascendant, conservatives such as Burke had been anxious to situate the balance of power within a context of the rule of international law, such that it should serve a higher purpose as 'an instrument for the European powers to express their unity against potential disintegrating forces' (Welsh 1995, 37). The preservation of the sovereignty of individual states was less important a function of the balance of power than the maintenance of the European public order considered as a whole. Balancing power thus became a potent *ideological* tool. This way of thinking not only persisted but actually flourished after the fall of Napoleon, when reaction once again appeared to hold the reins of state power, and when conservatives wished to employ that power to protect dynasties wherever they were under threat.

The result was widespread interventions by conservative powers in revolutionary situations abroad: 'French troops, for example, went into Spain in 1823; Belgium in 1832; the Papal States in 1849. Habsburg troops were regularly dispatched to the empire's Italian clients in the Age of Metternich. Russia sent entire armies into Persia and Turkey in the 1820s and Poland in 1831' (Showalter 2002, 31). And, in keeping with this, the diplomats such as Metternich who managed the Holy Alliance evolved a way of thinking about international politics where the formal balance of power was significantly less important than the need to maintain the unity of European powers in a struggle over the social question, where there still remained 'a precarious balance of forces' (Holbraad 1970, 30). In seeking to suppress their radical opponents in this way, however, the conservatives were conceding an important point to their more moderate liberal opponents: that international society was organized along ideological lines and for ideological purposes. Bereft of its defenders, the balance of power was increasingly isolated as an institution in an international society where the divisions along the 'social question' looked more and more important than political boundaries between states.

Partly in response to the cosmopolitan challenge presented by liberalism and radicalism, then, the concept of the balance of power was becoming less associated with the ideas of sovereignty or the states-system, and more attached to the conservative idea of the need for intervention at least to preserve monarchical and aristocratic power within societies. The concepts of the state and 'reason of state' were figuring less and less within conservative thinking about international politics, as the reactionary movement increasingly mimicked the liberal focus on the social underpinnings of international politics. Although conservatives violently disagreed with liberals' prescriptions for domestic order, the structure of their thought about international politics was thus rather similar: international peace and order required stable domestic societies, secured if necessary by concerted international action and intervention. But the conservative position lacked the philosophical sophistication of liberalism, substituting an out-dated religious theory of monarchical government for the liberals' scientific conception of human nature, and it had little to say about the social transformations that were at the centre of the liberal account of the difference between the ancient and modern worlds. In these crucial respects, conservatism presented only a very hollow threat to the emerging ascendancy of the liberal idea of civilization.

Hegel's philosophy of history: Staat, Volk *and* Weltgeist

We have seen history being used by conservatives to sustain their belief in the legitimacy of state sovereignty, the balance of power and dynastic monarchy, and by liberals to sustain their belief in the progressive character of modern European civilization. We have not yet, however, considered a third kind of narrative of European, and indeed world, history which cannot readily be consigned to either the conservative or the liberal camp, but which depends upon its own distinctive conceptual vocabulary: Hegel's philosophy of history, and especially his idea of history as the dialectical unfolding of the 'world-spirit' (*Weltgeist*), especially through the vehicle of the nation (*Volk*) embodied in its own particular state (*Staat*).

I said earlier that one of the great strengths of liberal thought about 'civilization' was that it offered a synthesis, on the liberals' own terms, of the main late eighteenth-century ideas about international politics. Obviously, it relied heavily on the idea of more or less uniform progress towards civilization associated with the sociological theories of the Scottish Enlightenment, but it also deployed Guizot's historical conceptualization of European civilization to harness an important element of the conservative world-view to the liberal cause, and it even claimed – although this remained, in a sense, liberalism's Achilles heel – to be able to accommodate diverse movements of national self-determination, and thus the idea of particular 'cultures', within an otherwise broadly universalistic 'civilized' world-view.

It is also possible to see in Hegel's project a similar, but differently realized, ambition to synthesize the Enlightenment's emphasis on the importance of universal reason in understanding and shaping human experience of the world with the romanticist and historicist emphasis on the particularity of that experience in different cultures and at different times. His resolution of the inherent tension between these two positions was not altogether dissimilar to Herder's or Humboldt's belief that the individuality of distinct nations contributed to a collective humanity. For Hegel, however, the culmination of the historical process of the development of human society lay in the emergence of rationally organized states, each of which represented a particular element of the world-spirit in its own unique national form: 'The nation state [*das Volk als Staat*] is the spirit in its substantial rationality and immediate actuality, and is therefore the absolute power on *earth*; each state is consequently a sovereign and independent entity in relation to others' (Hegel 1991, 366). This obviously attached enormous ethical and political importance to the sovereign state as an expression, and protector, of national culture. The state, in other words, having been relegated to the background of conservative thinking about intervention in international politics, was emerging into the foreground of the romanticist world-view. Whereas Herder had confined himself largely to thinking about the *Volk* in linguistic, aesthetic and cultural terms, Hegel's philosophy developed the *political* implications of his position in a highly statist direction.

Liberalism depended on the notion that the spread of commerce had produced a decisive transformation in world politics that heralded the possibility of a more peaceful era in which an essentially homogeneous mass of humanity, albeit administratively divided between different states, would enjoy the fruits of civilization. Partly in response to the interventionist strategies of the conservative Holy Alliance, partly thanks to a growing awareness of the opportunities presented by imperial suzerainty, liberals were increasingly prepared to harness the new power potential of the state, not least in its ability to call upon the products of newly industrialized economies and so to bring the benefits of this civilization to other, less fortunate peoples around the world. Hegel's philosophy suggested, by contrast, that the awesome new powers of the state might have a different world-historical role to play. Rather than building a universal civilization rooted in economic development and the materialistic pursuit of happiness, each state was realizing the ideal, rational purpose of humanity through its *own* development. For liberals, the state should either get out of the way of civilization altogether – in the extreme Cobdenite view – or promote the civilizing mission through the provision of good government, especially for those unfortunate peoples still labouring under barbarism. Hegel, by contrast, saw the state itself as the end of a process of human development, harnessing 'reason', a vital natural human capacity in all Enlightened and liberal thought, to the *national* development of a particular *Volk* within the context of a rationally organized state.

As in Herder's thought, what linked this to a more cosmopolitan world-view was the idea that the various national cultures were united in a single, harmonious whole:

> The principles of the spirits of nations [*Volksgeister*] are in general of a limited nature . . . and their deeds and destinies in their mutual relations are the manifest dialectic . . . [through which] the *universal* spirit, *the spirit of the world*, produces itself in its freedom from all limits, and it is this spirit . . . which is the highest right over all – over finite spirits in *world history* as the *world's court of judgement*. (Hegel 1991, 371)

A crucial difference from Herder, though, lay in Hegel's belief that this 'world-spirit' could be seen working through different national cultures at different times. History, according to Hegel, 'is the process whereby the spirit assumes the shape of events and of immediate natural actuality', and he believed that, of the various manifestations of the world-spirit, '*one of them is allotted to each nation* in its *geographical* and *anthropological* existence' (Hegel 1991, 374). Some nations, then, were carriers of the 'world-spirit' at a particular time, while others were not; the former possessed an 'absolute right as bearer of the present stage of the world-spirit's development', while 'the spirits of other nations are without rights, and they, like those whose epoch has passed, no longer count in world history' (ibid.). In effect, this amounted to a historicization of the principle of *Humanität* itself, which allowed Hegel to privilege European civilization in a way that Herder did not, and allowed Hegel's later interpreters to attach his philosophy to a much more aggressive kind of Eurocentric attitude towards non-Europeans, and within Europe a more militant nationalism, than Herder's. In spite of this, however, Hegel still followed Herder in keeping the concept of *Kultur* or *Geist* essentially distinct from the concept of race, although linked of course to the concept of the *Volk*: Europe's historical superiority was cultural rather than racial. That point of view, however, was about to change.

Race, class, culture and power

In chapter 1, we saw that Herodotus identified four main axes along which the identity of Greeks might be conceived as different from that of 'barbarians': blood, language, religion and custom. Language acquired a peculiar importance to the Greeks, and religion to the spiritual communities of the Middle Ages, while custom, especially if understood in a broad sense to include 'moral' causes of different national characters, had been of constant importance throughout the history of international political thought, and continued to be so in the nineteenth century. 'Blood', however, has thus far played a surprisingly small role in our story. Indeed, while recognizing that ethnic differences exist, the people whose thought we have been studying have generally been loath to attach overwhelming importance to ethnicity in and of itself. When they have made judgements that one particular ethnic group had certain characteristics, they have usually explained the fact with reference to the time-honoured argument of the effects of climate. Race or ethnicity *in itself* has seldom been used as an originating source of difference, even though it might serve as a powerful indicator of difference, and perhaps sometimes as a convenient shorthand indicator for a particular cluster of attributes or characteristics which are to be extolled or criticized.

Even the most obvious instance of racism before the nineteenth century – the mass enslavement of Africans and their transportation to work in the Americas – may lend support to this general lack of importance attached to race as an ethically or politically significant source of difference. As Frank Snowden comments, when slavery became linked exclusively to one particular ethnic group, and thus defined and defended in racial terms, it began to lose its general legitimacy as an institution after centuries of being widely accepted (Snowden 1983, 70–1). One reason for this may well be that prevailing religious sentiments, especially monotheistic ones, had prevented people from attaching much significance to ethnic difference. The idea that all people are divine creations suggests that it would be insulting to God to imply that certain people were made in a defective way. Although the argument was sometimes advanced that God had made different types of people to serve different purposes (Noah's sons were often used as 'prototypes' for different races), it was not until 1870 that categories of race for the first time 'became an almost universal or standardized key for the interpretation of human history, as well as for the understanding of contemporary society and its future evolution' (MacMaster 2001, 6), and for the first time began to become a prominent theme within European attitudes towards each other. There may well be some connection between the development of secularism in the late nineteenth century and a greater willingness to entertain the belief that race is an important source of differences between communities. Both were closely linked to the idea of adopting a more 'scientific' approach to the study of humanity, and both followed the development of Darwin's theory of natural selection, which had obvious and immediately controversial implications for Christian beliefs about the divine creation of man.

Race, Darwinism and geopolitics

The main contributor to the new centrality of the concept of race was a conservative French nobleman, Arthur de Gobineau. His principal theme, picking up the biological imagery so prevalent in conservative political thought, was the inevitable 'degeneration', and thus death, of all civilizations. This decline was not something that could be avoided indefinitely, as the liberals might hope, by reforming the educational or political system in order to offset the negative effects of mass society. Gobineau insisted that it was wrong to argue that civilizations were 'destroyed only by luxury, effeminacy, misgovernment, fanaticism, and the corruption of morals' (Gobineau 1915, 4). These were all things which, unless checked, could potentially kill off a civilization before its time. Moral education and good government, then, might prevent a civilization from dying a 'violent death'; but Gobineau's point was that nothing could prevent it from dying a 'natural death'.

To explain how he came to this view, we need to look more closely at how Gobineau conceptualized 'race' and 'civilization'. In his theory of race, he attached overwhelming importance to 'blood' as giving a people certain racial characteristics. He thought, for example, that all peoples are driven by two instincts: the desire for material prosperity (the 'male' principle, according to Gobineau's adaptation of a Hindu concept) and the desire to pursue intellectual development (the 'female' principle: Gobineau 1915, 86). The balance of these principles within a particular people, and therefore its national character, was entirely given by its racial characteristics. Crucially, Gobineau dispensed utterly with explanations for this difference rooted in moral factors, such as political or religious institutions, or physical ones, such as climate. He was quite clear that differences between peoples were 'not due to the fiercer action of the sun ... the sole cause is the influence of blood' (ibid., 92). Explicitly disagreeing with the eighteenth-century *philosophes*, he made race the sole cause of a nation's character (ibid., 5).

On civilization, Gobineau was a sharp critic of Guizot's definition of the concept, which was, he argued, too narrow. Neatly capturing the homogenizing character of the liberal idea of civilization, he complained that, if forced to accept Guizot's definition, 'I should be driven to consider only one nation, of all that have ever lived, as truly civilized – the English' (Gobineau 1915, 81; compare with Mann 1983, 23). Gobineau proposed an alternative formulation, but one which still spoke to the familiar liberal notion of civilization as involving the combination and coordination of social forces. For him, the only kinds of peoples who could ever become civilized were ones 'which understand that if they wish to increase their power and prosperity, they are absolutely compelled, either by war or peaceful measures, to draw their neighbours within their sphere of influence' (Gobineau 1915, 28). This inevitably involved some kind of racial mixture, and thus, while 'the human race in all its branches has a secret repulsion from the crossing of blood', it is those elements of the human race who can overcome this who are the 'only members of our species who can be civilized at all' (ibid., 29–30). The original peoples who founded the civilization would be ones who possessed, thanks to their innate racial character, a capacity to dominate their neighbours, 'in which the racial elements are so strong that they grip fast everything which comes within their reach, and draw it into themselves' (ibid., 86).

The civilization would thus originally bear the stamp of their particular orientation to the 'male' and 'female' principles, and one could discern these in many existing civilizations and thus understand their laws and governing institutions. This would change over time, however, as a result of the mixture of blood which, as we saw, Gobineau viewed as integral to the process of conquest and expansion of dominion that is required to build a civilization at all. Gradually, the vital core of the civilization – the original, civilizing race – is diffused and loses its animating power. On the one hand, 'its blood becomes merged in that of all the tributaries which it had attracted to its own stream'; on the other, 'the more personal part they take in the affairs of the State make them the chief mark for attack after a disastrous battle, a proscription or a revolution' (Gobineau 1915, 32). On the surface, the civilization may remain intact for a while, 'for while the blood of the civilizing race is gradually drained away by being parcelled out among the peoples that are conquered . . . the impulse originally given to those people still persists' (ibid., 33). But eventually even this impulse will work itself out; 'the civilization is dead' (ibid.).

Darwin's theory of natural selection (Darwin 1859) was thus part of a larger philosophical outlook that explicitly challenged key elements of the way of thinking that nineteenth-century liberals had inherited from the Enlightenment, and which – like the Enlightened world-view – depended on a specific 'configuration of assumptions concerning nature, time and human nature' (Hawkins 1997, 30). As we saw in the previous chapter, the Enlightened position had originally relied on a particular conception of human nature as uniform through time and space, and composed primarily of the ability to reason and the pursuit of certain passions. Darwin, by contrast, stressed the necessity of competition for the means of survival in a world of scarcity, and the importance of inherited characteristics as determining success in the resulting struggle for existence. Despite its obvious debts to the image of *laissez-faire* competition, the new theory of natural selection therefore transformed the Enlightenment science of man on which the liberal idea of civilization ultimately rested. It is difficult to exaggerate the implications for social and political thought of this change. As one leading social Darwinist, Benjamin Kidd, wrote in 1895:

> the principal result of the application of the principles of Darwinian science to human affairs must be, not the rationalistic interpretation of the scheme of development at work in the world, but the final deposition of Reason from the central place we had come to assume it occupied in the process of evolution the race is undergoing. (cited in Crook 1984, 92)

The application of Darwinian science to human affairs helped to demolish much of the ethical and progressive dimension that the concept of civilization had given to the structure of international order. It became much harder to see international politics in terms of a benevolent process leading towards this end goal, and the international system – much like Darwin's view of the natural world – became an arena of competition with no *telos* whatsoever.

How exactly were the implications of social Darwinism for international politics developed in the late nineteenth and early twentieth centuries? Obviously, Darwin's – or, more accurately, Herbert Spencer's – notion of the 'survival of the fittest' implied that the security of the state was an existential problem, especially once Darwinism became linked with the increasing use of racial categories to describe differences between European peoples, as opposed to their previous use to discriminate in the imperial context between Europeans and the rest. For example, Ernst Haeckel, a leading popularizer of Darwin's ideas in Germany, developed the concept of German Aryanism as a distinct racial group within Europe, and one moreover that had proved able to 'outstrip all other branches in the career of civilization' (cited in MacMaster 2001, 39). Notably, this made civilization a much more *competitive* endeavour than hitherto, where the 'lower' races seemed more dispensable, and where racial hierarchies were beginning to colour relations even within the 'family of civilized nations' in the European political system. The need to fight for white supremacy in the struggle for existence was also becoming a powerful motivation for imperialist expansion, although often advanced in conjunction with more traditional liberal ideas about the civilizing mission (Kidd 1898). Altogether, it is hard to overstate the intellectual significance of the Darwinian move in international political thought that took place in the late nineteenth century, although that impact was felt in many different ways (see Crook 1994 for an excellent analysis).

Before we move on, however, we need to take account of another major development in international political thought during this period: the rise of 'geopolitical' thinking, a term coined in 1899, although it should be noted that the German geographer Friedrich Ratzel had published a work in 1897 entitled *Politische Geographie*, and accordingly is usually granted the title of the 'father of geopolitical thought' (Parker 1985, 11). Again, this new concept was closely linked to social Darwinism, especially the idea of the necessity of the struggle for existence. In this case, though, it coincided with another development of acute importance to the British and American conception of their environment: the apparent 'closing in' of the world. This process essentially began with the official closing of the American frontier in 1890. The frontier had long been seen as a kind of safety-valve within American society, allowing large numbers of immigrants to be settled on the land, and so converted into the kinds of property-owning citizens that were deemed essential to any civilized society (see Turner 1986; Gates 1996). The closing of the frontier was therefore immediately perceived as a rather threatening development, and helped to fuel racist fears about the influx of new immigrants, who would not be so easily assimilated into American society.

In a more obviously international context, the same kind of idea arose from the growing awareness that, with the 'scramble for Africa' now largely complete, there were few if any opportunities for imperial expansion left. As Halford Mackinder put it in a celebrated 1904 lecture entitled 'The Geographical Pivot of History', the world was now a 'closed political system', in which 'every explosion of social forces, instead of being dissipated in a surrounding circuit of unknown space and barbaric chaos, will be sharply re-echoed from the far side of the globe' (in Ó Tuathail et al. 1998, 27). The ability to redirect social tensions so that their consequences were played out in the 'barbaric' spaces beyond the family of civilized nations was now no longer an option. Again, as with racist theories, British and American thinkers were now displaying their nervous awareness of the importance of divisions within the European political system, and less of the confident early nineteenth-century expectation of being able not only to handle such divisions but to overcome them and ensure the steady progress of civilization. More than ever, they were becoming concerned about the need for *power* to protect the civilization that they had already achieved in the brutal struggle for existence that, entrenched in a Darwinian world-view, they now anticipated. At the same time, with their resources for its defence diminished, they confronted a new and more penetrating array of criticisms of their cherished concept of civilization.

Critics of the liberal idea of civilization

The impact of Gobineau's racism and Darwinian theories about natural selection forced liberals to rethink their ideas about the role of competition, and even war, in their concept of how the family of civilized nations operated. Many others, however, developed sharp criticisms of the very idea of civilization itself. There are too many to examine in detail here. Some important lines of argument that I will not, for reasons of space, go into here include Sigmund Freud's analysis of the psychological consequences of the repression involved in civilizing people. Although he acknowledged that this could have positive social consequences, he warned that unless a less repressive form of civilization could be developed there were dangers (illustrated by the First World War) of a build-up and eventual explosion of psychological tensions (Freud 1961). Another powerful criticism was contained in Max Weber's 'cultural science' (*Geisteswissenschaft*) of the forms of economic conduct involved in Anglo-American civilization. As Weber saw it, this rested on an old Protestant idea of work in a 'calling' which had once, in more spiritual times, provided people with a powerful sense of purpose in their lives but which, in the 'disenchanted' modern world, had become a trap of meaningless toil and the accumulation of wealth for its own sake (Weber 1930). Without wanting to suggest that these are unimportant lines of argument, here I will pay rather more attention to three other attacks against the liberal idea of civilization, drawing upon the concepts of class, culture and power respectively.

Marx's attitude towards the liberal idea of civilization does display a certain degree of ambivalence. He did not conceal his appreciation of the world-historical significance of the bourgeois achievements which, like Constant and Mill, he recognized had transformed the ancient world into something distinctively modern. It had caused mankind to shake off the 'dull indolence' of the Middle Ages, and 'Uniquely it has demonstrated what human activity can accomplish' (Marx 1996, 4). And yet at the same time he recognized that this extraordinary intensification of the human ability to control and extract value from nature had led to great inequality and instability. On the latter point, Marx noted the persistence of commercial crises within the capitalist economic system which resulted from the fact that 'there is too much civilization, too many goods, too much industry, too much commerce' (ibid., 6); capitalist overproduction necessitated the continual destruction of productive resources, pushing societies back into conditions of 'temporary barbarism', and the continual expansion of capital to find new opportunities for the exploitation of human and material resources and thus the increase of its value. At the same time, civilization was associated with obvious and growing social and economic inequalities, rendering the liberal concern with the rights of man hypocritical. Constant may have been correct that the growth of commerce offered increased means with which individuals might pursue happiness, and that for some this would provide an agreeable trade-off for the loss of 'ancient liberty', but Marx realized that the means of pursuing private happiness were hardly equally shared under capitalist economics. While that problem of class stratification persisted, bourgeois capitalism was creating the agent of its own downfall.

Of perhaps greater significance to international political thought, though, is the fact that Marx turned another aspect of the liberal idea of civilization against itself: its drive to homogeneity and inter-dependence. 'National divisions', Marx noted, 'and conflicts between peoples increasingly disappear with the development of the bourgeoisie, with free trade and the world market, and the uniform character of industrial production and the corresponding circumstances of modern life' (Marx 1996, 17–18). This both demanded and enabled that 'united action, at least in the civilized countries' which was 'one of the first conditions for freeing the proletariat' (ibid., 18). Just as liberals embraced the homogenizing influence of commerce, so Marx even sought to accelerate it, arguing that national divisions would 'disappear even faster' once the rule of the proletariat was achieved. And all the desirable international consequences, in the form of the increased prospect of peace, which liberals had thought would flow from their bourgeois civilization would in fact be even greater under communism. In this way Marx ingeniously borrowed much of the conceptual vocabulary of nineteenth-century liberalism and turned it on its head, directing it against the capitalist economy that under-pinned *bourgeois* civilization, to conjure a new synthesis that was to prove just as compelling.

Another key intellectual challenge that Marx posed for the prevailing liberal conceptual synthesis was in its use of ideas about human nature as a justificatory tool for its ideas about progress towards civilization. Capitalism thus 'appears to the bourgeois intellect to be as much a self-evident necessity imposed by Nature as productive labour itself' (Marx 1965, 81). This line of argument had its roots in classical political economy, and, as well as exposing the political, social and economic consequences of capitalism, Marx set out to unravel the intellectual coherence of the liberal position. His key thesis here concerned the 'fetishization' of the commodity. Under capitalism, the goods that people produce take on the 'mysterious' form of commodities to be bought and sold in the market, and as such it appears to workers as if the 'social character' of their labour – the social relations between classes involved in the production process – is objectively given by the relationship between commodities in the market-place. Or, as Marx succinctly put it: production 'is a definite social relation between men, that assumes, in their eyes, the fantastic form of a relation between things' (ibid., 72). The social relations of production are thus obscured, and it is this which makes the laws governing them appear to be as much of a necessity as the natural laws that govern the physical world. The practical con-sequence of this is that it makes it hard to envisage how a revolutionary transformation of society might be effected, since something as 'natural' as the free exchange of commodities in the market is presumed to be immutable. The thesis of commodity fetishism was an immensely powerful line of argument, exposing one of the key dimensions of the liberal world-view – the purportedly 'natural' character of modern civilization – as a historically contingent product of a particular way of organizing society. It bears comparison with the achievement of Darwin, because in a similar way it tore apart this crucial conceptual join between civilization and human nature that had played such a pivotal role in stabilizing and sustaining the liberal intellectual synthesis.

Whereas Marx sought to transform the social aspects of liberal civilization and so restore alienated individuals to their full selves, Nietzsche, as Keith Ansell-Pearson observes, 'envisaged a cultural revolution in which our appreciation of language and our conceptions of truth and knowledge would undergo a fundamental transformation' (Ansell-Pearson 1994, 34). One of his principal targets here was the materialistic ideal of the pursuit of happiness, the growth of which liberals saw as such an important element of the achievement of civilization. For Nietzsche, this was antithetical to the true spiritual basis of 'high culture': as he scornfully remarked, 'He who wants to harvest happiness and contentment from life has only to avoid acquiring a higher culture' (Nietzsche 1986, 130). The 'civilization' proffered by liberals was not a form of higher culture; it was rooted in a 'slave morality' appropriate to the herd (Nietzsche 1994, 20). While pampering its adherents through material plenty, it weakened them spiritually, leading ultimately to sickness and degeneration. In its place, Nietzsche advanced an alternative, 'aristocratic' vision of 'higher culture' founded on a conception of nature where he also, unsurprisingly, parted company with the liberals. In contrast with the orthodox Enlightened thesis of a uniform human nature, Nietzsche's conception of nature was of something unequal and uneven, where the 'order of castes' was 'the supreme law of life', so that 'the privilege of each is determined by the nature of its being' (cited in Ansell-Pearson 1994, 41). Like Marx, he confronted the liberal synthesis along each of its conceptual axes and, like Marx, he offered a powerful critique of its incoherence, while advancing a compelling alternative synthesis of his own. These two critiques, combined with the growing fragility of liberalism's own sense of certainty after the Darwinian revolution, were to have the most dramatic political consequences in the following decades, as they informed strong ideological movements working for the downfall of the social and international order associated with the 'family of civilized nations'.

A final challenge was presented by Heinrich von Treitschke, whose *Politics* begins with the state as a natural necessity. Like the social historians of the Scottish Enlightenment, Treitschke stressed the naturalness of human social and political association, but he employed this to insist upon the necessary particularism of humanity: 'the assertion that mankind in the beginning looked upon itself as one, is the opposite of the truth. Humanity at the first cannot be otherwise conceived than as constituted in small groups', and he found historical evidence for this in anthropological studies of non-European peoples, which showed evidence of the ubiquity of government even in the most 'primitive' forms of human society (Treitschke 1916, 1.9, 6). In classically Herderian fashion, Treitschke asserted the inevitability and desirability of the political division of the world:

> the ideal of one universal empire is odious – the ideal of a state co-extensive with humanity is no ideal at all. In a single State the whole range of culture could never be fully spanned. . . . All nations, like all individuals, have their limitations, but it is exactly in the abundance of these limited qualities that the genius of humanity is exhibited. The rays of the Divine light are manifested, broken by countless facets among the separate peoples, each one exhibiting another picture and another idea of the whole. (Treitschke 1916, 1.19)

The most important conclusion of Treitschke's argument for international politics, however, and an issue on which he parted company decisively with Herder, was the inevitability of conflict between nations and the states that represented and embodied them.

'Any political community', Treitschke warned, 'not in a position to assert its native strength as against any given group of neighbours will always be on the verge of losing its characteristics as a State' (Treitschke 1916, 1.33). This point of view was encapsulated in the famous idea of the *Machtstaat* or power-state: 'The State is power, precisely in order to assert itself as against other equally independent powers', and it was only through power that any state 'realizes its own idea' (ibid., 1.19, 34). And a natural corollary of this is that war is an inevitable feature of international affairs, with the shifting bases of power, and is even to be welcomed as providing an expression for national identity. 'War is justified because the great national personalities can suffer no compelling force superior to themselves, and because history must always be in constant flux; war therefore must be taken as part of the divinely-appointed order' (ibid., 2.597–8). This reflects not only the Clausewitzian belief in the cultural significance of war, but even more Treitschke's appreciation of the situation

188 *The Liberal Idea of Civilization and its Critics*

in which Germany found herself in Europe: fragmented into small states – all of which contained an 'undeniably ridiculous element' (ibid., 1.34) – and so at the mercy of the will of greater powers and unable to develop their own national 'idea'. The welding together of the German *Reich* under Prussian leadership profoundly influenced Treitschke's view of the state as an independent force in its own right, literally an expression of power in a world that knew no other truth.

Treitschke's idea of the *Machtstaat* could be seen as the logical consequence of the combination of Hegel's statist formulation of Herderian nationalism with the idea of the international environment as a ruthlessly competitive struggle to create and sustain one's own civilization. In that form, especially as the influence of racist theories of competition inspired by Gobineau spread around Europe, it is fairly easy to see the roots of one of the most destructive theories of international politics of the twentieth century: Adolf Hitler's National Socialism. It is important to realize, though, that nineteenth-century liberalism did not fail simply because it was excessively 'utopian' in its belief that commerce would inevitably create a harmony of interests around the world which would underpin a more peaceful world order (see Carr 2001). Liberals certainly hoped such an outcome might come about, but, as we have seen, they were not unaware that civilization contained its own problems, and thought seriously about how they might be addressed through, for example, the development of educational institutions.

Conclusion: the impact of the two world wars

The First World War, of course, was a further major blow to liberal optimism, especially liberal beliefs that education and commerce were moving the world in the direction of greater rationality and more peaceful ways of solving international problems. During the war, however, liberals offered a vigorous defence of their idea of civilization, and after the war it continued to inform the new pattern of international order established by the Covenant of the League of Nations. They recognized, however, that the often easy confidence of the earlier nineteenth-century liberals would no longer suffice, and moved instead towards a more rationally directed image of social coordination as integral to the further development of civilization. Although traces of this are still evident in contemporary international organizations, I will close this chapter by considering an attack on interwar liberal assumptions about civilization that proved devastating in the context of the newly emerging academic discipline of international relations: the idea of political 'realism' associated with thinkers such as E. H. Carr and Hans Morgenthau.

Responding in 1915 to German criticisms about British imperialism, Alfred Zimmern replied with one of the most robust assertions of the core liberal doctrine in all its nineteenth-century glory:

> There is no such thing as English justice, English liberty, English responsibility. The qualities that go to the making of free and ordered institutions are not national but universal. They are no monopoly of Great Britain. They are free to be the attributes of any race or any nation. They belong to civilized humanity as a whole. They are part of the higher life of the human race. (Zimmern 1915, 364)

The purpose of the British imperial presence in India, Zimmern maintained, was not to spread 'English culture', and indeed he acknowledged that 'England has to learn from Indian culture as much as India from ours' (Zimmern 1915, 364). Nevertheless,

> to have laid for India the foundations on which alone a stable society could rest, to have given her peace from foes without and security within, to have taught her, by example, the kinship of Power and Responsibility, to have awakened the social conscience and claimed the public services of Indians in the village, the district, the province, the nation, towards the community of which they feel themselves to be members, to have found India a continent, a chaos of tribes and castes, and to have helped her become a nation – that is not a task of English culture: it is a task of civilization. (Zimmern 1915, 364)

The League of Nations continued to uphold the idea of a 'sacred trust of civilization', to be discharged by civilized imperial powers on behalf of those countries 'not yet able to stand by themselves under the strenuous conditions of the modern world' (Keene 2002, 132; and see also Bain 2003).

Not all of Zimmern's contemporaries were so sure, however, and the interwar period reflects something of a crisis of confidence among liberals in the imperial mission (see, for example, Hobhouse 1994, 21; Woolf 1998, 352–3; see also Herman 1997, 257–8), and even Zimmern after the war demonstrated a shrewd awareness of some of the obstacles facing the civilizing project (see Rich 1995; Zimmern 1936). Many liberals came to believe that civilization could no longer be expected to protect or regulate itself, and their concerns now went further than Mill's earlier worries about the dangerous by-products of the development of civilization, such as the emergence of mass societies. The war, for example, had powerfully reaffirmed Constant's fears about the dangers of a civilized society, in the sense of its technological and economic development, coming under the rule of a belligerent and uncivilized leadership. One response was to argue for the need for a more rationally directed form of social organization, both domestically and internationally, a position often associated with the 'new liberalism' developing in Britain. The general thrust of the new way of thinking reflected a concern, as Harold Laski put it, that 'The activities of a civilised community are too complex and too manifold to be left to the blind regulation of impulse' (Laski 1930, 17). This point of view was shared by new liberals such as J. A. Hobson, who employed an 'organic analogy' for thinking about social development – a concept we have seen earlier appearing as a staple of conservative thought – and deployed it, in effect, to reintroduce reason after its displacement by social Darwinists such as Kidd (see Long 1996).

While the First World War produced this general rethinking of liberalism, however, the second produced a crisis of faith in the sustainability of liberal civilization. This was exemplified by two of the most influential books on international politics written in the twentieth century, which together constitute the foundation of what is now usually called 'realism': Hans Morgenthau's *Politics Among Nations* and Edward Hallett Carr's *The Twenty Years' Crisis*. Morgenthau's text became the standard work on international relations in American universities (Thompson 1994); Carr's dialectical analysis of 'realism' and 'utopianism' similarly helped to frame the central problems of international politics for British scholars in the post-war era (Dunne 1998).

The touchstone of Morgenthau's realism – and not only his (see Lippmann 1982, 133–43; Syed 1963, ch. 1) – was the concept of human nature, and one which borrowed from Hume the old idea of the basic uniformity of human nature as a precondition for an objective enquiry into the political world. As Morgenthau succinctly put it, 'Social forces are the product of human nature in action' (Morgenthau 1949, 4). In that respect, of course, he was effectively agreeing with one of the central themes of liberal thought: the idea that a theory of international politics needs to be built upon and consistent with the concept of human nature. He parted company with the liberals, though, because he believed that their rationalist philosophy has misunderstood the nature of man, the nature of the social world and the nature of reason itself. It does not see that man's nature has three dimensions: biological, rational and spiritual. By neglecting the biological impulses and spiritual aspirations of man, it misconstrues the function reason fulfils within the whole of human existence; it distorts the problem of ethics especially in the political field; and it perverts the natural sciences into an instrument of social salvation for which neither their own nature nor the nature of the social world fits them. (Morgenthau 1946, 5)

Morgenthau's realism, in other words, was built upon accepting the realities of human nature as it really is, rather than (he claimed) the idealistic conception of human nature adopted by pre-war liberals, which exaggerated the role of reason at the expense of human nature's other dimensions. Not without a certain irony, Morgenthau's picture of the real place of reason in human nature looked a great deal like the dichotomy between reason and passion presented by the Enlightenment's 'science of man' (Morgenthau 1946, 154). 'Reason', Morgenthau said, 'is like a light which by its own inner force can move nowhere. It must be carried in order to move. It is carried by the irrational forces of interest and emotion to where those forces want it to move, regardless of what the inner logic of abstract reason would require' (ibid., 155). The true function of reason was much more humble than liberalism realized; it was merely to harmonize conflicting impulses, and bring the irrationally chosen ends of human action into harmony with each other and with the available means. Reason was purely instrumental. Thus Morgenthau sought to demolish what he perceived as liberalism's idealistic faith in rationally inspired progress towards civilization.

Carr shared Morgenthau's view that one of the central flaws in liberal theories of international politics was the mistaken belief that 'the moral law of nature could be scientifically established; and rational deduction from the supposed facts of human nature took the place of revelation or intuition as the source of morality' (Carr 2001, 25). But it is worth noting that Carr's version of the realist alternative to this position did not depend on a different conception of human nature in the way that Morgenthau's did. In fact, when discussing realist thought, Carr hardly mentioned 'human nature' at all. He did refer to Machiavelli as 'the first important political realist', and noted Machiavelli's belief that men 'are kept honest by constraint', implying that 'politics are not (as utopians pretend) a function of ethics, but ethics of politics' (ibid., 62).

But in his account of 'modern realism', Carr chose to stress the 'relativity of thought' as its key element because it was this which could 'demolish the utopian concept of a fixed and absolute standard by which policies and actions can be judged' (Carr 2001, 65, 71). Drawing on typical nineteenth- and early twentieth-century sentiments about white supremacy and the civilizing virtues of empire, he acidly demonstrated that the universal 'harmony of interests' posited by liberals concealed an underlying national interest expanded to cover the whole of humanity, and concluded that 'Theories of international morality are . . . the product of dominant nations or groups of nations' (ibid., 74). His version of political realism, in short, was based not upon the clash in human nature between reason and passion so much as on a belief in the inevitability of conflicting national interests in the world, and the consequent relativism that this introduced into all attempts to judge different patterns of international order, such as inflated claims for the 'sacred trust of civilization' embodied in the League of Nations. Social Darwinism he explicitly rejected as little more than a liberal attempt to find a new justification with which to prop up the *laissez-faire* system in the later nineteenth century (ibid., 46–9).

Despite their differences, Morgenthau's and Carr's realist theories were symptomatic of the wider attack upon the crucial concept of civilization which had underpinned nineteenth-century liberal thinking about international politics, and which continued to be the main goal of liberal theorists in the interwar years. After the Second World War, it very quickly became apparent that the old division of the world into a 'family of civilized nations' and the 'barbarians' beyond was no longer acceptable. When the British tried to use wording similar to that employed in the League Covenant in the United Nations Charter, for example, they were brusquely dismissed on the grounds that it did not properly respect the fact that 'among dependent peoples there were . . . peoples with a long heritage of civilization' (cited in Keene 2002, 139). A key difference between the League and the United Nations, then, was that the two organizations reflected very different attitudes towards the liberal idea of civilization. The former was still predicated on the notion that a select group of nations were already civilized, and so entitled to recognition as sovereigns, but were under a duty to spread the benefits of their civilization to the rest of the world. The latter was based on the rejection of this conception of civilization, and on the contrasting insistence that there was a plurality of different civilizations in the world, which should imply the recognition of the sovereignty of a wide range of peoples currently labouring under imperial domination. For the first time in human history, the idea of state sovereignty attained universal extension, and thus in the two decades after 1945 world politics as a whole came to be formally organized around the principle of the illegitimacy of imperialism. One of the major intellectual implications of this change, as we will see in the next and final chapter, was a shift in the conceptual vocabulary of what was increasingly called 'international relations theory': the move towards the ideas of a system or a society of states.

Further reading

To get a feel for political and sociological thought in the period more widely, Holmes 1984 and Bellamy 1990 are very useful, as is Collini et al. 1983. Brown et al. 2002 contains an unusually good selection of readings from nineteenth-century writings on international politics. Knutsen 1992 includes an excellent study of nineteenth-century international political thought, covering an admirably broad range of different thinkers in a single chapter. Holbraad 1970 is another excellent work and, despite its focus on theories about the Concert of Europe, is a useful introduction to the period as a whole. Something similar might be said for Gat 1992, which is also able to range widely around its core concern with military thought. For international political thought during the early twentieth century, Long and Wilson 1995 is indispensable. Crook 1994 is a fine study of the international political implications of Darwinism, while MacMaster 2001 is a good introductory study of the development of racist thought, leading on well into the wider scholarly literature.

Conclusion:
International System
and International Society

The development of the realist attack on liberal thinking about civilization might well be seen as an appropriate moment at which to end a survey of the history of international political thought. Nevertheless, to conclude the book, I want to look very briefly at some of the major developments in the conceptual vocabulary of international political thought which have taken place since 1945, in order to offer some suggestions for a framework through which one might connect the history presented here with the ways in which scholars currently think about the world. The period since 1945 may with good reason be treated as a distinct phase in the history of international political thought in large part because, for the first time, speculation about international politics, law and organization has been consolidated within an academic discipline that is now usually referred to as 'international relations', with its own departments in universities, its own academic journals and so on. The main stimulus to the formation of the new discipline was, of course, the crisis of the First World War – although, at least in America, it does have roots in the political science discipline at the turn of the century (as Schmidt 1998 shows) – and for a long time experts on international relations laboured under the stigma of belonging to a 'new' discipline which lacked a clear consensus as to exactly what its terms of reference were (see Schmidt 1998, 11–16). One consequence was that academic professionals in the field were anxious to emphasize how the study of international relations was distinct from other fields of enquiry which might want to 'poach' on the new discipline's terrain, such as politics or social science more generally. In international relations, this often took the form of an assertion of the uniquely anarchical character of international order, and therefore the inadvisability of making an argument from a 'domestic analogy' (Bull 1977, 46–51). Thus, although experts on international relations might borrow methods and sometimes even substantive insights from other fields, they had their own set of problems and questions about which they could speak with authority.

In the process of 'separating' international relations out in this way, theories gradually came to be clustered around two different concepts: the ideas of an 'international system' and an 'international society'. The first of these was especially popular in the United States, where it was associated with a scientific method devoted to the precise identification of concepts, actors and variables, the statement of testable hypotheses about relations between variables, and the rigorous, objective assessment of those hypotheses using quantitative or qualitative data (Kaplan 1957; Waltz 1979). The concept of an 'international society', by contrast, was more popular in the United Kingdom, where it became linked with a 'traditionalist' approach based on the humanities and involving evaluative judgement as an indispensable element of the study of international relations (Bull 1969). As a result of this methodological dispute, which was perhaps surprisingly bitter, the discipline effectively divided into two camps, one carrying on a broadly scientific research programme into the dynamics of the international system and its actors, the other concerned with philosophical, historical, legal and ethical speculation about the norms that constitute international 'sociability'. Elements of this division are still clearly present in contemporary international relations theory.

The idea of an international system

In the early 1950s, David Easton made a powerful attack on the way in which political science was conducted in the United States at the time. His main point was that political science was lagging behind the other social sciences to an alarming degree because it was too 'traditionalist' in its outlook (Easton 1953, 50). Political scientists were excessively attached to simply gathering and relating facts ('hyperfactualism'), and the field as a whole suffered from 'an immoderate neglect of general theory' (ibid., 47). To cure the problem, political scientists needed carefully defined 'orienting concepts', to specify exactly what members of the discipline were trying to discover when they were studying politics. Political scientists therefore should abstract from the whole social system some variables which seem to cohere more closely than others, much as price, supply, demand and choice among wants do in economics, and to look upon them as a subsystem which can be profitably examined, temporarily, apart from the whole social system. (Easton 1953, 97)

A 'systematic theory' of politics, in short, would consist of precisely defined concepts 'corresponding to the important political variables', and 'statements about the relations among these concepts' (Easton 1953, 98). This approach was taken up principally by 'structural-functionalist' theories of politics (for example, Almond and Powell 1967), which identified certain key 'structures' within the political system (parties, bureaucracies, legislatures, etc.) and developed statements about their respective political 'functions' (aggregating interests, formulating policies, distributing resources, etc.).

Easton's appeal for a 'systematic theory' of politics had an immense influence on the development of political science both in the US and elsewhere. Because the discipline of international relations often existed within or in close proximity to university departments of political science, this had an obvious knock-on effect, but it was perhaps particularly important because many theorists of international relations felt that Easton's concerns were unusually relevant to them, since their new discipline was still having difficulty defining exactly what it was they were trying to analyse, and what they were trying to say about it. Moreover, Easton's attack on 'hyperfactualism' also seemed pertinent to the discipline of international relations, especially given the attachment of political realists such as Morgenthau to the historical analysis of the facts of international life. Morton Kaplan, one of Easton's colleagues at Chicago University, put this latter point especially forcefully: 'A history . . . continually brings in "facts" which are believed relevant as a story is told. But histories are never explicit concerning the variable categories within which "facts" should be placed nor with respect to how a "fact" as a variable is related to other variables' (Kaplan 1957, xii). As we have seen from Easton's exposition, this was precisely what systematic theory was for: it would specify concepts to describe the variables, thus permitting the proper organization of factual data, and it would contain a body of statements about the relations between variables, which could be tested in terms of whether the distribution of facts across variables did indeed correspond to the presumed relationships (see ibid., 6–12).

From Kaplan's point of view, then, Easton's criticisms of political science applied, if anything, even more strongly to international relations, and he concluded that the most urgent task was to develop a clear understanding of the 'international system'. This project helped to define the boundary between international relations and political science because, Kaplan argued, in a way which might at first sight seem rather surprising, the international system was fundamentally different from the political system; indeed, 'the international system may be characterized as a null political system' (Kaplan 1957, 14). To explain this point, Kaplan noted that an essential function performed within political systems was to 'specify the areas of jurisdiction for decision-making units and provide methods for settling conflicts of jurisdiction'; a government is therefore 'an unambiguous sign of a political system since governments are hierarchical in organization ... and they arbitrate jurisdictional disputes between other subsystems of the society' (ibid.). This was precisely what was lacking in international relations, however: 'In the present international system, the nation states have political systems, but the international system itself lacks one' (ibid.). What, then, is the 'international system'? Kaplan's early work did not actually develop a proper theory of one in general, but rather, as he later observed, sought to move 'from general theory to comparative theories of different systems' (Kaplan 1979, 131), examining six instances of a possible, but theoretically unspecified, 'international system', such as a 'balance of power system' or a 'loose bipolar system'.

Another important proponent of this new approach was Karl Deutsch, who contended that mechanistic, organicist and historicist models were all inadequate to capture scientific thought after the 1940s. Each had its own problems: 'Mechanism and the equilibrium concept cannot represent growth and evolution. Organisms are incapable of both accurate analysis and internal rearrangement; and models of historical process lacked inner structure and quantitative predictability' (Deutsch 1963, 79). In their place, he proposed the use of models derived from 'cybernetic' systems that stressed the importance of *communication*. He claimed that 'It is communication, that is, the ability to transmit messages and to react to them, that makes organizations; and it seems that this is true of organizations of living cells in the human body as well as of organizations of pieces of machinery in an electronic calculator, as well as of organizations of thinking human beings in social groups' (ibid., 77). In part, this new focus on techniques of communication in cybernetic systems was driven by the experience of new forms of communication technology and their impact on social life and international politics. But it was also driven partly by the desire to escape the pessimism of the early political realists. One of the salient features of cybernetic systems, Deutsch explained, was their capacity to be 'self-controlling', to adapt to their environment as well as to their own past behaviour, and that 'they have, in some cases, a limited capacity to learn' (ibid., 80).

The most influential single statement of the concept of an international system, though, was provided by Kenneth Waltz, who identified three key elements to a political system in general: an organizing principle, the different functions which the units within the system performed, and their different capabilities. Like Kaplan, and drawing upon the ideas of Morgenthau and other realists, Waltz argued that the organizing principle of the international system had been anarchy, and that consequently the idea that the units might perform different functions within the system 'dropped out' of consideration, since it is only in hierarchic systems where units have differential functions, with some subordinated to others (Waltz 1979). In itself, this clearly reflected the political changes that had taken place since the interwar period, since most liberal thinkers of those earlier decades would have automatically assumed the existence of hierarchy in their conceptualization of the idea of a restricted 'family of civilized nations'. Waltz's conceptualization of the international system, then, provided a neat bridge between the realists' rejection of the imperialistic civilizing mission of the nineteenth-century liberals and the scientific project outlined by Kaplan, where the analysis of the structure of the system could now be reduced to the apparently readily operationalizable question of the distribution of the capabilities of the units. Waltz's formulation of the idea of an international system remains one of the basic categories with which theorists of international relations operate today, albeit within the context of controversies about the nature of power (see, for example, Keohane and Nye 1989), a critical attack on Waltz's decision to drop the issue of the differentiation of units out of his model (see Ruggie 1998), and a new focus on the way in which the construction of the identities of actors may influence the outcomes of international relations (Wendt 1999).

The idea of an international society

One possible reason why 'traditionalism' proved more tenacious in the field of international relations was that that discipline had never simply been associated with political science, but had deep roots in international law and diplomatic history; international *politics* was only ever one part of the subject matter of international relations, albeit probably the most important part. Traditionalist theorists appealed to these roots in their response to the new demands for a more systematic approach to the study of international relations. Hedley Bull, for example, called it a 'classical approach' to the subject 'that derives from philosophy, history and law' (Bull 1969, 20).

Partly thanks to Bull's continuing defence of traditionalism, political realism developed in a quite different direction in Britain, under the auspices of a group of theorists organized around the 'British committee for the theory of international politics' (see Dunne 1998). The first characteristic feature of this group's approach to the subject was its decision to adopt a 'comparative-historical' approach, borrowing from Arnold Toynbee's study of the rise and fall of different civilizations (itself heavily influenced by a sense of the decline of the West). As one of its first acts, the British committee 'decided to make a prolonged study of States-Systems in various parts of the globe throughout the ages' (Butterfield 1975, 6), with the initial intention of producing a common work on the subject. Accordingly 'the committee set out to compare the historical evidence, and see what the systems in various parts of the globe have in common and how they differ' (Watson 1992, 3).

The committee's research programme was not, however, exhausted by this monumental comparative-historical task. Wight also posed a key question that reveals its members' sensitivity to the normative issues raised by this choice of historical programme: 'For what reasons are we inclined (as I think we probably are) to judge a states-system as *per se* a more desirable way of arranging the affairs of a great number of men than the alternatives, whatever these may be?' (Wight 1977, 44). On this crucial normative question, although the school was principally interested in the modern states-system as a historical phenomenon, it was also more generally interested in the meaning and role of 'Western values' in international relations (see Wight 1966b). The idea that the members of the British committee should concern themselves with the study of 'Western values' was very forcefully suggested by Butterfield in an early committee paper. He argued that the major issue of the time, the Cold War, 'has of necessity to be conducted henceforward as a war of ideas and ideals' (Butterfield 1959, 15). As he saw it, 'the stage is now set for a conflict of ideals in the world at large', and one in which the basic issue was the international spread of Western liberal-democratic values (ibid.,

12, 17). Obviously, this made it important for the committee to understand the meaning of 'Western values' and their place in international relations.

Wight provided a catalogue of those 'Western values' which he believed to be relevant to modern international relations: individual positive liberty, toleration or open-mindedness, constitutionalism, moderation, resistance and responsibility or prudence (Wight 1966b, 88, 89, 91, 122, 128). He placed most emphasis on the fact that 'it is a characteristic of medieval and modern Europe that ... it has cultivated [the] middle ground, and developed the conception of a political morality distinct equally from personal morality and from *Realpolitik*' (ibid., 127). This middle ground rejects appeals to individual moral sentiment or articles of faith, and yet it nevertheless 'upholds the validity of the ethical in the realm of politics', making, in effect, an 'accommodation between moral necessity and practical demands' (ibid., 128). This understanding of 'Western values', which is both tellingly different from *Realpolitik* and echoes Carr's earlier account of the need for a balance between realism and utopianism, is very closely associated with Wight's conception of the rationalist tradition, which he also saw to be concerned to occupy the '*via media*' in international relations theory, between the revolutionist and realist traditions, balancing the revolutionists' moral sentiment with a characteristically realist awareness of the role of power politics.

In their historical researches, the committee's approach was powerfully influenced by the conservative historians' idea that the European society of sovereign states and balance of power diplomacy represented the key mechanisms of modern international order. This was predicated on three classically Rankean propositions: that Europe had held predominance in the universal history of mankind since 1492; that European history between 1492 and 1798 could essentially be viewed in terms of the development of the modern state; and, finally, that these European states formed a society, based on common culture, religion and moral outlook (Butterfield 1955, 110–11). The second and third of these were especially crucial to the further development of the English school's historical conceptualization of modern international society. The historiography that the English school adopted therefore compelled a focus on the juridico-constitutional history of the absolutist, territorial state as the basis for the construction of the European, and subsequently international, society, leading to the basic proposition that 'Among the regional systems into which the world was divided that which evolved in Europe was distinctive in that it came to repudiate any hegemonial principle and regard itself as a society of states that were sovereign or independent' (Bull and Watson 1984, 6). This explains, among other things, the constitutive importance attached to the Peace of Westphalia within the English school's historical narrative of international society. Wight, despite his reservations, argued that the Peace represented 'the legal basis of the states system' (Wight 1977, 113). That this is so is almost a signature of the English school. Bull took 1648 to mark 'the emergence of an international society as distinct from a mere international system' (Bull 1992, 75). For Watson, 'The concept of independence for a similar multitude of small states in our present international society . . . has evolved from the Westphalian settlement and bears an inherited resemblance to it' (Watson 1992, 196). Overall the result was, as Watson puts it, that 'The European system since Westphalia – that is, during most of its existence – has theoretically been a society of independent states who all recognise each other as such. The committee accepted the theory' (Watson 1990, 103).

The historical narrative which the English school developed, on the basis of their conservative historiographical assumptions, thus led them towards a particular account of the origins and expansion of the modern international society. Most tellingly, this was based on a rejection of naturalist arguments about the universal and progressive character of human reason, and instead concentrated on a historicist sensitivity to the differences and peculiarities of particular cultural formations. This led the English school to prioritize the pluralistic principle of toleration as the basis for peaceful coexistence as the foundation of modern international society, and their normative reflections on international justice essentially came to revolve around the questions of whether greater 'solidarity' might be created without jeopardizing this basic pluralism (see Bull 1966 and, for a recent statement of the position, Jackson 2000). Heavily influenced by Carr and Toynbee, and then by Butterfield and Wight, scholarship on international society developed an abiding scepticism about traditional liberal claims to be able to develop a genuinely cosmopolitan global culture or civilization (Bull 1977). Not all share this point of view, of course, and one of the central lines of contemporary English school theorizing concerns the effort to discern whether or not an extension of moral community might be possible, which would permit a more cosmopolitan sense of obligation to be added to the limited, statist framework of the view of international justice advanced by Bull (for one of the leading examples, see Linklater 1990 and 1998).

Conclusion

International system and international society are such deeply
embedded concepts in international political thought today that the
scholars who use them, while paying a great deal of attention to
defining their meaning, seldom reflect on how historically unusual it
is to think of political relations between communities in these terms
rather than, as we have seen in this book, the many other ways which
have been employed in the past. Indeed, especially in the English
school's work on international society, but also to some extent in theories of the international system (where Hobbesian thought about
the state of nature as a state of war plays a prominent role), the tendency of contemporary theorizing, connected with the continuist and
traditionalist methods noted in the introduction, has been to re-
interpret the history of international political thought as if everyone
had thought in these terms. People whose thought patently cannot be
reduced to this logic are, more often than not, dismissed as not
having any awareness of the distinctively *international* character of
some political relations at all.

Of course, the whole thrust of my presentation of the history of
international political thought has been to highlight the differences
between the conceptual vocabulary we use today and that which has
been used in the past. Some of the problems we face may be timeless
– at least nothing I have said in the book rules out that possibility –
but it has become very clear that the language within which we
attempt to build solutions to our current problems is not timeless.
Studying the history of international political thought does not present
us, then, with a stockpile of particularly excellent answers to our
questions, but rather with a better sense of the limitations under
which we labour, and an idea, perhaps, of how things might be
otherwise. In this respect, it is vital to appreciate the novelty and, one
might almost say, the peculiarity of the ideas of an international
system and international society, which may appear to be such fundamental parts of everyday speculation about international relations
at present that it is tempting to treat them as natural concepts that
everyone has always used. They are not; there are no such concepts.

References

Alcock, Susan, D'Altroy, Terence, Morrison, Kathleen, and Sinopoli, Carla (eds), 2001, *Empires: Perspectives from Archaeology and History* (Cambridge: Cambridge University Press).

Alexandrowicz, Charles, 1967, *An Introduction to the History of the Law of Nations in the East Indies* (Oxford: Clarendon Press).

Almond, Gabriel, and Powell, G. Bingham, 1967, *Comparative Politics: A Developmental Approach* (Boston: Little, Brown).

Al-Tafahum, 'Abd, 1969, 'Doctrine', in A. J. Arberry (ed.), *Religion in the Middle East: Three Religions in Concord and Conflict* (Cambridge: Cambridge University Press), pp. 365–412.

Althusius, Johannes, 1964, *The Politics of Johannes Althusius*, trans. Frederick Carney (Boston: Beacon Press).

Ansell-Pearson, Keith, 1994, *An Introduction to Nietzsche as Political Thinker: The Perfect Nihilist* (Cambridge: Cambridge University Press).

Aquinas, Thomas, 1966, *The Political Ideas of St. Thomas Aquinas: Representative Selections*, trans. Dino Bigongiari (New York: Hafner).

Aristotle, 1957, *The Physics*, trans. Philip H. Wicksteed and Francis M. Cornford, rev. edn, 2 vols (Cambridge, MA: Harvard University Press).

Aristotle, 1958, *The Politics of Aristotle*, trans. Ernest Barker (New York and London: Oxford University Press).

Aristotle, 1968, *The Nicomachean Ethics*, trans. H. Rackham (Cambridge, MA: Harvard University Press).

Armitage, David (ed.), 1998, *Theories of Empire, 1450–1800* (Aldershot: Ashgate).

Armitage, David, 2000, *The Ideological Origins of the British Empire* (Cambridge: Cambridge University Press).

Arneil, Barbara, 1996, *John Locke and America: The Defence of English Colonialism* (Oxford: Oxford University Press).

Arnold, Matthew, 1993, *Culture and Anarchy and Other Writings* (Cambridge: Cambridge University Press).

Aron, Raymond, 1966, *Peace and War: A Theory of International Relations* (Garden City, NY: Doubleday).

Arrian, 1933, *History of Alexander*, trans. E. Iliff Robson, 2 vols (London: Heinemann).

Ashcraft, Richard, 1968, 'Locke's State of Nature: Historical Fact or Moral Fiction?', *American Political Science Review*, 62, pp. 898–915.

Augustine, 1957–72, *The City of God against the Pagans*, various translators, 7 vols (Cambridge, MA: Harvard University Press).

Bacon, Helen, 1961, *Barbarians in Greek Tragedy* (New Haven, CT: Yale University Press).

Bagby, Philip, 1963, *Culture and History: Prolegomena to the Comparative Study of Civilizations* (Berkeley: University of California Press).

Bain, William, 2003, *Between Anarchy and Society: Trusteeship and the Obligations of Power* (Oxford: Oxford University Press).

Balsdon, J. P. V. D., 1979, *Romans and Aliens* (Chapel Hill: University of North Carolina Press).

Barnard, F. M., 1965, *Herder's Social and Political Thought: From Enlightenment to Nationalism* (Oxford: Clarendon Press).

Barnard, F. M., 2003, *Herder on Nationality, Humanity and History* (Montreal: McGill-Queen's University Press).

Bederman, David, 2001, *International Law in Antiquity* (Cambridge: Cambridge University Press).

Bedford, David, and Workman, Thom, 2001, 'The Tragic Reading of the Thucydidean Tragedy', *Review of International Studies*, 27, pp. 51–67.

Belch, Stanislaus, 1965, *Paulus Vladimiri and his Doctrine Concerning International Law and Politics*, 2 vols (London: Mouton).

Bellamy, Richard, 1990, *Victorian Liberalism: Nineteenth-Century Political Thought and Practice* (London: Routledge).

Bentham, Jeremy, 1843, *The Works of Jeremy Bentham*, vol. 2 (Edinburgh: William Tait).

Bentham, Jeremy, 1960, *A Fragment on Government and An Introduction to the Principles of Morals and Legislation* (Oxford: Blackwell).

Berlin, Isaiah, 1992, *The Crooked Timber of Humanity: Essays in the History of Ideas* (New York: Knopf).

Berridge, G. R., Keens-Soper, Maurice, and Otte, T. G., 2001, *Diplomatic Theory from Machiavelli to Kissinger* (London: Palgrave).

Berry, Christopher, 1982, *Hume, Hegel and Human Nature* (The Hague: Martinus Nijhoff).

Berry, Christopher, 1997, *Social Theory of the Scottish Enlightenment* (Edinburgh: Edinburgh University Press).

Bethel, Slingsby, 1680, *The Interest of Princes and States* (London: John Wickins).

Black, Antony, 2001, *The History of Islamic Political Thought: From the Prophet to the Present* (Edinburgh: Edinburgh University Press).

Bodin, Jean, 1965, *Method for the Easy Comprehension of History*, trans. Beatrice Reynolds (New York: Columbia University Press).

Bodin, Jean, 1992, *Political Writings*, trans. Julian Franklin (Cambridge: Cambridge University Press).

Bohman, James, and Lutz-Bachmann, Matthias (eds), 1997, *Perpetual Peace: Essays on Kant's Cosmopolitan Ideal* (Cambridge, MA: MIT Press).

Borschberg, Peter, 1994, *Hugo Grotius Commentarius in Theses XI: An Early Treatise on Sovereignty, the Just War and the Legitimacy of the Dutch Revolt* (Berne: Peter Lang).

Botero, Giovanni, 1956, *The Reason of State and The Greatness of Cities*, trans. P. J. Waley, D. P. Waley and Robert Peterson (New Haven, CT: Yale University Press).

Boucher, David, 1998, *Political Theories of International Relations* (Oxford: Oxford University Press).

Braudel, Fernand, 1994, *A History of Civilizations*, trans. Richard Mayne (London: Allen Lane).

Bresciani, Edda, 1990, 'Foreigners', in Sergio Donadoni (ed.), *The Egyptians*, trans. Robert Bianchi, Anna Lisa Crone, Charles Lambert and Thomas Ritter (Chicago: University of Chicago Press), pp. 221–53.

Briant, Pierre, 2002a, *From Cyrus to Alexander: A History of the Persian Empire* (Winona Lake, IN: Eisenbrauns).

Briant, Pierre, 2002b, 'History and Ideology: The Greeks and "Persian Decadence"', trans. Antonia Nevill, in Thomas Harrison (ed.), *Greeks and Barbarians* (Edinburgh: Edinburgh University Press), pp. 193–210.

Brown, Chris, 1992, *International Relations Theory: New Normative Approaches* (Brighton: Harvester Wheatsheaf).

Brown, Chris, 2002, *Sovereignty, Rights and Justice: International Political Theory Today* (Cambridge: Polity).

Brown, Chris, Nardin, Terry, and Rengger, Nicholas (eds), 2002, *International Relations in Political Thought: Texts from the Ancient Greeks to the First World War* (Cambridge: Cambridge University Press).

Brundell, Barry, 1987, *Pierre Gassendi: From Aristotelianism to a New Natural Philosophy* (Dordrecht: Reidel).

Buckle, Stephen, 1991, *Natural Law and the Theory of Property: Grotius to Hume* (Oxford: Clarendon Press).

Bull, Hedley, 1966, 'The Grotian Conception of International Society', in Herbert Butterfield and Martin Wight (eds), *Diplomatic Investigations: Essays on the Theory of International Politics* (London: Allen and Unwin), pp. 51–73.

Bull, Hedley, 1969, 'International Theory: The Case for a Classical Approach', in Klaus Knorr and James Rosenau (eds), *Contending Approaches to International Politics* (Princeton, NJ: Princeton University Press), pp. 20–38.

Bull, Hedley, 1977, *The Anarchical Society: A Study of Order in World Politics* (London: Macmillan).

Bull, Hedley, 1992, 'The Importance of Grotius in the Study of International Relations', in Bull, Benedict Kingsbury and Adam Roberts (eds), *Hugo Grotius and International Relations* (Oxford: Clarendon Press), pp. 65–93.

Bull, Hedley, Kingsbury, Benedict, and Roberts, Adam (eds), 1992, *Hugo Grotius and International Relations* (Oxford: Clarendon Press).

Bull, Hedley, and Watson, Adam (eds), 1984, *The Expansion of International Society* (Oxford: Clarendon Press).

Burke, Peter, 1991, 'Tacitism, Scepticism, and Reason of State', in J. H. Burns (ed.), *The Cambridge History of Political Thought, 1450–1700* (Cambridge: Cambridge University Press), pp. 479–98.

Burns, Vincent, 1994, *Romanization and Acculturation: The Rhineland Matronae* (Ann Arbor, MI: University Microfilms International).

Butterfield, Herbert, 1955, *Man on his Past* (Cambridge: Cambridge University Press).

Butterfield, Herbert, 1959, 'Misgivings about the Western Attitude to World Affairs', *British Committee Papers*, Royal Institute of International Affairs.

Butterfield, Herbert, 1975, 'Raison d'Etat', in Butterfield (ed.), *Martin Wight Memorial Lectures 1–8* (Brighton and London: University of Sussex, London School of Economics and Royal Institute of International Affairs).

Buzan, Barry, and Little, Richard, 2000, *International Systems in World History: Remaking the Study of International Relations* (Oxford: Oxford University Press).

Campbell, John, 1752, *The Present State of Europe, Explaining the Interests, Connections, Political and Commercial Views of its Several Powers*, 3rd edn (London: Longman).

Canning, Joseph, 1996, *A History of Medieval Political Thought, 300–1450* (London: Routledge).

Cardini, Franco, 2001, *Europe and Islam*, trans. Caroline Beamish (Oxford: Blackwell).

Carlyle, A. J., and Carlyle, R. W., 1962, *A History of Medieval Political Theory in the West*, 6 vols (London: William Blackwood and Sons).

Carr, E. H., 2001, *The Twenty Years' Crisis, 1919–1939: An Introduction to the Study of International Relations*, 2nd edn, reissued with a new introduction by Michael Cox (Basingstoke: Palgrave).

Ceadel, Martin, 1987, *Thinking about Peace and War* (Oxford: Oxford University Press).

Christensen, Johnny, 1962, *An Essay on the Unity of Stoic Philosophy* (Copenhagen: Munksgaard).

Church, William, 1972, *Richelieu and Reason of State* (Princeton, NJ: Princeton University Press).

Cicero, 1933, *De natura deorum*, trans. H. Rackham (London: Heinemann).

Cicero, 1956, *De officiis*, trans. Walter Miller (London: Heinemann).

Cicero, 1959, *De re publica and De legibus*, trans. Clinton Walker Keyes (London: Heinemann).

Cobden, Richard, 1995, *The Political and Economic Works of Richard Cobden*, 6 vols (London: Routledge).

Coleman, John, 1997, 'Ancient Greek Ethnocentrism', in Coleman and Clark Walz (eds), *Greeks and Barbarians: Essays on the Interactions between Greeks and Non-Greeks in Antiquity and the Consequences for Eurocentrism* (Bethesda, MD: CDL Press), pp. 175–220.

Collingwood, R. G., 1945, *The Idea of Nature* (Oxford: Clarendon Press).

Collini, Stefan, Winch, Donald, and Burrow, John, 1983, *That Noble Science of Politics: A Study in Nineteenth-Century Intellectual History* (Cambridge: Cambridge University Press).

Condorcet, Marquis de, 1795, *Outlines of an Historical View of the Progress of the Human Mind* (London: Johnson).

Constant, Benjamin, 1988, *Political Writings*, ed. and trans. Biancamaria Fontana (Cambridge: Cambridge University Press).

Cook, J. M., 1983, *The Persian Empire* (New York: Schocken).

Cornell, Vincent, 1999, 'Fruit of the Tree of Knowledge: The Relationship between Faith and Practice in Islam', in John Esposito (ed.), *The Oxford History of Islam* (Oxford: Oxford University Press), pp. 63–105.

Crook, D. P., 1984, *Benjamin Kidd: Portrait of a Social Darwinist* (Cambridge: Cambridge University Press).

Crook, D. P., 1994, *Darwinism, War and History: The Debate over the Biology of War from the 'Origin of the Species' to the First World War* (Cambridge: Cambridge University Press).

Darwin, Charles, 1859, *On the Origin of Species by Means of Natural Selection* (London: J. Murray).

Davies, Anna Morpurgo, 2002, 'The Greek Notion of Dialect', in Thomas Harrison (ed.), *Greeks and Barbarians* (Edinburgh: Edinburgh University Press), pp. 153–71.

Descartes, René, 1983, *Principles of Philosophy*, trans. Valentine Rodger Miller and Reese Miller (Dordrecht: Reidel).

Deudney, Daniel, 1995, 'The Philadelphian System: Sovereignty, Arms Control, and Balance of Power in the American States-Union, circa 1787–1861', *International Organization*, 49, pp. 191–228.

Deutsch, Karl, 1963, *The Nerves of Government: Models of Political Communication and Control* (New York: Free Press).

Diderot, Denis, 1992, *Political Writings*, ed. and trans. John Hope Mason and Robert Wokler (Cambridge: Cambridge University Press).

Donelan, Michael, 1990, *Elements of International Political Theory* (Oxford: Clarendon Press).

Doyle, Michael, 1983, 'Kant, Liberal Legacies and Foreign Affairs', *Philosophy and Public Affairs*, 12, pp. 205–35, 323–53.

Doyle, Michael, 1997, *Ways of War and Peace: Realism, Liberalism and Socialism* (New York: W. W. Norton).

Dumont, Jean, 1726, *Corps universel diplomatique du droit des gens . . . depuis la règne de l'empereur Charlemagne*, 6 vols (Amsterdam: La Haye).

Dunn, Ross, 1986, *The Adventures of Ibn Battuta: A Muslim Traveller of the 14th Century* (London: Croom Helm).

Dunne, Timothy, 1993, 'Mythology or Methodology? Traditions in International Theory', *Review of International Studies*, 19, pp. 305–18.

Dunne, Timothy, 1998, *Inventing International Society: A History of the English School* (London: Macmillan).

Easton, David, 1953, *The Political System: An Enquiry into the State of Political Science* (New York: Knopf).

Elias, Norbert, 1994, *The Civilizing Process: Sociogenetic and Psychogenetic Investigations*, trans. Edmund Jephcott (Oxford: Blackwell).

Erasmus, Desiderius 1997, *The Education of a Christian Prince*, trans. Neil Cheshire and Michael Heath (Cambridge: Cambridge University Press).

Ferguson, Adam, 1995, *An Essay on the History of Civil Society* (Cambridge: Cambridge University Press).

Forsyth, M., Keens-Soper, H. M. A., and Savigear, P., 1970, *The Theory of International Relations: Selected Texts from Gentili to Treitschke* (London: Allen and Unwin).

Franceschet, Antonio, 2002, *Kant and Liberal Internationalism: Sovereignty, Justice and Global Reform* (London: Palgrave).

Franklin, Julian, 1963, *Jean Bodin and the Sixteenth-Century Revolution in the Methodology of Law and History* (Westport, CT: Greenwood Press).

Franklin, Julian, 1973, *Jean Bodin and the Rise of Absolutist Theory* (Cambridge: Cambridge University Press).

Franklin, Julian, 1991, 'Sovereignty and the Mixed Constitution: Jean Bodin and his Critics', in J. H. Burns (ed.), *The Cambridge History of Political Thought, 1450–1700* (Cambridge: Cambridge University Press), pp. 298–328.

Freud, Sigmund, 1961, *Civilization and its Discontents*, trans. James Strachey (New York: W. W. Norton).

Fukuda, Anhiro, 1997, *Sovereignty and the Sword: Harrington, Hobbes and Mixed Government in the English Civil Wars* (Oxford: Clarendon Press).

Gaius, 1946, *The Institutes of Gaius*, trans. Francis de Zulueta, 2 vols (Oxford: Clarendon Press).

Gat, Azar, 1989, *The Origins of Military Thought: From the Enlightenment to Clausewitz* (Oxford: Oxford University Press).

Gat, Azar, 1992, *The Development of Military Thought: The Nineteenth Century* (Oxford: Oxford University Press).

Gates, Paul Wallace, 1996, *The Jeffersonian Dream: Studies in the History of American Land Policy and Development* (Albuquerque: University of New Mexico Press).

Gay, Peter, 1966, *The Enlightenment: An Interpretation*, vol. 1: *The Rise of Modern Paganism* (New York: W. W. Norton).

Gay, Peter, 1969, *The Enlightenment: An Interpretation*, vol. 2: *The Science of Freedom* (New York: W. W. Norton).

Gierke, Otto von, 1966, *The Development of Political Theory*, trans. Bernard Freyd (New York: H. Fertig).

Gilbert, Allan, 1938, *Machiavelli's 'Prince' and its Forerunners* (Durham, NC: Duke University Press).

Gobineau, Arthur de, 1915, *The Inequality of Human Races*, trans. Adrian Collins (London: Heinemann).

Gong, Gerrit, 1984, *The Standard of 'Civilization' in International Society* (Oxford: Clarendon Press).

Grant, Michael, 1995, *Greek and Roman Historians: Information and Misinformation* (London: Routledge).

Gratian of Bologna, 1993, *The Treatise on Laws: The Decretum, Distinctions 1–20*, trans. Augustine Thompson and James Gordley (Washington, DC: Catholic University of America Press).

Grewe, Wilhelm, 1988, *Fontes historiae iuris gentium*, vol. 1 (Berlin: Walter de Gruyter).

Grotius, Hugo, 1925, *De jure belli ac pacis*, 2 vols, trans. F. Kelsey (Oxford: Clarendon Press).

Grunebaum, G. E. von, 1970, *Classical Islam: A History, 600–1258*, trans. Katherine Watson (London: Allen and Unwin).

Guicciardini, Francesco, 1949, *Ricordi*, trans. Ninian Hill Thomson (New York: S. F. Vanni).

Guicciardini, Francesco, 1994, *Dialogue on the Government of Florence*, trans. Alison Brown (Cambridge: Cambridge University Press).

Guizot, François, 1864, *Memoirs of a Minister of State, from the Year 1840* (London: R. Bentley).

Guizot, François, 1878, *The History of Civilization: From the Fall of the Roman Empire to the French Revolution*, trans. William Hazlitt (New York: D. Appleton).

Guizot, François, 1997, *The History of Civilization in Europe*, trans. William Hazlitt (London: Penguin).

Gusdorf, Georges, 1971, *Les Sciences humaines et la pensée occidentale 4: Les Principes de la pensée au siècle des lumières* (Paris: Payot).

Gustafson, Lowell (ed.), 2000, *Thucydides' Theory of International Relations* (Baton Rouge: Louisiana State University Press).

Guthrie, W. K. C., 1969, *A History of Greek Philosophy*, vol. 3: *The Fifth-Century Enlightenment* (Cambridge: Cambridge University Press).

Haakonssen, Knud, 1985, 'Hugo Grotius and the History of Political Thought', *Political Theory*, 13, pp. 239–65.

Haakonssen, Knud, 1990, 'Natural Law and Moral Realism: The Scottish Synthesis', in Michael Stewart (ed.), *Studies in the Philosophy of the Scottish Enlightenment* (Oxford: Clarendon Press), pp. 61–85.

Hall, Edith, 1989, *Inventing the Barbarian: Greek Self-Definition through Tragedy* (Oxford: Clarendon Press).

Hampsher-Monk, Ian, 1998, 'Speech Acts, Languages or Conceptual History?', in Hampsher-Monk, Karin Tilmans and Frank van Vree (eds), *History of Concepts: Comparative Perspectives* (Amsterdam: Amsterdam University Press), pp. 37–50.

Harrison, Thomas (ed.), 2002, *Greeks and Barbarians* (Edinburgh: Edinburgh University Press).

Hart, Marjolein 't, 1993, *The Making of a Bourgeois State: War, Politics and Finance during the Dutch Revolt* (Manchester: Manchester University Press).

Hauterive, Alexandre Maurice Blanc de Lanautte, 1800, *De l'état de la France à la fin de l'an VIII* (Paris: Henrics).

Hawkins, Mike, 1997, *Social Darwinism in European and American Thought, 1860–1945: Nature as Model and Nature as Threat* (Cambridge: Cambridge University Press).

Heeren, A. H. L., 1834, *Manual of the History of the Political System of Europe and its Colonies, from its Formation at the Close of the Fifteenth Century to its Re-establishment upon the Fall of Napoleon*, trans. from 5th German edn, 2 vols (Oxford: D. A. Talboys).

Hegel, G. W. F., 1991, *Elements of the Philosophy of Right*, trans. H. B. Nisbet (Cambridge: Cambridge University Press).

Henshall, Nicholas, 1992, *The Myth of Absolutism: Change and Continuity in Early Modern Europe* (London: Longman).

Herder, Johann Gottfried, 2002, *Philosophical Writings*, trans. Michael Forster (Cambridge: Cambridge University Press).

Herman, Arthur, 1997, *The Idea of Decline in Western History* (New York: Free Press).

Herodotus, 1987, *The History*, trans. David Grene (Chicago: University of Chicago Press).

Hinsley, F. H., 1963, *Power and the Pursuit of Peace: Theory and Practice in the History of Relations between States* (Cambridge: Cambridge University Press).

Hinsley, F. H., 1986, *Sovereignty*, 2nd edn (Cambridge: Cambridge University Press).

Hirschman, Albert, 1977, *The Passions and the Interests: Political Arguments for Capitalism before its Triumph* (Princeton, NJ: Princeton University Press).

Hobbes, Thomas, 1996, *Leviathan* (Cambridge: Cambridge University Press).

Hobhouse, L. T., 1994, *Liberalism and Other Writings* (Cambridge: Cambridge University Press).

Holbraad, Carsten, 1970, *The Concert of Europe: A Study in German and British International Theory, 1815–1914* (London: Longman).

Holmes, Stephen, 1984, *Benjamin Constant and the Making of Modern Liberalism* (New Haven, CT: Yale University Press).

Holmes, Stephen, 1995, *Passions and Constraint: On the Theory of Liberal Democracy* (Chicago: University of Chicago Press).

Holzgrefe, J. L., 1989, 'The Origins of Modern International Relations Theory', *Review of International Studies*, 15, pp. 11–26.

Hovden, Eivind, and Keene, Edward (eds), 2002, *The Globalization of Liberalism* (London: Palgrave).

Howell, James, 1646, *Lustra Ludovici, or, The Life of the Late Victorious King of France, Lewis the XIII (and of his Cardinal de Richelieu)* (London: Humphrey Moseley).

Humboldt, Wilhelm von, 1963, *Humanist Without Portfolio: An Anthology of the Writings of Wilhelm von Humboldt*, trans. Marianne Cowan (Detroit: Wayne State University Press).

Hume, David, 1902, *Enquiries Concerning the Human Understanding and Concerning the Principles of Morals*, ed. L. A. Selby-Bigge, 2nd edn (Oxford: Clarendon Press).

Hume, David, 1967, *A Treatise of Human Nature* (Oxford: Clarendon Press).

Hume, David, 1994, *Political Essays* (Cambridge: Cambridge University Press).

Huntington, Samuel, 1996, *The Clash of Civilizations and the Remaking of World Order* (New York: Simon and Schuster).

Hurrell, Andrew, 1990, 'Kant and the Kantian Paradigm in International Relations', *Review of International Studies*, 16, pp. 183–205.

Israel, Jonathan (ed.), 1991, *The Anglo-Dutch Moment: Essays on the Glorious Revolution and its World Impact* (Cambridge: Cambridge University Press).

Jackson, Robert, 2000, *The Global Covenant: Human Conduct in a World of States* (Oxford: Oxford University Press).

Jahn, Beate, 1999, 'IR and the State of Nature: The Cultural Origins of a Ruling Ideology', *Review of International Studies*, 25, pp. 411–34.

Jolowicz, H. F., 1939, *Historical Introduction to the Study of Roman Law* (Cambridge: Cambridge University Press).

Kamali, Mohammad Hashim, 1999, 'Law and Society: The Interplay of Revelation and Reason in the Shariah', in John Esposito (ed.), *The Oxford History of Islam* (Oxford: Oxford University Press), pp. 107–53.

Kant, Immanuel, 1960, *Observations on the Feeling of the Beautiful and the Sublime*, trans. John T. Goldthwait (Berkeley: University of California Press).

Kant, Immanuel, 1991, *Political Writings*, trans. H. B. Nisbet, 2nd edn (Cambridge: Cambridge University Press).

Kaplan, Morton, 1957, *System and Process in International Politics* (New York: Wiley).

Kaplan, Morton, 1979, *Towards Professionalism in International Theory: Macrosystem Analysis* (New York: Free Press).

Keene, Edward, 2002, *Beyond the Anarchical Society: Grotius, Colonialism and Order in World Politics* (Cambridge: Cambridge University Press).

Kelley, Donald, 1973, 'The Development and Context of Jean Bodin's Method', in *Proceedings of the International Conference on Bodin in Munich* (Munich: C. H. Beck), pp. 123–50.

Kelly, J. M., 1992, *A Short History of Western Legal Theory* (Oxford: Clarendon Press).

Keohane, Robert, and Nye, Joseph, 1989, *Power and Interdependence*, 2nd edn (New York: Harper Collins).

Kidd, Benjamin, 1898, *The Control of the Tropics* (London: Macmillan).

Kidd, Benjamin, 1902, *Principles of Western Civilization* (New York: Macmillan).

Knutsen, Torbjörn, 1992, *A History of International Relations Theory* (Manchester: Manchester University Press).

Koch, Christophe-Guillaume de, and Schoell, Maximilien Frédéric, 1817, *Histoire abrégé des traités de paix, entre les puissances de l'Europe, depuis la paix de Westphalie*, rev. edn (Paris: Gide).

Koebner, Richard, 1965, *Empire* (New York: Grosset and Dunlap).

Koenigsberger, H. G., Mosse, George L., and Bowler, G. Q., 1989, *Europe in the Sixteenth Century*, 2nd edn (London: Longman).

Kokaz, Nancy, 2001, 'Moderating Power: A Thucydidean Perspective', *Review of International Studies*, 27, pp. 27–49.

Kratochwil, Friedrich, 1995, 'Sovereignty as "Dominium": Is there a Right of Humanitarian Intervention?', in Michael Mastanduno and Gene Lyons (eds), *Beyond Westphalia? National Sovereignty and International Intervention* (Baltimore: Johns Hopkins University Press).

Kristeller, Paul Oskar, 1979, *Renaissance Thought and its Sources* (New York: Columbia University Press).

Kuhn, Thomas, 1976, *The Structure of Scientific Revolutions*, 2nd edn (Chicago: University of Chicago Press).

Kuhrt, Amélie, 2001, 'The Achaemenid Persian Empire (c. 550–c. 330 BCE)', in Susan Alcock, Terence D'Altroy, Kathleen Morrison and Carla Sinopoli (eds), *Empires: Perspectives from Archaeology and History* (Cambridge: Cambridge University Press), pp. 93–123.

Kuttner, Stephan, 1982, 'The Revival of Jurisprudence', in Robert L. Benson and Giles Constable (eds), *Renaissance and Renewal in the Twelfth Century* (Cambridge, MA: Harvard University Press), pp. 299–323.

Lapid, Yosef, and Kratochwil, Friedrich (eds), 1996, *The Return of Culture and Identity in IR Theory* (Boulder, CO: Lynne Rienner).

Las Casas, Bartolome de, 1974, *In Defense of the Indians*, trans. Stafford Poole (DeKalb: Northern Illinois University Press).

Laski, Harold, 1930, *A Grammar of Politics*, 2nd edn (New Haven, CT: Yale University Press).

Lebovics, Herman, 1986, 'The Uses of America in Locke's *Second Treatise of Government*', *Journal of the History of Ideas*, 47, pp. 567–81.

Lefkowitz, Mary, 1996, 'Ancient History, Modern Myths', in Lefkowitz and Guy MacLean Rogers (eds), *Black Athena Revisited* (Chapel Hill: University of North Carolina Press), pp. 3–23.

Lewis, Bernard, 1982, *The Muslim Discovery of Europe* (New York: W. W. Norton).

Lewis, Bernard, 1988, *The Political Language of Islam* (Chicago: University of Chicago Press).

Linehan, Peter, 2001, 'At the Spanish Frontier', in Linehan and Janet Nelson (eds), *The Medieval World* (London: Routledge), pp. 37–59.

Linklater, Andrew, 1990, *Men and Citizens in the Theory of International Relations*, 2nd edn (London: Macmillan).

Linklater, Andrew, 1998, *The Transformation of Political Community* (Cambridge: Polity).

Lintott, Andrew, 1993, *Imperium Romanum: Politics and Administration* (London: Routledge).

Lippmann, Walter, 1982, *The Essential Lippmann: A Political Philosophy for Liberal Democracy* (Cambridge, MA: Harvard University Press).

Lisola, François Paul de, 1667, *The Buckler of State and Justice* (London: James Fisher).

Liverani, Mario, 2001, *International Relations in the Ancient Near East, 1600–1100 BC* (Basingstoke: Palgrave).

Lloyd, Geoffrey, 1979, *Magic, Reason and Experience: Studies in the Origin and Development of Greek Science* (Cambridge: Cambridge University Press).

Long, A. A., 1986, *Hellenistic Philosophy: Stoics, Epicureans, Sceptics*, 2nd edn (London: Duckworth).

Long, A. A., and Sedley, D. N., 1987, *The Hellenistic Philosophers*, vol. 1: *Translations of the Principal Sources with Philosophical Commentary* (Cambridge: Cambridge University Press).

Long, David, 1996, *Towards a New Liberal Internationalism: The International Theory of J. A. Hobson* (Cambridge: Cambridge University Press).

Long, David, and Wilson, Peter (eds), 1995, *Thinkers of the Twenty Years' Crisis: Inter-War Idealism Reassessed* (Oxford: Oxford University Press).

Machiavelli, Niccolò, 1988, *The Prince*, trans. Russell Price (Cambridge: Cambridge University Press).

Machiavelli, Niccolò, 1996, *Discourses on Livy*, trans. Harvey Mansfield and Nathan Tarcov (Chicago: University of Chicago Press).

MacIntyre, Alasdair, 1966, *A Short History of Ethics* (London: Routledge and Kegan Paul).

MacMaster, Neil, 2001, *Racism in Europe, 1870–2000* (Basingstoke: Palgrave).

Maistre, Joseph de, 1977, *Essay on the Generative Principle of Political Constitutions* (New York: Delmar).

Mann, Thomas, 1983, *Reflections of a Nonpolitical Man*, trans. Walter Morris (New York: Frederick Ungar).

Mapel, David, and Nardin, Terry (eds), 1998, *International Society: Diverse Ethical Perspectives* (Cambridge: Cambridge University Press).

Marshall, P. J., and Williams, Glyndwr, 1982, *The Great Map of Mankind: Perceptions of New Worlds in the Age of Enlightenment* (Cambridge, MA: Harvard University Press).

Marx, Karl, 1965, *Capital: A Critical Analysis of Capitalist Production*, trans. Samuel Moore and Edward Aveling (Moscow: Progress Publishers).

Marx, Karl, 1996, *Later Political Writings*, ed. and trans. Terrell Carver (Cambridge: Cambridge University Press).

Mayall, James, 1990, *Nationalism and International Society* (Cambridge: Cambridge University Press).

Meinecke, Friedrich, 1970, *Cosmopolitanism and the National State*, trans. Robert Kimber (Princeton, NJ: Princeton University Press).

Meinecke, Friedrich, 1984, *Machiavellism: The Doctrine of Raison d'Etat and its place in Modern History*, trans. Douglas Scott (Boulder, CO: Westview Press).

Meyer, John, 2001, *Political Nature: Environmentalism and the Interpretation of Western Thought* (Cambridge, MA: MIT Press).

Mill, John Stuart, 1882, *Dissertations and Discussions: Political, Philosophical, and Historical*, 4 vols (New York: Henry Holt).

Mill, John Stuart, 1946, *On Liberty and Considerations on Representative Government* (Oxford: Blackwell).

Mill, John Stuart, 1985, *Essays on French History and Historians*, vol. 20 of *Collected Works of John Stuart Mill*, ed. John Robson (Toronto: University of Toronto Press).

Moles, John, 1996, 'Cynic Cosmopolitanism', in R. Bracht Branham and Marie-Odile Goulet-Caze (eds), *The Cynics: The Cynic Movement in Antiquity and its Legacy* (Berkeley: University of California Press), pp. 105–20.

Momigliano, Arnaldo, 1987, *On Pagans, Jews, and Christians* (Middletown, CT: Wesleyan University Press).

Montaigne, Michel de, 1991, *The Complete Essays*, trans. M. A. Screech (London: Allen Lane).

Montesquieu, Charles, 1989, *The Spirit of the Laws*, trans. Anne Cohler, Basia Carolyn Miller and Harold Samuel Stone (Cambridge: Cambridge University Press).

Moorhead, John, 2001, *The Roman Empire Divided, 400–700* (London: Longman).

Morgenthau, Hans, 1946, *Scientific Man versus Power Politics* (Chicago: University of Chicago Press).

Morgenthau, Hans, 1949, *Politics Among Nations: The Struggle for Power and Peace* (New York: Knopf).

Morkot, Robert, 2001, 'Egypt and Nubia', in Susan Alcock, Terence D'Altroy, Kathleen Morrison and Carla Sinopoli (eds), *Empires: Perspectives from Archaeology and History* (Cambridge: Cambridge University Press), pp. 227–51.

Muldoon, James, 1972, 'The Contribution of the Medieval Canon Lawyers to the Formation of International Law', *Traditio*, 28, pp. 483–97.

Muldoon, James, 1979, *Popes, Lawyers, and Infidels: The Church and the Non-Christian World, 1250–1550* (Philadelphia: University of Pennsylvania Press).

Muldoon, James, 2000, *Empire and Order: The Concept of Empire, 800–1800* (Basingstoke: Macmillan).

Muthu, Sankar, 1999, 'Enlightenment Anti-Imperialism', *Social Research*, 66, pp. 959–1007.

Myers, Henry, and Wolfram, Herwig, 1982, *Medieval Kingship* (Chicago: Nelson-Hall).

Nardin, Terry, 1992, 'Ethical Traditions in International Affairs', in Nardin and David Mapel (eds), *Traditions of International Ethics* (Cambridge: Cambridge University Press), pp. 1–22.

Nederman, Cary, 1988, 'Nature, Sin and the Origins of Society: The Ciceronian Tradition in Medieval Political Thought', *Journal of the History of Ideas*, 49, pp. 3–26.

Neillands, Robin, 1990, *The Hundred Years War* (London: Routledge).

Nietzsche, Friedrich, 1986, *Human, All Too Human: A Book for Free Spirits*, trans. R. J. Hollingdale (Cambridge: Cambridge University Press).

Nietzsche, Friedrich, 1994, *On the Genealogy of Morality*, trans. Carol Diethe (Cambridge: Cambridge University Press).

Nill, Michael, 1985, *Morality and Self-Interest in Protagoras, Antiphon and Democritus* (Leiden: E. J. Brill).

Nisbet, Robert, 1980, *History of the Idea of Progress* (New York: Basic Books).

Nussbaum, Arthur, 1947, *A Concise History of the Law of Nations* (New York: Macmillan).

Nussbaum, Martha, 1997, 'Kant and Cosmopolitanism', in James Bohman and Matthias Lutz-Bachmann (eds), *Perpetual Peace: Essays on Kant's Cosmopolitan Ideal* (Cambridge, MA: MIT Press), pp. 25–57.

Nussbaum, Martha, 2001, *The Fragility of Goodness: Luck and Ethics in Greek Tragedy and Philosophy*, rev. edn (Cambridge: Cambridge University Press).

Nye, Joseph, 2000, *Understanding International Conflicts: An Introduction to Theory and History*, 3rd edn (New York: Longman).

O'Connor, Mary, 1955, *The Historical Thought of François Guizot* (Washington, DC: Catholic University of America Press).

Oestreich, Gerhard, 1982, *Neostoicism and the Early Modern State*, trans. David McLintock (Cambridge: Cambridge University Press).

Olivecrona, Karl, 1974, 'Appropriation in the State of Nature: Locke on the Origin of Property', *Journal of the History of Ideas*, 35, pp. 211–30.

Onuf, Nicholas Greenwood, 1998, *The Republican Legacy in International Thought* (Cambridge: Cambridge University Press).

Onuf, Peter, and Onuf, Nicholas, 1993, *Federal Union, Modern World: The Law of Nations in an Age of Revolutions, 1776–1814* (Madison: Madison House).

Oresko, Robert, Gibbs, G. C., and Scott, H. M. (eds), 1997, *Royal and Republican Sovereignty in Early Modern Europe* (Cambridge: Cambridge University Press).

Osiander, Andreas, 1991, *Peacemaking and International Legitimacy: Stability and Consensus in the States-System of Europe* (Oxford: Clarendon Press).

Ó Tuathail, Gearóid, Dalby, Simon, and Routledge, Paul, 1998, *The Geopolitics Reader* (London: Routledge).

Pagden, Anthony (ed.), 1987, *The Languages of Political Theory in Early Modern Europe* (Cambridge: Cambridge University Press).

Pagden, Anthony, 1990, *Spanish Imperialism and the Political Imagination: Studies in European and Spanish-American Social and Political Theory, 1513–1830* (New Haven, CT: Yale University Press).

Pagden, Anthony, 1995, *Lords of All the World: Ideologies of Empire in Spain, Britain and France c. 1500–1800* (New Haven, CT: Yale University Press).

Pangle, Thomas, and Ahrensdorf, Peter, 1999, *Justice Among Nations: On the Moral Basis of Power and Peace* (Lawrence: University Press of Kansas).

Parker, Geoffrey, 1985, *Western Geopolitical Thought in the Twentieth Century* (London: Croom Helm).

Parkinson, F., 1977, *The Philosophy of International Relations: A Study in the History of Thought* (London: Sage).

Parry, Clive (ed.), 1969, *Consolidated Treaty Series* (Dobbs Ferry, NY: Oceana Publications).

Parry, J. H., 1940, *The Spanish Theory of Empire in the Sixteenth Century* (Cambridge: Cambridge University Press).

Pennington, Kenneth, 1993, *The Prince and the Law, 1200–1600: Sovereignty and Rights in the Western Legal Tradition* (Berkeley: University of California Press).

Phillips, J. R. S., 1998, *The Medieval Expansion of Europe*, 2nd edn (Oxford: Clarendon Press).

Plato, 1997, *Complete Works*, various translators (Indianapolis and Cambridge: Hackett).

Pocock, J. G. A., 1972, *Politics, Language and Time: Essays on Political Thought and History* (London: Methuen).

Pocock, J. G. A., 1975, *The Machiavellian Moment: Florentine Political Thought and the Atlantic Republican Tradition* (Princeton, NJ: Princeton University Press).

Pocock, J. G. A., 1987, 'The Concept of a Language and the *Métier d'historien*: Some Considerations on Practice', in Anthony Pagden (ed.), *The Languages of Political Theory in Early Modern Europe* (Cambridge: Cambridge University Press), pp. 19–38.

Popkin, Richard, 1973, 'The Philosophical Basis of Eighteenth-Century Racism', in Harold Pagliaro (ed.), *Racism in the Eighteenth Century* (Cleveland: Case Western Reserve University Press).

Porter, Roy, and Teich, Mikuláš (eds), 1981, *The Enlightenment in National Context* (Cambridge: Cambridge University Press).

Post, Gaines, 1964, *Studies in Medieval Legal Thought: Public Law and the State, 1100–1322* (Princeton, NJ: Princeton University Press).

Pufendorf, Samuel von, 1991, *On the Duty of Man and Citizen according to Natural Law*, trans. Michael Silverthorne (Cambridge: Cambridge University Press).

Pütter, Johan Stephan, 1790, *An Historical Development of the Present Political Constitution of the Germanic Empire*, trans. Josiah Dornford, 3 vols (London; n.p.).

Ramsay, Paul, 1992, 'The Just War According to St Augustine', in Jean Bethke Elshtain (ed.), *Just War Theory* (Oxford: Blackwell), pp. 8–22.

Redfield, James, 2002, 'Herodotus the Tourist', in Thomas Harrison (ed.), *Greeks and Barbarians* (Edinburgh: Edinburgh University Press), pp. 24–49.

Reill, Peter, 1996, 'Herder's Historical Practice and the Discourse of Late Enlightenment Science', in Wulf Koepke (ed.), *Johann Gottfried Herder: Academic Disciplines and the Pursuit of Knowledge* (Columbia, SC: Camden House), pp. 13–21.

Reynolds, Susan, 1994, *Fiefs and Vassals: The Medieval Evidence Reinterpreted* (Oxford: Oxford University Press).

Reynolds, Susan, 1997, *Kingdoms and Communities in Western Europe, 900–1300*, 2nd edn (Oxford: Clarendon Press).

Rich, Paul, 1995, 'Alfred Zimmern's Cautious Idealism: The League of Nations, International Education, and the Commonwealth', in David Long and Peter Wilson (eds), *Thinkers of the Twenty Years' Crisis: Inter-War Idealism Reassessed* (Oxford: Clarendon Press).

Richter, Melvin, 1995, *The History of Political and Social Concepts: A Critical Introduction* (Oxford: Oxford University Press).

Robertson, John, 1998, 'Empire and Union: Two Concepts of the Early Modern European Political Order', in David Armitage (ed.), *Theories of Empire, 1450–1800* (Aldershot: Ashgate), pp. 11–44.

Robertson, William, 1972, *The Progress of Society in Europe: A Historical Outline from the Subversion of the Roman Empire to the Beginning of the Sixteenth Century*, (ed.) Felix Gilbert (Chicago: University of Chicago Press).

Robinson, James, 1929, *Civilization* (London: Encyclopaedia Britannica).

Robson, John, 1998, 'Civilization and Culture as Moral Concepts', in John Skorupski (ed.), *The Cambridge Companion to Mill* (Cambridge: Cambridge University Press), pp. 338–71.

Rohan, Henri de, 1995, *De l'intérêt des princes et des états de la chrétienté*, (ed.) Christian Lazzeri (Paris: Presses Universitaires de France).

Rosenberg, Justin, 1994, *The Empire of Civil Society: A Critique of the Realist Theory of International Relations* (London: Verso).

Rousseau, Jean-Jacques, 1991, *Rousseau on International Relations*, (ed.) Stanley Hoffmann and David Fidler (Oxford: Clarendon Press).

Rousseau, Jean-Jacques, 1997, *The Discourses and other Early Political Writings*, trans. Victor Gourevitch (Cambridge: Cambridge University Press).

Ruggie, John Gerard, 1998, *Constructing the World Polity: Essays on International Institutionalization* (London: Routledge).

Russell, Frank, 1936, *Theories of International Relations* (New York: Appleton-Century).

References

Russell, Frederick, 1975, *The Just War in the Middle Ages* (Cambridge: Cambridge University Press).

Sabine, George, 1961, *A History of Political Theory*, 3rd edn (Hinsdale, IL: Dryden Press).

Salmon, E. T., 1982, *The Making of Roman Italy* (Ithaca, NY: Cornell University Press).

Salter, Mark, 2002, *Barbarians and Civilizations in International Relations* (London: Pluto Press).

Sambursky, S., 1959, *Physics of the Stoics* (London: Routledge and Kegan Paul).

Sampson, Ronald, 1956, *Progress in the Age of Reason* (London: Heinemann).

Schacht, J., 1970, 'Law and Justice', in P. M. Holt, Ann Lambton and Bernard Lewis (eds), *The Cambridge History of Islam* (Cambridge: Cambridge University Press), pp. 539–68.

Schellhase, Kenneth, 1976, *Tacitus in Renaissance Political Thought* (Chicago: University of Chicago Press).

Schick, Edgar, 1971, *Metaphorical Organicism in Herder's Early Works: A Study of the Relation of Herder's Literary Idiom to his World-View* (The Hague: Mouton).

Schlegel, Friedrich, 1996, 'Essay on the Concept of Republicanism Occasioned by the Kantian Tract "Perpetual Peace"', in *The Early Political Writings of the German Romantics*, trans. Frederick Beiser (Cambridge: Cambridge University Press), pp. 93–112.

Schmidt, Brian, 1998, *The Political Discourse of Anarchy: A Disciplinary History of International Relations* (Boulder, CO: Westview Press).

Schofield, Malcolm, 1990, 'Ideology and Philosophy in Aristotle's Theory of Slavery', in Günther Patzig (ed.), *Aristotele's 'Politik': Akten des XI. Symposium Aristotelicum* (Göttingen: Vandenhoeck and Ruprecht), pp. 1–27.

Schofield, Malcolm, 1991, *The Stoic Idea of the City* (Cambridge: Cambridge University Press).

Shaban, M. A., 1979, 'Conversion to Early Islam', in Nehemia Levtzion (ed.), *Conversion to Islam* (New York: Holmes and Meier), pp. 24–9.

Shapin, Steven, 1996, *The Scientific Revolution* (Chicago: University of Chicago Press).

Shapin, Steven, and Schaffer, Simon, 1985, *Leviathan and the Air-Pump: Hobbes, Boyle and the Experimental Life* (Princeton, NJ: Princeton University Press).

Sheehan, Michael, 1994, *The Balance of Power: History and Theory* (London: Routledge).

Sherwin-White, A. N., 1967, *Racial Prejudice in Imperial Rome* (Cambridge: Cambridge University Press).

Sherwin-White, A. N., 1973, *The Roman Citizenship*, 2nd edn (Oxford: Clarendon Press).

Showalter, Dennis, 2002, 'Europe's Way of War, 1815–64', in Jeremy Black (ed.), *European Warfare, 1815–2000* (Basingstoke: Palgrave), pp. 27–50.

Skinner, Quentin, 1978, *The Foundations of Modern Political Thought*, 2 vols (Cambridge: Cambridge University Press).

Skinner, Quentin, 2002, *Visions of Politics*, 3 vols (Cambridge: Cambridge University Press).

Snowden, Frank, 1983, *Before Color Prejudice: The Ancient View of Blacks* (Cambridge, MA: Harvard University Press).

Spruyt, Hendrijk, 1997, *The Sovereign State and its Competitors: An Analysis of Systems Change* (Princeton, NJ: Princeton University Press).

Stokes, Eric, 1959, *The English Utilitarians and India* (Oxford: Oxford University Press).

Strugnell, Anthony, 1973, *Diderot's Politics: A Study of the Evolution of Diderot's Political Thought after the Encyclopédie* (The Hague: Martinus Nijhoff).

Syed, Anwar Hussain, 1963, *Walter Lippmann's Philosophy of International Politics* (Philadelphia: University of Pennsylvania Press).

Tacitus, 1920, *Dialogus, Agricola and Germania*, various translators (London: Heinemann).

Thomas, Rosalind, 2000, *Herodotus in Context: Ethnography, Science and the Art of Persuasion* (Cambridge: Cambridge University Press).

Thompson, Kenneth, 1994, *Fathers of International Thought: The Legacy of Political Theory* (Baton Rouge: Louisiana State University Press).

Thucydides, 1900, *Thucydides Translated into English*, trans. Benjamin Jowett, 2 vols (Oxford: Clarendon Press).

Thucydides, 1998, *The Peloponnesian War*, trans. Steven Lattimore (Indianapolis: Hackett).

Treitschke, Heinrich von, 1916, *Politics*, trans. Blanche Dugdale and Torben de Bille, 2 vols (New York: Macmillan).

Tribonian, 1987, *Justinian's Institutes*, trans. Peter Birks and Grant McLeod (Ithaca, NY: Cornell University Press).

Tuck, Richard, 1979, *Natural Rights Theories: Their Origins and Development* (Cambridge: Cambridge University Press).

Tuck, Richard, 1987, 'The "Modern" Theory of Natural Law', in Anthony Pagden (ed.), *The Languages of Political Theory in Early-Modern Europe* (Cambridge: Cambridge University Press), pp. 99–119.

Tuck, Richard, 1993, *Philosophy and Government, 1572–1651* (Cambridge: Cambridge University Press).

Tuck, Richard, 1999, *The Rights of War and Peace: Political Thought and the International Order from Grotius to Kant* (Oxford: Oxford University Press).

Tully, James (ed.), 1988, *Meaning and Context: Quentin Skinner and his Critics* (Cambridge: Polity).

Tully, James, 1993, *An Approach to Political Philosophy: Locke in Contexts* (Cambridge: Cambridge University Press).

Turner, Frederick Jackson, 1986, *The Frontier in American History* (Tucson: University of Arizona Press).

Ullmann, Walter, 1966, *Principles of Government and Politics in the Middle Ages* (London: Methuen).

Ullmann, Walter, 1975, *Law and Politics in the Middle Ages: An Introduction to the Sources of Medieval Political Ideas* (Ithaca, NY: Cornell University Press).

Van Caenegem, R., 1988, 'Government, Law and Society', in J. H. Burns (ed.), *The Cambridge History of Medieval Political Thought, c. 350–c. 1450* (Cambridge: Cambridge University Press), pp. 174–210.

Vattel, Emerich de, 1916, *The Law of Nations, or, The Principles of Natural Law Applied to the Conduct and to the Affairs of Sovereigns*, trans. C. G. Fenwick (Washington, DC: Carnegie Institution).

Viroli, Maurizio, 1992, *From Politics to Reason of State: The Acquisition and Transformation of the Language of Politics, 1250–1600* (Cambridge: Cambridge University Press).

Vitoria, Franciscus de, 1991, *Political Writings*, (ed.) Anthony Pagden and Jeremy Lawrance (Cambridge: Cambridge University Press).

Vyverberg, Henry, 1989, *Human Nature, Cultural Diversity and the French Enlightenment* (Oxford: Oxford University Press).

Walker, R. B. J., 1992, *Inside/Outside: International Relations in Political Thought* (Cambridge: Cambridge University Press).

Waltz, Kenneth, 1959, *Man, the State and War: A Theoretical Analysis* (New York: Columbia University Press).

Waltz, Kenneth, 1979, *Theory of International Politics* (Reading, MA: McGraw-Hill).

Watson, Adam, 1990, 'Systems of States', *Review of International Studies*, 16, pp. 99–109.

Watson, Adam, 1992, *The Evolution of International Society* (London: Routledge).

Weber, Max, 1930, *The Protestant Ethic and the Spirit of Capitalism*, trans. Talcott Parsons (London: Routledge).

Welch, David, 2003, 'Why International Relations Theorists Should Stop Reading Thucydides', *Review of International Studies*, 29, pp. 301–19.

Welsh, Jennifer, 1995, *Edmund Burke and International Relations: The Commonwealth of Europe and the Crusade against the French Revolution* (London: Macmillan).

Wendt, Alexander, 1999, *Social Theory of International Politics* (Cambridge: Cambridge University Press).

Whittow, Mark, 1996, *The Making of Orthodox Byzantium, 600–1025* (London: Palgrave).

Wight, Martin, 1966a, 'Why is There No International Theory?', in Herbert Butterfield and Wight (eds), *Diplomatic Investigations: Essays on the Theory of International Politics* (London: Allen and Unwin), pp. 17–34.

Wight, Martin, 1966b, 'Western Values in International Relations', in Herbert Butterfield and Wight (eds), *Diplomatic Investigations: Essays on the Theory of International Politics* (London: Allen and Unwin), pp. 89–131.

Wight, Martin, 1977, *Systems of States* (Leicester: Leicester University Press).

Wight, Martin, 1991, *International Theory: The Three Traditions* (Leicester: Leicester University Press).

Williams, Howard, 1992, *International Relations in Political Theory* (Milton Keynes: Open University Press).

Williams, Michael, 1989, 'Rousseau, Realism and *Realpolitik*', *Millennium*, 18, pp. 185–203.

Wolfers, Arnold, 1956, *The Anglo-American Tradition in Foreign Affairs: Readings from Thomas More to Woodrow Wilson* (New Haven, CT: Yale University Press).

Woodward, E. L., 1929, *Three Studies in European Conservatism. Metternich: Guizot: the Catholic Church in the Nineteenth Century* (London: Constable).

Woolf, Greg, 2001, 'Inventing Empire in Ancient Rome', in Susan Alcock, Terence D'Altroy, Kathleen Morrison and Carla Sinopoli (eds), *Empires: Perspectives from Archaeology and History* (Cambridge: Cambridge University Press), pp. 311–22.

Woolf, Leonard, 1998, *Empire and Commerce in Africa: A Study in European Imperialism* (London: Routledge).

Yates, Frances Amelia, 1975, *Astraea: The Imperial Theme in the Sixteenth Century* (London: Routledge).

Zammito, John, 2002, *Kant, Herder and the Birth of Anthropology* (Chicago: University of Chicago Press).

Zehfuss, Maja, 2002, *Constructivism in International Relations: The Politics of Reality* (Cambridge: Cambridge University Press).

Zimmerman, E. A. W. von, 1787, *A Political Survey of the Present State of Europe* (London: C. Dilly).

Zimmern, Alfred, 1915, 'German Culture and the British Commonwealth', in R. W. Seton-Watson, J. Dover Wilson, Zimmern and Arthur Greenwood, *The War and Democracy* (London: Macmillan), pp. 348–84.

Zimmern, Alfred, 1936, *The League of Nations and the Rule of Law, 1918–1935* (London: Macmillan).

Index

Lightning Source UK Ltd.
Milton Keynes UK
UKOW06f1229211015

261090UK00010B/187/P